The Real Deal

The Life of Bill Knapp

The Real Deal
The Life of Bill Knapp

WILLIAM B. FRIEDRICKS

bpc

Business Publications Corporation Inc.

ISBN-13: 978-0615852799
ISBN-10: 0615852793
LCCN: 2013946154

Business Publications Corporation Inc.
The Depot at Fourth
100 4th Street
Des Moines, Iowa 50309
(515) 288-3336

For Mom and Dad, again

Contents

Acknowledgments

I was supposed to interview Bill Knapp in 2001 for the book I was then writing, but for some reason, we had to cancel the meeting. Nine years passed before I finally met Bill, and because I had another project that required me to interview him, we arranged to get together. During our discussion, I said something about his many business dealings in Des Moines. That comment led to several more conversations and eventually this book.

Once I began, Bill told me in his no nonsense manner: "Tell the good with the bad; otherwise it won't be worth a damn." I have tried to do so. Bill sat through numerous interviews, conversations, and telephone calls, and gave me full access to his personal and company papers. Otherwise, however, he stayed completely out of the way. While he often inquired about my progress, he never tried to influence my point of view or asked to see anything I had written. I had complete editorial freedom from the project's inception to the book's completion.

Although research and writing is often a solitary experience, I incurred many debts along the way. People at Knapp Properties were especially helpful. Carly Fisher, Bill's executive assistant, was my go-to person and made the project a whole lot easier. Deb Gans generously dug through calendars and records for me; Dennis Galeazzi made financial records available; and the late Daryl Neumann graciously answered many questions in the last months of his life. Most important were Bill Knapp II and Gerry Neugent, who have worked with Bill since the 1970s. They opened records, sat for multiple interviews, suggested contacts I had not considered, and kept me from making mistakes in the manuscript.

Others generously assisted me as well. Susan Knapp, Irene Knapp, and Ginny Haviland, were invaluable. John Knapp helped with the photos, and Mike Knapp loaned me a number of useful Iowa Realty Scrapbooks. Marilyn Dailey provided insight into Iowa Realty's early history, Linda Birocci helped with property records, and Des Moines Register librarian Jo Ann Donaldson aided me with the newspaper's clip files and photos. A complete list of all the people I interviewed and/or opened personal papers to me is included at the end of the book. Thank you all.

ACKNOWLEDGMENTS

Simpson College granted me a sabbatical and then a leave so I could finish this book. Special thanks to Steve Griffith, the academic dean, for supporting the project and the history department—Nick Proctor, Becca Livingstone, Judy Walden, and Daryl Sasser—for covering classes in my absence. Once again, Linda Sinclair transcribed my interviews and helped with correspondence.

Everyone at Business Publications made the publishing process easy. Janette Larkin and Ashley Holter oversaw the project, copyeditor Linda Ross made the text more readable, and the production team created a great design for the book.

My family and close friends have been most important. John and Holly Burns, Chuck and Chris Korte, Owen Duncan and my daughters, Sarah and Emily, patiently listened to my all-too-frequent stories about Bill Knapp. My wife, Jackie, again gave me constant encouragement, read the entire manuscript, and made many valuable suggestions. She also came up with the book's title. Lastly, my parents, Burt and Ginny Friedricks have provided all kinds of support over the years, and as I did with my first book, I'd like to dedicate this to them.

Introduction

The Knapps' sumptuous 2010 holiday party was finally winding down. As Gerry Neugent, Knapp Properties president and chief operating officer, was leaving, he stopped to thank his close friend and partner Bill Knapp for the evening. With his arm around the eighty-four-year-old host, he jokingly asked, "How many deals did you close this evening?" "Only one," Bill replied. They chuckled, but it was more than just a laughing matter. Bill Knapp was the consummate dealmaker and was well known for doing deals anywhere and anytime.[1]

His negotiating tactics had come a long way from his childhood on a southern Iowa farm during the Great Depression. According to an often repeated story, Bill and his younger brother Paul had been sent to a nearby farm to buy a rooster. Their father told his sons they could pay as much as 60 cents for the bird. After a brief conversation, the neighbor told the Knapp boys he would sell them the rooster for 25 cents. "Oh no, young Bill responded, "We will go as high as 50 or 60 cents."[2]

He would eventually hone his bargaining skills, but that was well in the future. The lesson he took from his youth was more general; he did not want to farm. The Knapps scraped by, but they were poor. The uncertainty and insecurity of agrarian life gnawed at the family, and Bill hoped for a future where he could control his destiny.[3] This pushed him and large numbers of other rural residents to seek their fortunes elsewhere. Naval service during World War II first pulled Bill off the farm, and when he returned stateside, he became one of the many who abandoned the countryside for the city. He held several manufacturing jobs and tried the restaurant business before joining millions of veterans who took advantage of the GI Bill and went back to school. Vocational training, he hoped, would land him a better job.

But it was by accident that Bill found his calling. After hiring a real estate agent to sell his restaurant property, Bill showed and then sold the building himself but had to pay the sales commission. "Hell, I can sell real estate," he recalled thinking.[4] And he did. His determination and drive, coupled with an ability to read people, soon made him a leading salesman in Des Moines. He liked the freedom the job offered and quickly gained even more control in 1952, when he acquired Hollis Realty, the small firm where he had worked. Bill renamed the business Iowa Realty and built it into the state's largest real estate operation. At the same time, he diversified beyond the residential brokerage business. He used his budding deal-making ability to buy and sell land, move into commercial real estate, and develop property. Apartments, hotels, and restaurants were eventually added to his growing empire. Together, these endeavors made Bill one of Iowa's wealthiest and most influential individuals.

Of course, key hires were important to Iowa Realty's success as well. Ken Grandquist and Paul Knapp were especially significant, but there was no question that Bill was in charge. "He could put the fear of God in you," Iowa Realty training manager Tim Meline remembered, and agents jumped when he gave a directive. During the late 1970s, for instance, Bill grew increasingly upset when leisure suits, instead of the more standard business suits and ties, became the daily attire of many employees. One day his temper flared; he got on the office intercom system, identified himself, and growled, "It's 11:15 and I'm going to lunch. I'll be back here at 12 o'clock, and I don't want to see a goddamn leisure suit within three miles of this place." Word quickly spread to the branch offices as well, and the trendy apparel immediately disappeared from company facilities.[5]

Impatient and tough, Bill was propelled by a fierce competitiveness and fear of falling back into poverty, but it was his intelligence and vision that led to great success. Although not well educated, he had a very quick and agile mind. Businessman James (Jim) Cownie believed Bill was "as smart as anyone I know," while Knapp Properties' Gerry Neugent noted he could assimilate huge amounts of complex information rapidly and identify the key components. Moreover, Bill's ability to see the big picture fostered strategic thinking, often giving him the advantage of see possibilities where others did not. Roger Brooks, the retired chief executive officer of AmerUs (now part of Aviva), compared him to "a chess player who was several moves ahead of most people." Then there was his uncanny aptitude for envisioning the future use of land: in his mind's eye, he could see suburban homes and shopping centers on present-day farm fields; gleaming office buildings where decaying structures stood; or commercial parks on vacant ground. Equally important, Bill could push ideas into reality by bringing people together and negotiating and closing deals. He put it simply: "I like to make things happen."[6]

He clearly made things happen in downtown Des Moines. Others, such as banker John Fitzgibbon and trucking magnate John Ruan, had kicked off the city's downtown renaissance of the 1970s and 1980s, but Bill kept the revitalization going. He became especially interested in downtown in 1977, when he purchased the dilapidated Hotel Savery. Soon he was refurbishing the hotel and playing a leading role in downtown redevelopment projects. Bill pushed for the skywalk system, assembled land and wooed a developer for a major office complex, and brought both low-income housing and a luxury high-rise condominium to the city's core. He remains involved in downtown and is active in the Des Moines Redevelopment Company, an organization he helped assemble that is brokering land deals for the city's next wave of renewal. Such leadership led the late Iowa state senator, Elaine Szymoniak, to remark, "If you really want something done, you go to Knapp."[7]

Years earlier, Bill had begun making an impact in Iowa political circles. A lifelong Democrat, his association with the party grew in 1962, when he became acquainted with gubernatorial candidate Harold Hughes, who went on to serve as the governor of Iowa from 1963 to 1969 and then represented the state in the U.S. Senate until 1975. The two developed a close friendship. Through Hughes, Bill met other leading Democrats, and over the years became the chief fundraiser/donor and power broker among Iowa Democrats. Hughes was also pivotal in deepening Bill's empathy and understanding for the less fortunate. He came by this naturally, given his upbringing on a struggling farmstead. But it was Hughes's progressive influence and Bill's increased involvement in downtown—where he frequently encountered urban poverty firsthand—that led to a growing interest in philanthropy.

This generosity became more evident in the early 1980s. He believed he had a responsibility to the community and thought it important to know he was not "a taker." Attorney Roxanne Conlin called him a "very soft touch," although according to the *Des Moines Register*, many of his rivals at the time would have characterized the aggressive businessman differently. Nonetheless, Bill's early largesse reached a growing number of recipients. First were inner-city charities—homeless shelters, childcare facilities, and low-income housing projects. Besides making outright gifts, Bill was also using his skills and connections to raise funds on behalf of these and many other organizations. Then the scope of his giving broadened. He gave millions to Drake University and the Iowa State Fair, and became a major financial supporter of a variety of nonprofit groups throughout greater Des Moines. Late in life, Bill explained his activity: "Sure everyone wants to make money. You have to make money to give it away. But the satisfaction that you get making life better for people less fortunate—that's the only thing you take with you."[8]

Amidst his accomplishments, victories, and successes, there were failures, mistakes, and losses. Agreements collapsed, developments did not get off the ground, and relationships soured. He had a long-term extramarital affair, his first marriage crumbled, and he suffered the tragic death of his son. But he pressed on. Movement had always characterized Bill Knapp. When events in his life were over, they were over. He did not relive the good times or wallow in the bad but moved on to something new. There was a sense of urgency and immediacy about him. He lived very much in the present with his eye on the future. What was important was the project at hand, and there was always a project at hand. He could size up a deal quickly and understood that time was the enemy: "If a deal's going to happen, you have to get in and get it done, or it blows up." And he loved putting things together. Once he started making deals for a living, Bill never considered what he did work.[9]

Over the years, he became the epitome of a "mover and shaker." He conjured and cajoled, he pushed and pulled, guiding and shaping the greater Des Moines area into a bigger and better place. He continues to do so today.

The Real Deal

The Life of Bill Knapp

Chapter One

Down on the Farm

In the fall of 1935, nine-year-old Billy Knapp eavesdropped on a disturbing conversation emanating from downstairs. His parents and representatives from Union Central Life Insurance Company were seated around the family's kitchen table discussing an all too common problem in rural America: the Knapps had fallen behind on their mortgage payments, and the insurance company was threatening foreclosure. Ultimately, the situation was resolved; the family secured a loan from the Federal Land Bank of Omaha, paid off Union Central Life, and avoided losing their land. This was not the first time the Knapps had struggled financially, but the overheard exchange made an impression on young Billy. He already knew that farming was tough and yielded little, but now he learned just how precarious it could be. A depression had engulfed American agriculture since the 1920s, and commodity prices tumbled at the beginning of the decade. They remained relatively flat until 1929 when, with the onset of the Great Depression, these prices fell again. In the midst of this dismal economy, farmers were always at the mercy of the weather and fluctuations in the market, so hard physical labor did not guarantee a decent living. This was certainly the situation for the Knapp family. Endless work, little control over their destiny, and going without were the harsh realities for Billy, his siblings, and his parents. "We knew what was going on," Bill Knapp later recalled. "I've never forgotten about just how tough it can be when you don't have anything."[1]

Billy did not yet know what he wanted to do with his life, but he imagined a future beyond the farm. He already understood that farming meant constant chores with little or no reward. It was a life where success was determined by forces beyond one's control, and it was not the life for him. Early on, Billy decided to flee the countryside and pursue anything that would get him off the farm and away from the control of his father. Ideally, he would find a livelihood where he could direct his own future.

Because of the difficult life on the Knapp family farm, located outside of Allerton in Wayne County about 100 miles south of Des Moines, William Clair Knapp (Billy) was actually born in Detroit, Michigan. The Knapps had been in Iowa since the 1850s and had first purchased land in Wayne County in the 1870s, but the 200-acre farm Billy would come to know as the home place was a combination of two parcels acquired by his grandfather, William Knapp (Will) in 1892 and 1906. By the time Billy's father, William Newton Knapp, Jr. (Bill), graduated from Allerton High School in 1918, it was clear the farm could not support the entire family.[2]

Bill left the farm and worked a variety of jobs until 1920, when he took a position at the Chicago, Rock Island & Pacific Railway roundhouse in Trenton, Missouri, which was the firm's major repair facility for locomotives operating out of the Kansas City area. Soon though, Bill started looking for a better job. Several years earlier in 1914, automobile magnate Henry Ford had shaken up the business world by announcing the $5-a-day wage plan while reducing the workday from nine hours to eight. This more than doubled the maximum wage on the Ford factory floor, and thousands of workers sought jobs there. The plan succeeded in building a more reliable workforce. However, after five years, its attractiveness began to wane, so Ford upped the ante and created the $6-a-day wage. This caught Bill Knapp's eye, and in 1921, he headed for Detroit where he landed a job at Ford's Highland Park plant. Here he worked on the assembly line and in the tool crib, checking out equipment to machinists and mechanics.[3]

In December 1923, Clarence Colson, a foreman at the Ford factory, invited Bill Knapp home for Christmas dinner. Colson and his wife Marie-Louise had been hosting her sister, Anna, who was visiting from France, and the two had matchmaking in mind.

Anna Nissle Billen had been born in Strasbourg, France, in 1903. She was the third of six children born to a French father and a German mother, who ran a small café. At some point in Anna's childhood, the family lost the restaurant because of her father's gambling debts. They subsequently moved to Paris. The family struggled during World War I, and twelve-year-old Anna was forced to start working for a company that made maps for the French military. She continued to work at a number of jobs and sometime after the war she moved to Belgium to live with her sister Marie-Louise. Here eighteen-year-old Anna met Belgian Alphonse Billen at a dance, and after a brief courtship, the two married. Anna knew that her husband had served in the war but did not know of his exposure to mustard gas, which had damaged his lungs. A persistent cough grew worse, and Alphonse was eventually hospitalized. He understood he was dying and worried about his young bride's future, especially because his mother ran a brothel, and he did not want Anna to fall into a life of prostitution.[4]

To protect his wife, Alphonse contacted Marie-Louise, who by this time had married a former American soldier and was living in Detroit, asking her to invite Anna to come for an extended visit. Marie-Louise agreed and sent her sister money for passage. Anna arrived in Detroit in October 1923, thrilled to see her sister and a new country. Three weeks later, everything changed; Anna learned that her husband had died, and the twenty-year-old was now a widow with an unclear future.[5]

This was the young woman that Bill Knapp met when he went to the Colsons' house for Christmas dinner. The two were clearly opposites: Bill was stern, serious, and opinionated, while Anna was fun loving, engaging, and outgoing. Still, they were immediately attracted to each other, and although Anna spoke very little English, they began dating in early January. This continued into the spring, and after Anna's six month visa expired, Bill asked Marie-Louise for her sister's hand in marriage. Marie-Louise was delighted as this would allow her sister to remain in the United States. The wedding took place in May 1924, and the newlyweds settled into a basement apartment. They soon bought a small house next door to Marie-Louise and Clarence located just a couple of miles away from Ford's Highland Park factory, where the men continued working.[6]

In this Detroit house on Adeline Street on July 18, 1926, Billy Knapp was born. He was an energetic and happy child until that first winter when he developed a painful, red rash on his cheeks. His alarmed parents took him to a doctor who diagnosed the illness as erysipelas, a bacterial skin infection that would require the baby to be quarantined; but a second doctor believed Billy merely suffered from frostbite. Whatever the problem, it cleared up before Bill and Anna took any drastic action, and that spring, the nine-month-old was walking. By that time, Anna was pregnant again, and in December 1927, she gave birth to Paul Roger. She and husband Bill expected to raise their two boys in Detroit.[7]

But problems on the Knapp family farm in Iowa soon uprooted the young couple and their two children. Bill's parents, Will and Minnie, had struggled financially for years. Will was somewhat of a rogue who, without warning, would desert the family for long stretches of time, leaving Minnie and the children to manage as best they could. When in town, he often hatched schemes that sometimes put the family farm at risk. This instability was likely one of the reasons Bill had left the home place—he would be one less person for the farm to support, and when he landed a paying job, he could send money back to his family to help financially. Bill did just that, and while he was at the Ford factory, he regularly sent his mother $5 per week.[8]

Troubles for the Knapps began years earlier when World War I seemed to usher in opportunity for Will and thousands of other Iowa farmers. Agricultural prices soared, the federal government provided subsidies to encourage production, and farm incomes rose. Many farmers borrowed money to expand their operations or buy more equipment. Will took out an $11,000 mortgage on the farm and paid off two previous mortgages. From that point on, Will took out several additional mortgages on the farm, gambling that the strong agricultural market would continue. It did not. As Europe recovered from the war, American agricultural exports to the continent declined. This decline combined with the ending of federal price supports caused commodity prices to tumble in 1920. They remained flat throughout the decade. This put farmers in a difficult bind; while their income fell, their mortgage payments and interest rates remained stable, and prices for other goods rose. Their debts mounted, their standard of living declined, and a growing number faced foreclosure and bankruptcy. This was exactly the situation Will and Minnie faced. They could not make their mortgage payments nor meet their tax obligations, and other bills went unpaid. Farmers National Bank, the holder of the third mortgage on the Knapp land, foreclosed on the property in 1921, but Will had already absconded, eventually turning up in Long Beach, California. Meanwhile, the family declared bankruptcy and the farm was put up for sale, with the bank as the only bidder.[9]

Minnie and the children apparently remained on the farm as renters, but then in a strange twist, Farmers National Bank closed, and the trustee in charge of the bank's property sold the land back to Will Knapp, who had temporarily returned to Allerton. The land was still subject to the first $11,000 mortgage held by Union Central Life Insurance Company, and in 1928, it came due. This posed yet another financial crisis for the Knapps and appears to be the reason Bill moved back to his family's farm.[10]

Meanwhile, Bill's older brother Floyd, who lived in Des Moines at the time, loaned his parents $1,765 to pay the interest due on their mortgage, and with this payment, the Knapps obtained a five-year extension on the mortgage. Family lore, however, suggests that Floyd's other siblings all chipped in some money to save the farm. Whatever the case, Floyd held the note on the property, and evidently the plan was for Bill and his family to move to the farm and operate it.[11]

As these financial arrangements were being worked out, Bill sent Anna and the children to Allerton, a town of nearly 800 people, while he stayed in Detroit to put the house up for sale and to earn additional money to buy cattle. Anna had always lived in cities, and rural Iowa would prove to be quite a shock. Her surprise began almost immediately. Unlike the large and crowded urban train stations she had known, Anna and the boys arrived at the small Allerton depot in the summer of 1928. Except for Minnie Knapp, her two youngest daughters Hazel and Helen, her son Floyd and his wife who came to meet them, the tiny railway station was deserted. Anna's apprehensions grew when she reached the Knapp home and discovered that like much of rural America, it had no electricity, no indoor plumbing, and mice were a frequent nuisance. Ill at ease in crude surroundings, Anna had no choice but to endure, adapt, and wait several months for her husband to arrive. She and her boys moved into one of Minnie's upstairs bedrooms and slowly became familiar with the rhythms of farm life.[12]

Bill finally left Detroit and joined his family in Allerton that fall. Within a year, Anna was pregnant again, and it was sometime in that period that Minnie and her daughters moved out of the house and into town. In the spring of 1930, Anna gave birth to her third child, Mary Louise, named after her sister. The young family appeared to be doing well, but in December 1930, the legacy of financial instability returned, when Floyd sued his parents for the funds he had loaned them two years earlier. The money had never been repaid, his father Will was gone, and back taxes were due on the farm. Floyd ended up with a judgment lien on the Knapp land but could not make the required payments. He eventually sold the certificate to buy the land to the Union Central Life, the holder of the property's first mortgage. At this point, Bill put $500 down, took out a $4,500 mortgage from the life insurance company, and reacquired the farm. But Floyd's lawsuit against their parents seemed to have angered Bill, and the events it set in motion led to a permanent break between the two brothers.[13]

Nonetheless, Bill had saved the Knapps' farm, which resembled many others in Iowa at the time. When historian Dwight Hoover wrote of his own family's Mahaska County farm of the 1920s and 1930s, he could have been describing the Knapps'. It was a "a nineteenth century operation," explained Hoover, "a capitalistic enterprise overlaid on a subsistence occupation, a family farm that provided the residents with most of their food with crops that brought needed cash in a market economy."[14] The Knapps' general purpose farm had cattle and dairy cows, hogs, sheep, chickens, horses, a garden, an orchard, and field crops. Slightly more than half of the farm's 200 acres was devoted to pasture, with 45 acres of corn and soybeans. Oats and alfalfa were grown for livestock feed. These many aspects of the farm sustained the family and yielded commodities to sell, but they also meant there was always something to be done. Every year the crop cycle started again with harrowing, followed by planting, harvesting, threshing, and plowing. Farm animals, of course, required daily attention, fences were in need of constant mending, equipment had to be fixed, and buildings needed to be repaired. Until the early 1940s, when Bill Knapp bought a Farmall tractor, horses provided the motive power for field work. Prior to the Rural Electrification Administration (REA), which funded the stringing of power lines across Wayne County in 1940, chores such as milking the cows were done by hand.[15]

Until he joined the United States Navy in 1944, this farm was the center of Billy Knapp's universe. It was dominated by the oversized personality of his strict, controlling father; and Bill's demanding, severe temperament was likely shaped by the financial instability of his formative years, which had resulted from his father's failed money-making schemes and frequent desertions. A tireless and sturdy worker, he insisted on order and was a strict disciplinarian. Anna, meanwhile, was by all accounts charming and delightful, but intimidated by her husband's dominant character and, while in his presence, routinely complied with his wishes.

With a taskmaster father and a submissive mother, Billy, Paul, and Mary Louise grew up doing chores as soon as they were able. For many young, rural Iowans, the farm proved a veritable playground for exploration and activities such as fishing, hunting, and swimming in the summer and skating or sledding in the winter. For the Knapp children, however, it was largely work. As boys, Billy and Paul had regular duties; they helped with milking the cows, feeding the chickens, and slopping the hogs. By adolescence, they were shouldering much of the adult farm responsibilities, while their sister Mary Louise worked alongside her mother, caring for the chickens, separating the cream from the milk, tending the garden, and doing the housework. "All the Knapp kids worked a lot on the farm," Irene Knapp remembered, "but their father was particularly hard on Billy and Paul. During the summer months, they would work in the fields all day and then come in and milk the cows late into the evening."[16]

There were small acts of rebellion, although Billy never confronted his controlling father directly. Instead, he acted out quietly. One of the best examples of this involved smoking. Although his father smoked, he did not want his children to do so. Billy took the rule as a challenge. As a young teen, he started taking dried leaves from the yard, rolling them in cigarette paper, and smoking them. He quickly involved Paul in the illicit practice, but the contents of the homemade cigarettes soon changed: instead of leaves, the brothers began pulling bits of cotton stuffing from their father's Model A's upholstery. The boys never got caught, and they reveled in their big secret. [17]

All three Knapp children were close to one another, but Billy and younger brother Paul developed a particularly close bond, which would last until Paul died in 2008. Separated by only seventeen months, the two were quite different. Billy was short and scrappy, a tough youngster who was brash and outgoing. Paul, who would soon be taller and larger than his brother, was reserved and cautious. Early on, the two were nearly inseparable and, whether at work or play, Billy would lead and Paul would follow. This was evident on and off the farm, at school, or in their few outside activities. Billy rode his pony to and from the White Country School, about a mile south of the family property. Two years later, Paul joined his brother for the trek on a pony of his own. At school, the boys' differences were apparent. Feisty but amiable, Billy was an indifferent student, more interested in socializing than school work, while Paul was a reticent child who liked blending into the crowd and enjoyed arithmetic. Billy's sunny personality drew others to him. Childhood friend Wayne Hornocker remembered him "as a natural leader," while Reva Dixon Crooks, who grew up on a farm south of the Knapps', noted, "He was liked by all." Sometimes, though, his boisterous disposition led to fistfights with classmates. Here his father intervened, and in an effort to channel Billy's spirit, he taught him and then Paul to box. Billy remained interested in boxing through his service in the navy during World War II.[18]

His passion for boxing is telling. Athletic but never interested in team sports, Billy found boxing satisfying because of its individualistic nature. When he stepped into the ring, he controlled his own destiny; his skill and training generally determined whether he won or lost a bout. He was responsible to no one but himself, and it was in this situation he was most comfortable. This notion of control remained important for Billy, and later when searching for a career, it became essential: Billy Knapp wanted to be his own boss.

But a job search was years down the road for the youngster. Because of his ever expanding duties at the farm, Billy did not participate in many extracurricular activities. One rare exception was Boy Scouts. A troop had been established in Allerton in 1936, founded by the town's commercial club to keep area youth out of trouble by providing constructive activities. The new local troop was given a cabin in Chautauqua Park (South Park) for meetings and activities. Billy and Paul were only in the scouts for a few months, probably in 1937 or 1938, but it was long enough for the brothers to enjoy overnight camping. During that short time, Billy even earned a merit badge.[19]

Besides scouting, Billy regularly attended church with his mother, brother, and sister. Though not at all religious, his father insisted the family go to church, evidently hoping to provide a moral grounding for his children he himself had never had. Anna, who was raised Catholic, agreed. Beginning with her years in Detroit, she had gone to a Methodist church with her sister and brother-in-law. Over the years in Allerton, the family went to the Baptist church, the Methodist church, and later the Christian church. Bill drove his family to church, but instead of attending, he went down to the town pool hall or stopped by to visit his mother Minnie. This religious background led to a family ritual, where every night the children went into Bill and Anna's room to say their prayers before heading off to bed.[20]

Life remained difficult for the Knapps. The family always had food to eat but little else. Clothes were mended until they could not be, holes in the soles of shoes were patched with pieces of cardboard, and all but necessities were done without. Regardless of constant struggles, Bill very much wanted his sons to stay on the farm. This point was conveyed daily when the boys looked at the barn and saw the large sign "Wm Knapp & Sons" adorning a wall of the building. It is unclear whether Grandfather Will or Bill originally posted the placard, but the message was clear. To encourage the boys toward this destiny, Bill gave each son a cow and told them they could keep any money derived from their animals. Billy's cow gave birth to twins, and for a time he had his own small herd. Even though he enjoyed his animals, this and other efforts by his father were not enough to be convincing. Ironically, the twice-a-day chore of milking the cows was the job he most disliked, and not yet a teenager, Billy believed he "would rather do anything than farm."[21]

His father inadvertently encouraged Billy to leave the farm by giving him a taste of life beyond it. In addition to farming, Bill was always looking for money-making deals and opportunities. In 1938, he thought he saw one. Anna's sister Marie-Louise and her husband Clarence had left Detroit for Florida several years earlier. When Clarence died of cancer, Marie-Louise proposed the Knapps leave Iowa and move in with her in Miami. With the farm economy showing little sign of improvement, Bill thought it time for something else. He took up his sister-in-law's suggestion and decided to move the family to Florida. Bill sold his livestock, equipment, and some household items at auction, but because he received no bid on the farm, he rented it out for a year.[22]

When the Knapps arrived in Miami in the summer of 1938, they set up camp at Marie-Louise's; Billy and Paul slept in a tent in her backyard, while Bill, Anna, and Mary Louise moved into the house. Shortly after arriving, Bill started looking for work but instead found a restaurant and bar available. He leased the business, and soon he and Anna were hard at work in the café. Unfortunately, the restaurant required long hours and yielded little. Disillusioned by their lack of success, Bill and Anna realized life in Florida was not necessarily any easier than it was in Iowa; but for Billy, the excursion was an adventure. It was the first trip outside of Iowa he could remember, and he relished the time in Miami away from the farm chores. He could now imagine a life apart from agriculture.[23]

After six months, though, Bill had had enough. He packed up the family and returned to Allerton. Because the farm had been rented for a year, the Knapps initially moved in with Minnie until they could return to their home. Back on the farm, life returned to the familiar; Billy went back to his chores, but he continued thinking of a future off the farm. While working in the field one day, he told a neighbor, Dirl (Slim) Richardson, "Dad thinks I'm going to farm; well, he's got another think coming."[24]

If there was one event all the Knapps enjoyed together in rural Iowa, it was the weekly ritual of going into town on Saturday night. Merchants extended their hours and a carnival atmosphere pervaded the evening. Farm families and town residents alike headed to Allerton's Central Avenue, the town's main business district, which ran several blocks south from the Rock Island railroad tracks. Here they sold produce, purchased groceries and supplies, chatted with friends, and enjoyed various forms of entertainment. Each week, the Knapps took their eggs and cream to sell at Cawthorn Produce, then the family scattered. Billy, Paul, and Mary Louise headed with their friends to the movie theater or the roller skating rink, which was located on the second floor above the theater. During the spring and summer, they might enjoy a movie outdoors when the "Airdome" theater was set up "under the trees on the town hall grounds." Anna, meanwhile, took the money from the sale of the eggs and cream and went to Robinson's Grocery or Luther's Cash Store for groceries and staples and then visited with friends. Bill usually went to the pool hall or tavern and later met up with the family at the grandstand. There people caught up on the latest local news, snacked on ice cream, roasted peanuts, or popcorn, and listened to the town band perform. Although this once-a-week institution was a year-round event, many farm families, including the Knapps, often came to town to do their shopping earlier in the day when the weather turned colder.[25]

Market day lost some of its allure for Billy in the fall of 1940, because the fourteen-year-old was in town daily when he started attending Allerton High School. His time at the four-year high school brought him into contact with more teenagers from town, led him to think about a career that would keep him off the land, and introduced him to the young woman who would later become his first wife.

Billy remained a lackluster and unmotivated student, taking the general course of classes with no real goal in mind. He still won over friends easily, but his pugnacious streak led to fistfights from time to time, and he boxed whenever he had the opportunity. Now in Allerton on a regular basis, he became more aware of the town and country divide and saw that town teens seemed better off than those from the hinterland. This started him thinking about finding a career in town where the workload was more manageable than on the farm and where a better living could be made. Sometime during high school, Billy contemplated a future as a barber. The notion is illustrative. Much of barbering involved talking with customers, something Billy clearly enjoyed and came by naturally. Moreover, a barber could develop a regular clientele, and therefore the business seemed less subject to vagaries than the farm. This would allow for a much greater control over his own destiny, something Billy saw as important.[26]

The 1944 class prophecy section of the "Allerton Eye," a column that ran in the *Corydon Times-Republican* newspaper and covered Allerton school news, provided a snapshot, albeit a romantic one, of what Billy and his classmates dreamed about their future. It reported that Billy had become a "champion boxer" living in Chicago, who was "quite popular with the women." It concluded by explaining that he was "still engaged to Irene Hill, of course, but just hasn't gotten the nerve to take the final step."[27]

This statement about Irene Hill was based on reality. Irene was the second of three daughters born to Wayne and Lola Hill, who farmed outside of Woodland, Iowa, about twenty miles west of Allerton. In 1932, her family moved to a farm near Lineville in Wayne County, a half mile north of the Missouri state line and about twelve miles south of Allerton. When it was time for their daughters to attend high school, the Hills sent them to the larger high school in Allerton, but because of the distance, the girls roomed in town during the school year. Industrious and athletic, Irene excelled in her classes and played on the school's basketball team. It was at Allerton High that she met Billy, and like her classmates, she was drawn to his bright personality. The two started dating in 1942, when she was a sophomore and he a junior.[28]

As graduation neared, the two had become serious, but it was clear that World War II would interrupt any future plans the couple had considered. Similar to many other young men at the time, Billy was itching to get into the fight. He recalled feeling "it was my duty to serve," but there were perks as well; going off to war offered adventure and time away from the farm. He was just shy of his eighteenth birthday; however, he needed his parents' written consent to enlist. Bill and Anna gave their permission. In July 1944, with the entire family, which now included Carolyn, another daughter born two years earlier, his parents took Billy to Des Moines, where the following day he and the rest of the recruits boarded a train for the U.S. Naval Training Center in San Diego.[29]

Besides instruction in military drill, seamanship, firefighting, weapons and other skills, Billy's eight weeks of basic training also offered him a chance to box, something he would continue once aboard ship. When boot camp ended, he returned to Allerton for a short leave. He arrived in early October to a surprise homecoming party at his parents' house. He then spent the next couple of days visiting with family, friends, neighbors, and Irene, before taking the train back to San Diego, where he was assigned to the Landing Craft Vehicle Personnel (LCVP) school on Coronado Island. Here he learned to pilot the LCVPs or Higgins boats, which would transport up to thirty-six marines on amphibious assaults. In December, Billy was among a number of sailors assigned to the USS Catron, an attack transport, and trucked ninety miles north up the California coast to San Pedro, where the ship was docked.[30]

Once aboard, Billy and his shipmates readied the Catron for war and took it on a shakedown cruise to San Diego. In early January 1945, the ship returned to San Pedro, where Billy received a visit from his father. Not one given to displays of affection, Bill was clearly worried about his son going to battle and made the long train trip to southern California to see him off. Most telling during his brief stay was a conversation he had with Billy's division officer, Larry Graham. As the two men parted, Bill told the young ensign, "Take care of my son Billy."[31]

The Catron left port later that day and headed for the South Pacific. Soon, the sailors settled into a routine, and, like many other servicemen had discovered, boredom proved the first enemy. Fortunately, Billy found boxing a good way to pass the time. "It was something I enjoyed and a way to avoid calisthenics," he recalled. As long as the ship was in friendly waters, one of the most popular entertainments for the crew was watching fellow sailors spar in the boxing ring. Shipmate James Penney remembered Billy as a "friendly but feisty young man" who "was a talented boxer and won more fights than he lost."[32]

Life on the Catron turned more serious, however, when the ship joined a large flotilla off the coast of Okinawa in late March. The day before the planned invasion, the Catron and other assault ships sent a number of boat crews out on reconnaissance missions. Billy volunteered, but Ensign Graham remembered Bill Knapp's words and told him he would not be going.[33]

When the attack of Okinawa began on Easter Sunday, April 1, Billy Knapp joined the fight and began taking troops ashore. Back and forth he and the other boat pilots went, landing marines and equipment on the beach. That first afternoon, they also began the grim task of bringing injured and dead marines back to the Catron. Billy recalled how heavy the dead bodies were as he lifted them into his boat. A return to the Catron, however, did not necessarily guarantee safety. While anchored off the coast of Okinawa, the ship came under Japanese attack twice, once by a Kamikaze pilot, who was shot down before he could harm the ship, and once by a submarine, which fired a torpedo that just missed the Catron's bow. For seven days and nights, the Catron's crew supported the assault, and Billy performed capably. Ensign Graham recognized his service in a letter to his parents, writing, "The Navy and our ship could stand a few more like him."[34]

After a week in battle, the Catron headed back out to sea, and for the rest of Billy's deployment, it crisscrossed the Pacific transporting U.S. troops, supplies, and Japanese prisoners of war. The intensity of the wartime experience clearly had an impact on Billy. Although he "never feared dying," he realized "that life is pretty tenuous," and he looked forward to going home. Although praised for his service, Billy reacted to the navy's military discipline the same way he responded to the strict control of his father: he occasionally resorted to covert acts of rebellion. Sometime after Okinawa, Billy persuaded a carpenter aboard the Catron to build a shipping crate, which he promptly filled with three carbine rifles, a Thompson submachine gun, and ammunition. He shipped the box home, and surprisingly, it arrived without a hitch. Paul promptly used the machine gun for rabbit hunting, which alarmed area farmers and resulted in his father confiscating the guns, covering them with grease, wrapping them in burlap, and tossing them in their pond.[35]

But the offense went undetected, and by February 1946, the Catron docked in Pearl Harbor for a final time, where it was prepared for use as a target ship for the Bikini Atoll atomic tests that summer. Meanwhile, its crew members left Hawaii based on seniority and whenever they could find a spot on a ship headed for the states. Billy arrived in San Francisco in May and made his way back to Minneapolis, where he was honorably discharged at the end of the month.[36]

Immediately after he arrived home in early June, Billy's father and sister drove down to get Irene and bring her back for the homecoming celebration. When they reached her family's farm, Irene was mowing the yard with curlers in her hair. "Don't worry about your hair," they insisted, "just grab a change of clothes and come with us." She was not told that Billy was home, but the urgency of the trip left little doubt in Irene's mind. Once reunited, the young couple picked up where they had left off in high school.[37]

That summer, Billy and friend Wayne Hornocker went to the jewelry store to buy engagement rings. Irene accepted Billy's proposal, but there were a few rough spots for the newly engaged couple. Like many other boys who went off to war, Billy came back somewhat different: he was more mature on the one hand, but wilder on the other. He was anxious to get married and get started in life, but at the same time, he had developed a "live for the moment" attitude, which led to some drinking and carousing, habits he had picked up in the navy. Irene was dismayed by this behavior, which culminated one evening with Billy driving his father's car through a plate glass window of an Allerton café. The mishap literally and figuratively sobered Billy up, and after facing an angry father and disturbed fiancée, he gradually settled down.[38]

Somewhere along the line, he had dropped the idea of becoming a barber, but he was not going back to the farm. That fall, Billy landed a job at the Allerton Co-op Dairy facility. The plant separated butterfat from whole milk and then dried the skim milk to a powdered form for use in commercial bakeries. He worked the night shift, and spent most of his time cleaning the vats and machinery. It was dull, dirty work but it kept him from returning to the farm.[39]

Then in November, Billy and Irene were married in a small family wedding at Corydon Methodist Church. After the ceremony and reception that followed, the newlyweds settled into a small upstairs apartment in Allerton. Although Billy had his job at the milk plant and Irene was a secretary at the Wayne County treasurer's office, the young couple considered relocating in Chicago after the first of the year. The idea soon passed, however, and for a time Billy and Irene stayed in the small Iowa town.[40]

Billy's life had changed dramatically since high school. He had come of age serving his country in World War II, returned home to marry his high school sweetheart, and succeeded in getting off the farm. But he was living in a little rural community just two miles north of the family's acreage with a job he immediately disliked. He had no idea what he wanted to pursue, no real prospects, and still had a hankering for something that would give him a degree of control over his life.

Chapter Two

Finding His Niche

Over the next few years, Billy searched for a satisfying career: one where he could make some money, support his family, and enjoy financial security. Of course, the job also had to keep him off the farm and ideally allow him a great deal of autonomy.

The trouble was that tens of thousands of other World War II veterans were on similar job searches, and Billy was at a disadvantage. "I was impatient and eager to get started in life, but I wasn't prepared," he remembered, "and didn't have any real skills, so most of my first jobs involved working with my hands."[1] What Billy did have was a sparkling personality, a special way of dealing with people, and a drive to succeed. These traits made him perfectly suited for sales, but he did not realize it until he stumbled upon the real estate business. It was here he would finally find his niche.

Shortly after his wedding, Billy tired of his menial job at the milk plant and quit. Just as he started looking for something else, his father stepped in; if he could not keep his son on the farm, he was determined to have him remain in Allerton. He suggested Billy and Irene open a restaurant in town. The idea seemed sound: Billy could take out a low-interest GI loan to buy the building, the couple could probably save money by living above or behind the restaurant, and although the town was quite small, the railroad made steady business for the eatery likely. With no other opportunities on the horizon, Billy followed the advice. He obtained a $4,000 GI loan and in November bought a building on the west side of Central Avenue, the town's main street. After several weeks of preparation, the Knapps opened the I & B Café (the name was derived from the first initials of Irene and Billy's names) in January of 1947, and as envisioned, Billy and Irene moved into an apartment on the building's second floor. For a while, the restaurant business appeared ideal, as Billy and Irene's different personalities complemented each other in their new venture. The outgoing Billy worked the front, schmoozing with customers, pouring coffee, and seeing that the patrons' needs were met, while the quieter, detail-oriented Irene ordered the food and supplies, ran the kitchen, and kept the books. The couple was assisted by two young women; one waited tables, and the other worked in the kitchen.[2]

Townspeople readily patronized the place and as expected, Rock Island railroad personnel proved steady customers. Several times, in fact, railroad workers pounded on the door in the morning when the café was not opened early enough to suit their needs. Business was good, and the couple was making money. There were other positives as well: Billy enjoyed the work that involved talking and dealing with people, and he was his own boss. This afforded him the opportunity to shape his own destiny, and as he put it, he was not "subject to someone else's agenda." But the restaurant, which Billy later referred to as a "greasy spoon," was opened seven days a week and required constant attention. With the exception of a few hours off every Sunday afternoon, when Billy and Irene regularly went for drives with his parents, the couple worked all the time. The demands of the business were soon too much for them, and after six months, the two were ready for something else. Billy's father unsuccessfully tried to convince them to stay, but the two leased the restaurant to Gerald and Adene Linville and took the train to Denver, Colorado, where they looked for work.[3]

Irene landed a secretarial position, but Billy could not find a job. After about a month, the discouraged couple returned to Iowa, but instead of heading home, the Knapps chose to test the job market in Des Moines. They stayed with Gerald and Ruby Kint, old friends from Allerton, who had a small one-bedroom apartment on Grand Avenue about a mile east of the state Capitol. Two weeks later, the Knapps found their own apartment just down the street from the Kints, and Billy found a job at Iowa Packing Company. In some ways, the position was a step backward. It was a return to hard, dirty, manual labor; Billy was working along the carcass "disassembly" line. It was dangerous work, and he had no independence on the job. But working at Iowa Packing paid the bills and kept Billy in Des Moines, which clearly offered greater opportunities than Allerton.[4]

He stayed at the meatpacking firm about a month until he found a better job at Wood Brothers, a farm implement manufacturing company, where he worked on the assembly line. This was certainly better work than the packing plant but not something Billy saw himself doing for very long. He was quickly learning what he did not want to do with his life, but he still had no idea of what career path to pursue. While Billy and Irene's jobs were in Des Moines, the couple's social life was still closely tied to Allerton, where they spent most of their weekends visiting friends and family.

During one of these visits, Billy and his father began talking about the Allerton sales barn, which his father and partner Clell Cravens had recently purchased. The sales barn business, which bought and sold area livestock, indulged Bill Knapp's horse trader spirit. When he learned his son was unhappy with his work at Wood Brothers, he saw another opportunity to bring him back to Allerton and offered Billy a training position at the sales barn. Here Billy could learn the business, make some money, and because it was considered on the job training, he would then be eligible for a subsistence allowance of $65 per month under the GI Bill. Although the position would bring Billy back to Allerton, it was not manual labor and he would be involved with people and sales, two aspects of the restaurant business he had really enjoyed. Billy ultimately did not need much encouragement to quit Wood Brothers, and in the spring 1948, he took the job and the couple returned to Allerton.[5]

While Billy was learning all facets of the sales barn's operations, Irene sold Avon cosmetics and handled the paperwork for the livestock sales at the barn. Billy also soon started a side business making concrete blocks in the barn with a friend, Olin Edmundson. The problem was the two only had one concrete block form, which meant they could only make two concrete blocks at once. The partners quickly realized they could not make any money this way in the block business, and they soon stopped production.[6]

Unfortunately, Billy's stint at the sales barn did not suit him either, and he was again ready to try something else. College, a path made possible for World War II veterans with the GI Bill, "never entered my mind," he recalled. "I didn't know what I wanted to do....I just wanted to start making money. I didn't see college as a way to get a skill in anything I liked to do."[7] Yet, Irene was tiring of the instability caused by Billy's job hopping and thought some type of vocational training or education might help her husband find satisfying work and settle into a career. She urged him to attend the American Institute of Business (AIB) in Des Moines and take its program of business and court reporting courses. With good opportunities proving illusive and with the GI Bill, which would pay tuition and provide a living allowance, Billy had little to lose. The couple moved back to Des Moines. In the summer of 1948, they rented a room in a house on Pleasant Street, and Billy started classes at AIB, located in a building at Tenth Street and Grand Avenue.[8]

When classes started that fall, Billy was not the only Knapp at AIB. His brother Paul, who was back in Allerton after two years in the navy, was also struggling to find a good job. He was familiar with AIB because his girlfriend, Mary Lou Dougherty, had gone there to play for the Typists, the school's nationally regarded Amateur Athletic Union (AAU) women's basketball team. When he learned that Billy planned to attend the business school, he fell back into his childhood habit of following his older brother's lead: he moved to Des Moines and enrolled in AIB as well.

Irene found a bookkeeping position at the Packard and White Garage, and she and Billy moved into their own apartment at 1422 Sixth Avenue. Paul joined them there in the tiny rental until he found a place of his own. With Paul and Mary Lou in town, Billy and Irene spent much more time in Des Moines; and the two couples frequently ate dinner at the Y Not Grill, an all-night diner just down the street on Sixth Avenue. Billy and Paul's sister Mary Louise soon found a job in Des Moines and joined her brothers in the city. Life seemed more settled until the spring of 1949, when Bob and Darlene Cook, who were now renting Billy and Irene's Allerton building and café, wanted out and did not renew their lease. The Knapps were unable to find another tenant and had no desire to go back to the restaurant business, so they listed the building for sale with W. K. Brewer, a Des Moines real estate agent. They also decided that Irene and Mary Louise would return to Allerton to run the restaurant until it was sold.[9]

Meanwhile, Billy finished his yearlong AIB certificate program, which paid off immediately when he found a bookkeeping position at Kohles and Company Heating. Clearly, this was a better job than any he had held previously, but it was dull, and Billy never liked numbers. Then one day, Brewer called to say he had a prospective buyer for the Allerton property, but he had a conflict and asked Billy if he could take the client to see the building. Billy agreed, showed the property, and negotiated the deal. He was dismayed when he had done the work but Brewer still collected the commission on the sale. This led him to consider the real estate business.[10]

Billy talked at length with Brewer, who suggested that if he wanted to get into real estate, he should visit with Ed Northrup, a fellow agent who had an office across the hall from Brewer in the downtown Home Federal Building. Billy already knew a little about the industry through his uncle Floyd, who had left the family farm and Allerton for Des Moines in the 1920s, where he built and sold homes for a living. Aware that the business had kept his uncle off the farm and intrigued by his conversation with Brewer, Billy met with Northrup. The agent immediately took a liking to the young man and offered him a job. By this time, Irene had moved back to Des Moines and found a position in the accounting department of the Iowa Farm Bureau. Irene's income gave the couple some financial stability, and Billy decided he could afford to leave Kohles to give real estate a try.[11]

If ever there was a time to get into real estate, this was it. Following World War II, the nation faced an acute housing shortage, leading to a new residential construction boom. Historian Lizabeth Cohen explained: "One of every four homes standing in the United States in 1960 went up in the 1950s." By the time the 1960s opened, "62 percent of Americans could claim they owned their own homes, in contrast to 44 percent as recently as 1940, the largest jump in home ownership ever recorded." Now settled in Des Moines, Billy was soon one of the agents ready to help people into these homes.[12]

He joined Northrup, who until late 1949 had run a one-man operation. Here Billy learned the art of selling, obtained his real estate license, and sold a few properties. He loved the business from the start and immediately realized he belonged in real estate. It was clear that here Billy had finally found his niche. "It was not drudgery, like the earlier jobs I'd held," he recalled, and "never really seemed like work." He enjoyed working with clients, reveled in the independence accorded him, and loved negotiating the deal. He also appreciated the commission system and reaping the benefits of his own work.[13]

Northrup proved much more than a mentor to Billy. He and his wife Helen befriended the Knapps and frequently socialized with them. They also looked out for the young couple, and when Billy and Irene started house hunting in early 1950, the Northrups helped them find their first home, a small one-bedroom on Thirtieth Street. Also, because the Knapps had only a bedroom set, the Northrups provided odds and ends of furniture to outfit the rest of the house.[14]

Although Billy had sold a few homes, he realized greater success was possible if he was part of the multiple listing service (MLS), which allowed brokers access to one another's property listings. Northrup had not subscribed to the MLS, and Billy correctly believed this limited his sales. Thus, after about eight months, he began looking for another real estate job with MLS privileges. In the midst of his search, he was approached by Bill and Karl McCollough, two brothers who worked for Hollis & Company Real Estate. They invited him to join them at the Hollis firm, which was part of the multiple listing exchange. Billy readily accepted the offer.[15]

Located in the AIB Building at Tenth and Grand, Hollis & Company was a huge improvement over Northrup Real Estate. Besides access to the MLS, Billy benefitted from the camaraderie and advice of the several other agents who also worked at Hollis. In addition to owner Byron Hollis and the McCollough brothers, the other salesmen at the company included Harry Huddleson, John Luin, and Bob McCaughtry. Many in the industry were a bit older than Billy, and some resented the twenty-four-year-old. "At the time," he noted, "it was mostly older people in the business. Usually when you retired from your job, you went into real estate." Many of the Des Moines area agents were in their fifties or sixties, and some thought of young Knapp as a "flash in the pan." Billy clearly remembered, "There was a lot of animosity—everyone was shooting for you." His father, in fact, had tried to dissuade him from real estate because it was not a business for young men. Already driven to succeed and attain financial security, Billy now had to prove himself to his colleagues and his father. These challenges reinforced his competitive spirit and pushed him to work harder than others.[16]

This drive was important, but Billy's charm was too, and as always, he had a way of endearing himself to people. His new boss Hollis was no exception. Much like the Northrups, Hollis and his wife Betty became friendly with the Knapps outside of the office. The couples enjoyed each other's company and frequently dined together. In fact, it was Betty Hollis who hosted a baby shower for Irene in the late summer of 1950.[17] This blending of work and pleasure remained a lifelong pattern for Billy; business associates and friends were generally one and the same, and he rarely stopped thinking about the job.

Byron Hollis immediately realized what he had in Billy Knapp: "He was the most outstanding recruit ever to come into the Des Moines real estate street. He had rapport with prospects. He had the touch, the ability to get the confidence of investors...and keep them happy." One particular sale in 1951 suggested Billy's special touch. After selling a young couple their first home, Billy stopped by to check on them during move-in day. This was not something agents ordinarily did. While he was there, new furniture the couple had ordered arrived, but it had been disassembled for delivery. Billy retrieved pliers and a screwdriver from his car and helped reassemble the furniture.[18]

Interest in his customers, extra effort, and long hours soon made Billy the firm's top salesman. Hollis recalled that the young agent was sometimes selling three houses a day, which translated into an annual salary of $15,000 to $16,000 per year. If accurate, Billy's annual income was nearly four times that of the national household average, a sizeable salary for what had just become a young family. On September 21, 1950, Irene gave birth to Virginia (Ginny) Irene. A month before Ginny was born, Irene left her job at Iowa Farm Bureau and, like most married women of the era, stayed at home to raise her daughter.[19]

Another reason Billy's real estate star continued to rise was his growing knowledge of the area real estate. Whenever he had the opportunity, he drove around Des Moines and central Iowa, acquainting himself with the regional housing market. Through such tours, Billy developed a keen eye for trends in the business: he could spot areas that were in decline, areas that were up and coming, and directions the city seemed to be moving. This ability would prove invaluable down the road when Billy went into the land development business; but for now, a familiarity with the houses on the market gave him an edge with clients.[20]

Billy was also making important connections while at Hollis. Maybe the most significant was John R. Grubb, a young and, at this point, small-time Des Moines homebuilder, who used the Hollis firm to sell some of his homes. Much like Billy, Grubb had grown up poor, served in World War II, and tried a number of jobs before he came upon his career—home-building—by accident. The two men became fast friends and before long began socializing together with their wives. Over the next few years, this relationship would result in several very important and profitable business deals.[21]

But for the moment, Billy was content to sell homes, a lot of them. It was becoming clear he was no flash in the pan, and others tried recruiting him to their firms. Hollis even suggested that Billy start a branch office. But the young broker did not bite; he was happy selling for Hollis and not interested in management, although he did begin recruiting others to work for Hollis. One of his earliest hires was Paul Manley, a young man who had also attended AIB. Billy convinced him that there was greater potential in real estate sales, and Manley joined the firm in 1951. Late that year, however, Byron Hollis began coming up short when it came time to pay the commissions he owed his top agents. Never a good money manag-er, Hollis's debts mounted until mid-1952, when the amount he owed Billy in back commissions rose to nearly $8,000. The young agent wanted the money; Hollis could not pay it, and the two began negotiating. By August, they reached an agreement: in lieu of payment, Hollis turned over the real estate firm to Billy. Hollis bowed out, but the rest of the agents stayed with their new twenty-six-year-old boss.[22]

To kick-start the new company, Billy went after some new recruits. Because he resented the dismissive attitude of some of the older agents in town, he sought out other young men like Paul Manley. One such figure was Les Calvert, who had recently started working for a Des Moines bro-ker named Gerald Wright. Calvert was flattered by the offer but turned it down, telling Billy he "didn't plan to stay in the doggone business long." Ironically, Calvert remained active in the area real estate business for the next fifty years.[23] Then, in a seemingly curious move for someone who had always longed for independence, Billy sought help in running the firm. It actually made sense. He knew sales and wanted to continue selling homes and dealing with people, but he wanted to have someone else focus on the details of the operation. He offered a partnership to Billy McKain. McKain had worked for Bill and Karl McCollough—who had left Hollis to start their own real estate firm, McCollough Investment Company—before recently joining Hollis in July. He liked the idea of the partnership and readily accepted the offer.[24] Like most other real estate companies in Des Moines, the new operation was named after its proprietors, thus Knapp McKain. But the name was short lived. Billy had remembered what E. O. Fenton, the president of AIB, had said about company monikers. It was better to have a corporate entity named after something as opposed to someone because individual owners or partners might leave the business or die and that would open the door to a name change, which might hurt business. After a week, he renamed the venture Iowa Realty.[25]

Naming the company Iowa Realty proved fortuitous for a little more than a year later, it became obvious that the two owners were not getting along. Each believed he knew what was better for the firm, and there were growing clashes between the two headstrong partners. At the same time, McKain was having some misgivings about the real estate sector in general and believed a downturn in the market was likely. Eventually McKain wanted out, and Billy was more than happy to oblige. He bought back McKain's interest in the business, and Iowa Realty continued without a hitch.[26]

Now in complete control of his company, the brash, forceful owner told Paul Manley, one of his young salesman, that he "wanted to make Iowa Realty the biggest [real estate company] in the city."[27] Billy had taken the Des Moines real estate market by storm but he was just getting started.

Bill's parents, Bill and Anna Knapp
on their wedding day, 31 May 1924.
Courtesy of Bill Knapp.

The Knapp brothers on horseback, Bill (right) on Diamond, and Paul on Sparkle, ca.
1935. Courtesy of Bill Knapp.

Knapp family farm in Allerton, Iowa. Courtesy of Nancy Jones.

Paul on tractor, Bill on planter at Knapp farm, Allerton, Iowa, ca. 1943. Courtesy of Irene Knapp.

Knapp family photo, 1944. Standing from left to right are Bill and his siblings Paul and Mary Louise. Seated from left to right are Bill's father Bill, baby sister Carolyn, and his mother Anna. Courtesy of Nancy Jones.

With shipmates aboard the USS Catron, 1945. Bill is fourth from the right. Courtesy of Bill Knapp.

Bill (left) boxing on the USS Catron, 1945. Courtesy of Bill Knapp.

Bill and Irene Knapp with two employees in front of their restaurant, the I&B Café, Allerton, Iowa, 1947. Courtesy of Irene Knapp.

Bill as a young real estate agent in front of Hollis & Company, his employer, ca. 1949. Courtesy of Irene Knapp.

Bill and his team at Iowa Realty, ca. 1955. Standing from left to right: Stu Berkey, Bill Knapp, Bob McCaughtry, Bob Deitz, and D. D. Whisler. Seated from left to right: Ernie Roush, Kirk Fowler, Kenny Grandquist, Harold Knapp, Herman Miller, and Paul Manley. Courtesy of Irene Knapp.

Iowa Realty sign in front of the office at 3617 Beaver, ca. 1962. Courtesy of Irene Knapp.

Bill with his children, Ginny and Roger, 1961. Courtesy of Cindy Grandquist.

Bill and tennis buddies. Note Paul Knapp (second from left), Roger Cleven (fifth from left), Kenny Grandquist (second from right), and Bill Knapp (third from right), 1963. Courtesy of Irene Knapp.

Advertisement for John Grubb Homes, from Iowa Realty Buyers Guide, ca. 1962.
Courtesy of Iowa Realty.

Iowa Realty office building after second fire, 1967. Courtesy of Cindy Grandquist.

Governor Harold Hughes and Bill Knapp visit with President Lyndon Johnson in the White House, 1967. Courtesy of Bill Knapp.

The Hotel Savery when Bill purchased it in 1977. Photo by Chuck Anderson. Copyright 1977, The Des Moines Register and Tribune Company. Reprinted with permission.

Roger Knapp in tournament in Germany, 1978. Courtesy of Bill Knapp.

Bill with tennis pro Pancho Segura, 1981. Courtesy of Susan Knapp.

Iowa Realty billboard using well-known image of Iowa Realty yard sign, ca. 1980. Courtesy of Bill Knapp.

Chapter Three

Becoming Bill Knapp

Ever since Billy Knapp returned to Des Moines in 1949, he was on the move. Insecure about his foothold in the city and nagged by a constant fear of backsliding to the unpredictable, hard life of farming, he worked long hours at breakneck speed selling homes and commercial properties. Once, Paul Knapp recalled, Billy got a client out of bed at 1:30 a.m. to finalize a deal. But being a top salesman was not enough. His ambition was great, and the pugnacious owner of Iowa Realty was determined to make his small company the largest in the city. If persistence and hard work were essential to Billy's success, a growing economy, good hires, good timing, and vision were the others.[1]

Billy had the fortune of entering the business during the post–World War II boom and a rapidly expanding marketplace. While most others merely rode the wave of good times, Billy's impatience regularly led to action, often propelling him in directions which made Iowa Realty distinctive. These included concentrating on new home sales—a niche where few other Realtors focused—obtaining special financing to ease the sales process, and revamping its classified advertising, which set Iowa Realty apart from the competition. There were setbacks of course, but Billy recruited talented people and gave them wide rein in their jobs. This hands-off approach worked well, the company grew quickly, and Billy could look beyond day-to-day operations for new opportunities.

And look he did. In the early 1950s, Billy identified prospects others did not and took action. While most real estate agents waited for business to come to them, Billy persistently went after new business. It was during this period that he honed his bargaining skills and became adept at making deals, putting together arrangements with builders and bankers to bolster Iowa Realty sales. Agreements, arrangements, and compacts continued for the next several years, and by decade's end, Billy signed a deal taking him into land acquisition and development, a new direction which would set the tone for the rest of his career. But it was the art of the deal, seeing it, negotiating it, and closing it, that would define the man for the rest of his life. Billy Knapp, the young, upstart Realtor, transformed himself into Bill Knapp, the successful wheeling and dealing businessman.

For a little over a year, Bill and his partner McKain put up with each other, and because both were good salesmen, the company grew. By December 1952, Iowa Realty had more business than it could handle, and Bill recruited more agents by hiring people he knew. First, he added family members, Harold Knapp and Herman Miller. Knapp was a cousin, a son of Floyd Knapp who knew the real estate and construction business through stints with his father's operation. Miller was a son-in-law of Floyd who also had experience in construction. Knapp was a good salesman but from the start, Miller was exceptional. After selling a home at his first open house, he soon became one of the firm's most productive agents.[2]

Bill's most important hire, though, was Kenny Grandquist. When Bill first met him in 1949, Grandquist owned and operated a gas station at the corner of Thirtieth Street and Hickman Road. Bill had called the station about getting his stalled car started. Grandquist complied, but always the salesman, he asked Bill if the car ever needed gas. From then on, Bill bought all his gas at Grandquist's Phillips 66 service station. As the two became friendly, Bill recognized Grandquist's natural sales ability and began pressing the station owner to join Iowa Realty. Grandquist finally took the offer, got his real estate license, and began working for Bill in July 1953. "From then on," Grandquist recalled, "things started going well. I was selling like hell." Garrulous and well liked, Grandquist quickly became the firm's top salesman and would soon prove to be essential to Iowa Realty's growth and success.[3]

Bill now had a solid team of nine aggressive agents. As the size of his operation grew, he sold fewer and fewer homes himself but provided support and encouragement for his agents. "Bill was a pusher," remembered Realtor Les Calvert, and he expected results from his salesmen. Those who sold homes were treated well at Iowa Realty. Because of the bad experience he had had with Hollis, Bill paid his agents' commissions immediately after deals closed, and he offered incentives to promote sales. If agents met monthly company goals, Bill took them and their wives for steak dinners in downtown Des Moines. Once after a particularly good year in the mid-1950s, he treated his salesmen and their wives to a weekend trip to Chicago. Those who failed to produce, however, did not remain with the company long.[4]

Occasionally, Bill's driving attitude seemed counterproductive. At the time, the Des Moines area real estate board held a luncheon every Thursday in downtown Des Moines. The popular weekly gathering generally brought together 100 to 120 brokers and agents and provided a good place for real estate people to become acquainted and build relationships. But Bill only saw the immediate bottom line. Because agents were not buying or selling anything at the lunch, he considered it a waste of time. He preferred his salesmen to be out drumming up business and discouraged them from attending the weekly event. Even though the real estate business was competitive, cooperation among agents was important for property transactions to proceed smoothly, and such collaboration was usually better between agents who knew one other. Bill's position on the lunch probably hurt his business, but one would not know it. By the summer of 1954, the company advertised it had sold a home a day, claiming this was a sales record, "NEVER EQUALLED in Des Moines."[5]

Overseeing people, however, was not Bill's forte, and as soon as Grandquist's skill in dealing with the other salesmen became apparent, he assumed the informal role of the company's sales manager. Fun loving and genial, Grandquist got along well with the other men in the office and developed a real bond with them. In fact, he and the other agents frequently played poker on Friday nights. Bill, however, rarely participated. He was, in the words of former agent Roger Cleven, "totally committed to business," and in these early years, he rarely took time to socialize. When he did, gambling was not something he enjoyed. Although he had played a little poker aboard ship during World War II, it was just to pass the time.

Bill hated the idea of losing money to chance. It was too difficult to come by, and early on, any extra cash he earned went back into Iowa Realty.[6]

This focus on business was what defined Bill during the 1950s. A bundle of energy, Bill moved with celerity, and he could not stand idleness. He regularly worked late into the night filling up his appointment book to avoid wasted time the following day. According to longtime Des Moines Realtor Lew Clarkson, "Bill was always busy. He often used to walk by our office with an abstract in his hand. Nobody sold that many homes, but he always looked busy. And if he wasn't, he'd take the abstract down to the savings and loan and make contacts." Actually, this was how Bill spent a lot of his time: meeting people and making connections, promoting Iowa Realty, and learning the minutiae of the market.[7]

His activity and go-getter attitude was noticed by others as well. One morning in the early 1950s, builder Wayne Warren and grandson Robert Underwood were meeting with William Cotton, vice president at State Federal Savings and Loan, about a loan. In the midst of their conversation, Bill Knapp strolled through the building and waved at Cotton. The banker returned the gesture and then told Warren and Underwood, "Keep an eye on Bill Knapp; that young man is going places."[8]

Meanwhile, company growth required that Bill consider new office space. At the time, most major Des Moines area real estate firms were located downtown on Grand Avenue, from Fourth Street to the east to Tenth Street, where Iowa Realty was situated. As Bill began looking for a new location, Olaf Grandquist, a builder and Kenny Grandquist's father, was in the process of completing an office building north and west of downtown on Beaver Avenue. The new structure offered several advantages over the downtown AIB Building including ample parking, space, which could be configured especially for his business, room for additional growth, and most importantly, location in a rapidly expanding residential area near customers. Of course, there was also the Kenny Grandquist connection, and at the end of August 1953, Bill leased the building and moved Iowa Realty into its new Beaver Avenue office.[9]

The move occurred amidst the post–World War II economic expansion and with the mass exodus from central downtowns taking place across the country. As historian Jon Teaford explained, "Both commerce and population migrated outward from the urban core, escaping from the anachronistic downtown and the decaying neighborhoods."[10] This coincided with high marriage and birth rates following the war, which resulted in the baby boom. A large number of these young families sought housing, fueling a demand for homes on the peripheries of these cities. Unfortunately because of the Great Depression and then the war, few homes had been built over the past fifteen years and by 1947, there was a serious housing shortage, with more than six million American families living with relatives. In Des Moines, more 900 families found temporary shelter at Fort Des Moines, while in other areas, some found housing possibilities in reconfiguring existing structures. In Omaha, for instance, an advertisement offered: "Big Ice Box, 7 × 17 feet, could be fixed up to live in," while in North Dakota, grain bins were converted into apartments.[11]

The federal government addressed the problem in two ways. It began by pouring billions of dollars into the Federal Housing Administration (FHA), a New Deal agency established in 1934, which insured low-interest, long-term private mortgage loans. Bankers who participated had their loans guaranteed by the FHA in case of default, and because of the more generous terms, a whole new market of home buyers was opened. Up to that point, mortgage loans were generally given for as much as 50 percent of the appraised value of the home, interest rates were usually between 5 and 9 percent, and the repayment period was three to five years. Loans backed by the FHA, on the other hand, could be written for as much as 80 percent of a home's value, interest rates were 5 to 6 percent, and the repayment period was stretched to twenty years. This lowered monthly payments significantly and made the purchase of a home possible for people of more modest means.[12]

Then in 1944, as part of the GI Bill of Rights, the government created the generous Veterans Administration (VA) mortgage guarantee program. Run by the FHA, the program allowed veterans to borrow the entire appraised value of the home with little or no down payment. Low interest rates and a long repayment period were included as well. Together, FHA and VA loan programs underwrote 31 percent of all first mortgages nationally in 1950. By 1960, the figure had risen to 42 percent.[13]

These federal mortgage guarantees also took much of the risk out of homebuilding and touched off a building boom. Single-family housing starts soared from 114,000 in 1944 to 1,183,000 in 1948 and to 1,692,000 by 1950. Rapid construction of homes continued throughout the decade, cooling a bit by 1960, when 1,252,000 homes were started. Des Moines mirrored national trends, where housing starts jumped from a mere 15 in 1944 to 938 in 1948 and to 1,842 by 1950. Ten years later the figure stood at 988. This expansion in new homes coincided with a 17 percent increase in the city's population, rising from 178,000 to 209,000. Suburban growth was even more rapid: Ankeny and West Des Moines more than doubled over the course of the decade, while Urbandale and Windsor Heights increased by more than three times.[14]

Like many in the industry, Bill Knapp had taken advantage of this favorable real estate market, sold a number of homes, and done well. But it was also here in the mid-1950s that he began separating himself from the pack by taking his company in novel directions. Initially, this meant a move into selling new construction and making arrangements to ensure that customers would receive financing. Late in the decade, Bill took initial steps into land acquisition and development. Several factors pushed him into these areas. His status as a veteran made him keenly aware of other young veterans' wants and needs in housing. Connections and frequent conversations with Realtors, builders, and developers provided him a sense of where the market was heading, and Bill's impatience moved him to action. For Realtor Lew Clarkson, Bill's ability to read the market and act accordingly was his special aptitude. "He had the gift and the guts," Clarkson recalled, "That's what made Bill Knapp."[15]

While Bill understood that selling existing homes would remain important for business, he believed the continuing housing shortage meant a particularly strong market for new homes. This led to sweeping changes in the industry. Prior to 1945, most contractors across the country built up to five homes a year; usually, they built a home, sold it, moved on to erect another, and repeated the process. For instance, shortly after World War II, a Des Moines builder John Grubb, borrowed money, built two homes, sold them, and with the profits bought a lot and built a third home. But because of the hot market for new homes, contractors expanded their operations, and at the end of the 1950s, the median single-family home-builder was constructing twenty-two houses a year. At the same time, subdivisions were becoming much more prevalent and by mid-decade, three of every four new homes were erected in such developments.[16]

Bill tapped into this new home market by convincing builders that he and Iowa Realty had the sales expertise and experience to move their homes quickly. Not surprisingly, the first two contractors he signed on were Olaf Grandquist and John Grubb, a young builder he had become acquainted with while working for Byron Hollis. In 1954, Iowa Realty's sales force acted as the exclusive agent for Grandquist's new construction in the Harding Heights subdivision and Grubb's homes in the Windsor Manor development, both of which were located north and west of downtown Des Moines.[17]

Occasionally, builders came to Bill. Such was the case with Bob Canine, who approached Bill about listing his new homes with Iowa Realty after Chamberlain, Kirk & Cline, which generally focused on homes in the elite "South of Grand" district, turned him down. Usually though, it was Bill who went after new builders. He was just as likely to reel one in at the office or at an after-hours haunt, such as the Zodiac Club in the basement of the Commodore Hotel at Thirty-fifth Street and Grand Avenue. The lounge was a favorite gathering spot for those in the real estate industry. Bill and his agents frequented the place so regularly, in fact, that the menu featured an item called the Iowa Realty sandwich. It was here at the Zodiac that Bill often schmoozed, persistently selling himself and his firm. The aggressive sales pitch worked, and by the end of 1957, Iowa Realty was representing twenty-three of the city's leading homebuilders. In addition to Grandquist and Grubb, the list included Lloyd Clarke, Charles Colby, Jr., W. Reed Davisson, Robert Erikson, James Izzolena, William Miksich, and Robert Underwood. Again, this blending of business and leisure would become a trademark of his, as Bill was always looking for opportunities and ready to cut deals.[18]

Sometimes, amid these evenings of drinking and bragging, Bill's belligerent personality rubbed people the wrong way. This proved the case one evening in 1957. Jim Cedarstrom, an agent who worked for the smaller Lew Clarkson Realty, was angered by something that Bill had said and called him outside to fight. Not eager to take on the much bigger man— Cedarstrom had played basketball for Northwestern University—Bill declined, but Cedarstrom egged him on, shoving him until he agreed. Once outside, Bill's boxing skills kicked in. With the first punch he downed Cedarstrom, who broke his wrist when he hit the ground. The blow left Bill's hand swollen for days, but the brawl only added to his reputation as a tough, aggressive man on the move.[19]

And moving he was. In addition to signing on new builders, Bill made purchasing a home as easy as possible. The FHA and VA mortgage programs had opened the doors for many more prospective buyers, but sometimes local lenders did not have the funds available for such financing. To avoid this situation and ensure his customers had access to these loans, Bill approached several area lenders. "He spent a lot of time with bankers," former Iowa Realty agent Roger Cleven remembered, but it was clearly time well spent. Bill persuaded them that Iowa Realty had a strong track record of selling homes and could sell even more if financing was readily available. Several bankers, including Elmer Miller of Des Moines Savings and Loan and James Camp and Joe Strasser of United Federal Savings, agreed to help. Each institution set aside funds specifically for use by Iowa Realty home buyers intent on taking out FHA or VA loans. In return, Iowa Realty paid the bankers a fee whether or not the funds were used. Iowa Realty now could advertise, "Ample financing is also available," and this gave the growing company another powerful tool to attract customers. Bill remembered, "We pioneered in that area [ensuring availability of funds for government-backed loans]. At the time, it was quite a deal to get the lenders' confidence. I tried to be very persuasive—that I could develop what I said I could, and do what I said I could do....In those early years it meant a lot. It wasn't easy to make loans at that time."[20]

Bill also broke new ground in marketing. When he acquired what became Iowa Realty, real estate companies in Des Moines did most of their advertising in the classified sections of the morning *Des Moines Register* and/or its sister publication, the evening *Des Moines Tribune.* Traditionally, these firms ran larger advertisements in the Sunday issue of the *Register* because open houses were held that afternoon, but even here, the classified ads were essentially unadorned, text-only announcements of available homes on the market. Such classifieds were grouped by listing company, had brief descriptions of the properties for sale, and included contact information of agents showing the homes. Then in mid-March 1953, Jester & Sons Real Estate set its classified apart by including several photos of homes it had for sale and surrounding the advertisement with a black border. Bill immediately followed suit and the next Sunday, Iowa Realty's listings were distinct from all the others with a double column design surrounded by a border. Jester went back to its standard format of classified listings, but from late March on, Iowa Realty's Sunday listings were always distinguished by the border and stood out from the competition.[21]

By 1955 other Realtors used borders around their classified advertising, but by that time, Bill had gone a step further. In September 1954, he differentiated Iowa Realty from the others with a large, visually appealing ad in the *Sunday Register*'s classified section. Rather than merely stating the facts about properties the company had available, the ad highlighted the Iowa Realty name in a bold, large font and offered persuasive text about why people should use the company's services. This was followed by photographs of all its agents, a list of the new builders Iowa Realty represented, and then descriptions of some of the homes it had for sale. From this point on, Iowa Realty often ran similar large, attractive ads in the *Sunday Register*'s classified section. Over the next few years, these were sometimes supplemented with more targeted advertisements focused on new construction or homes in a particular subdivision.[22]

All was going well for Bill and Iowa Realty, but then came a couple of bumps in the road. Kenny Grandquist, who had been acting more or less as the sales manager, was finally named to the position in mid-1956. However, Bob McCaughtry, an agent who had been with the company longer than Grandquist, thought the position should have gone to him. In the meantime, top salesmen Herman Miller, Harold Knapp, and Paul Manley began considering leaving Iowa Realty because they wanted more independence. Together with McCaughtry, the three agents decided to go out on their own; but, because that would require a six-month waiting period before they could be part of the important multiple listing service (MLS), they chose to buy into an existing firm, which meant their access to the MLS continued uninterrupted. Ironically, they became partners with Kenny Bunsness and his Central Realty firm, which was just down the street on Beaver Avenue.[23]

Bill was initially angered. He hated to see some of his top salesmen leave, which accounted for about a third of his agents, but he moved quickly to rebuild the firm. Two of the most important hires were again family members. First was Clair Niday, a brother-in-law. Bill recruited him while Niday and his wife Doris, a sister of Irene's, were visiting the Knapps at Clear Lake, about 100 miles straight north of Des Moines. Niday had considered leaving his farm, and Bill sold him on the advantages of joining Iowa Realty. Niday eventually agreed and started with the company three months later in November 1956. Bill's eye for talent was on the mark again, and Niday soon became a top producer who went on to win the company's salesman of the year award a number of times.[24]

A month later, Bill's brother Paul joined the firm. He had earned his real estate license in 1950 and sold houses part time before landing a sales job at farm implement maker Massey Harris (a merger led to the name being changed to Massey Ferguson in 1958) in Des Moines. In 1951, Paul's career was interrupted when he was recalled by the navy to serve during the Korean War. Once he returned in 1953, Paul occasionally sold homes for Iowa Realty and resumed work at Massey Harris, eventually becoming a zone sales manager. But when he was transferred to the Oskaloosa office, Paul started looking for jobs that would bring him back to Des Moines. When Grandquist learned this, he suggested Iowa Realty hire Paul. Bill liked the idea. He and his brother had always been close, and Bill believed he and Paul could work well together. The belief proved correct. If Bill's hiring of Grandquist was the most important of his career, bringing in his brother Paul was a very close second.[25]

Paul's years of experience in sales made an immediate impact; he helped fill the void left by the four agents who had recently departed. Grandquist recalled, "Paul was a real crack salesman, and concentrated especially on some of the higher-priced houses. He got a lot of the top guys at Massey Ferguson who had a lot of money to buy from him." Paul remained a leading salesman for the next sixteen years before becoming even more important to Bill as the company's general sales manager.[26]

Shortly after hiring Paul in 1956, Bill faced another setback. Bookkeeper Jo Ann Burman had been embezzling funds from the company, but the theft was not known until early 1957, when a small localized fire in the Iowa Realty building destroyed much of her desk and work area. Fortunately, the rest of the office was undamaged, and business continued in a near normal fashion. Burman had set the fire in advance of the upcoming year-end audit hoping the flames would cover up her crime. Instead, the fire aroused suspicion. Robert Timmins, the McGladrey, Hansen, Dunn & Company accountant, who had done Iowa Realty accounting work since 1953, sifted through remaining records and discovered evidence of embezzlement. With proof in hand, Bill confronted Burman, who confessed to stealing and starting the blaze. She was fired, but Bill chose not to press charges because he thought the publicity might be bad for business. In addition, her parents had come forward, apologized for their daughter's actions, and agreed to pay restitution.[27]

In the wake of the theft and fire, Bill tightened controls over company finances by having his wife Irene, who had previous experience as a bookkeeper, take over Burman's duties. Other than that, the affair proved little more than an annoyance to Iowa Realty's continuing expansion. At a time when a Des Moines real estate firm of six or seven agents was a sizeable operation, Iowa Realty more than doubled its sales force from eight in 1954 to twenty-one in 1957. Over the same period, annual property sales jumped from an estimated 360 homes worth $4.5 million to 511 homes valued at $7.85 million. It was now apparent, though, that Bill had established a distinct division of labor: Grandquist was in charge of the sales side of the company, while Bill developed new business.[28]

One of the first changes Grandquist instituted was a weekly sales meeting. When the company was small, irregular ad hoc meetings and casual conversations were adequate for disseminating necessary information, but as the firm grew, a formal means of communicating with the sales force became essential. Here Grandquist shined, for he could be a mentor, cheerleader, and communicator. An outstanding salesman and great deal closer, Grandquist used the meetings to pass along sales tips, encourage and cajole the sales force to move homes, keep staff informed of company policy and direction, and field questions or complaints.[29]

With his core business running smoothly, Bill searched for new opportunities. One move was a natural outgrowth of the real estate business; Bill added insurance sales to Iowa Realty's services. It made sense. When the company sold houses and clients became homeowners, they needed insurance, and this offered Iowa Realty another sales opportunity. Usually it was Joe Clay, the company's closing manager, who made the insurance pitch. If home buyers were interested, Clay called Bill's wife Irene, who served as Iowa Realty's initial insurance agent. She ran the operation out of the Knapp home and handled all the paperwork. When Irene moved to the office and assumed the firm's bookkeeping duties in early 1957, Clay took over the insurance department. A number of other local Realtors, such as Chamberlain, Kirk & Cline, Darwin Lynner, and Beaverdale Realty, offered insurance as well, but Iowa Realty had a real advantage. Its ever increasing volume of home sales brought more and more people into the office and provided an ever increasing pool of potential insurance customers. Eventually, Iowa Realty added auto, fire, and business insurance to its offerings.[30]

Bill also went after more customers by opening a branch office on the south side of Des Moines. In late 1956, Des Moines Realty, a three-person operation on Southwest Ninth Street, had sold all its listings, and Jim Cooper, the company's salesman, began looking for other work. Bill had heard of the situation and thought it provided a chance for Iowa Realty to get a foothold in the south side market. With the two broker-owners, Harold Teater and Bill Kirkman, he arranged a deal, which called for Iowa Realty to take over their office lease payment and buy the firm's meager office furnishings. He then proposed that the two brokers and their agent continue working at the office, to be operated under the Iowa Realty name. Kirkman and Cooper stayed, while Teater left and started working for builder John Grubb. Kirkman soon left as well. Still, the deal proved worthwhile for Bill. He now had Jim Cooper, an experienced agent who already knew the south side Des Moines real estate market, on the Iowa Realty team, and the office was inexpensive to run. Even as other salespeople were added to the branch, they were all on straight commission, and the outpost was run without secretarial help or support staff. Anything requiring such assistance was taken over to the main office. Thus for a minimal outlay, Iowa Realty expanded its reach into another part of the city.[31]

Besides adding to the company's offerings, Bill worked with the Home Builders Association of Des Moines to encourage people to buy homes. In spring of 1957, the association held its first "School for Home Buyers" at the Des Moines Art Center. It was a two-day affair, which offered free sessions about buying or remodeling a home. Speakers ran the gamut from builders and inspectors, to real estate agents and appraisers. Interest was high, and with 150 people attending the first session, the Home Builders Association made the school an annual event. It is unclear whether Bill was involved in this first program, but because he was closely associated with many of the city's builders, it is most likely. Given his company's rapid rise in the central Iowa market, Bill understood that what was good for Des Moines real estate was good for Iowa Realty. The following year, he was on the event's planning committee with, among others, builder and good friend John Grubb. The 1958 school for home buyers was much larger than the previous year and consisted of a number of programs over four days, including new topics such as decorating, financing, home design, landscaping, and maintaining the value of a home.[32]

While the impact of the school is uncertain, 1958 was a good year for Des Moines real estate. In July, the number of home building permits in the city was up from 81 in 1957 to 118, reflecting a 47 percent increase. Iowa Realty enjoyed record sales as well; sales volume rose 40 percent over the previous year to $11 million, while the company sold more than two houses per day. Despite this achievement, Bill took little time to reap the benefits of his success and remained in the words of Realtor Roger Cleven, "one hundred percent business." If there were one perk he did enjoy, it was in obtaining the biggest, most ostentatious automobile possible. Like many Americans of the era, Bill moved up through the General Motors brands as he became more successful. In 1949, he drove a used 1940 Chevrolet, an entry-level automobile. When his company began to take off in the early 1950s, Bill upgraded to an Oldsmobile, and in 1956, he bought the ultimate symbol of status, a new, flashy, convertible Cadillac in a bright shade of purple.[33]

Soon though, the car's garish color was too much for Bill, whose friends had dubbed the monstrosity "the purple ghost." In 1958, Bill ordered a new, more subdued Cadillac, but a strike at General Motors had delayed its arrival. Meanwhile, his good friend John Grubb had already ordered a new Cadillac. When his arrived, he drove over to the Iowa Realty office on Beaver to show off his new car and tease Bill about still having the purple ghost. He took Bill for a ride in the new car, and Bill asked his friend how much it would take for him to trade his new Cadillac for the purple ghost and then trade that in when Bill's new car arrived. Grubb thought his friend was joking and picked the outlandish figure of $2,500. Bill agreed, and when they were at a stop sign, he leaned over, pulled the keys out of the ignition, and told Grubb to get out of his car. Grubb was dumbfounded, but Bill persisted that a deal was a deal. Grubb finally complied, got out of the car, and walked back to Bill's office where he took possession of the ugly purple ghost. He had it for several months before the new Cadillac arrived.[34]

The two friends laughed about that episode for years, but it was illustrative. Bill loved making deals and took them very seriously. His ability to size up situations and make quick decisions often gave him an edge in such transactions, and he cut deals with friends as often as he did with business associates. From the mid-1950s to 1960, Bill negotiated some important deals that set his future in motion.

Not surprisingly, the first big deal involved John Grubb. He was developing his first subdivision, and since Iowa Realty had been successful in selling many of his homes, Grubb asked Bill to handle the home and lot sales in Zelda Acres, a West Des Moines development directly south of Resthaven Cemetery, named after his wife. Before the sale, Grubb had arranged for Elmer Miller and Des Moines Savings and Loan to offer GI loans for these homes with no down payment. Although this had been done in other parts of the country, it had not been the practice in Des Moines. With such financing available, Bill ran a half-page advertisement in the *Des Moines Register* initially offering the sixty-eight three-bedroom, brick homes for $17,000 to $21,000. Soldiers and veterans could qualify for a low, fixed-rated GI loan with no down payment. The splashy ad was followed by a two-day open house, held on a Saturday and Sunday in early April 1958. With balloons decorating the completed show homes, a carnival atmosphere prevailed, and a number of Iowa Realty agents, including Jim Cooper, Roger Cleven, Pat Greene, and Roy Riley, sold nineteen homes over the weekend. A couple more open houses followed, and by late June, all the development's homes that had been completed or were under construction had been sold, and all but a handful of the subdivision's homes yet to be built had been presold as well.[35]

The success of Zelda Acres boosted John Grubb's esteem as a builder, enhanced Bill's reputation as a Realtor, and encouraged the friends to work together. In February 1959, Grubb announced the development of a new subdivision northeast of downtown Des Moines called Sheridan Park, north of Sheridan Avenue between East Thirty-eighth Street and East Forty-second Street. Much larger than anything he had done previously, the plans ultimately called for 550 modest homes throughout the 160-acre project. Again, Bill handled the sales as the first plats opened that summer and, much like Zelda Acres, the deal proved lucrative for both Grubb and Iowa Realty.[36]

Deals like these added to Iowa Realty's inventory of homes available, which by 1959 totaled over 200 and was, according to company advertising, "the largest selection of homes [offered by a realty firm] in Des Moines." That same year, Iowa Realty began calling itself "Iowa's Largest Realtor." It is not clear whether this claim was based on sales volume, which the firm boasted was record breaking, on its large number of listings, or the size of its sales force, which numbered twenty-five by 1959. Unfortunately, because sales records for the period no longer exist, the statement is difficult to substantiate. Among those in the business, there was some debate at the time whether or not Iowa Realty had surpassed Chamberlain, Kirk & Cline as the largest in the city. Nonetheless, Iowa Realty's rapid growth was impressive, and clearly, it was the firm on the rise. Equally important, the company had transformed the industry by aggressively marketing new construction, establishing deals with local banks to guarantee the availability of financing for its customers, and using bold, new designs in its newspaper advertising.[37]

Building Iowa Realty to a leading position in its market was a major achievement, but Bill kept pressing, and two other deals pointed him in a brand new direction; one involved a partner, a long-term commitment, and land development, while in the other, Bill acted alone, bought property, and quickly turned around and sold it at a profit.

In January 1959, Bill bought Stuart Hills, a thirty-acre parcel immediately west of the new forty-seven-acre Merle Hay Plaza, which was scheduled to open in August and would be Iowa's largest shopping center. It was a sizeable purchase; Bill paid $160,000 for the land, but it is likely he was already in discussions with John Grubb about jointly developing this property. These talks led to the establishment of Allied Development, a fifty-fifty partnership designed to hold prime real estate owned by the two businessmen. A month later, Bill transferred Stuart Hills to Allied Development. The valuable land was bounded by Douglas Avenue to the south, Sixty-sixth Street to the west, Aurora Avenue to the north, and Sixty-fourth Street to the east. In some ways, this was a natural move, for owning land to be developed offered many more opportunities than merely brokering sales, and this would be the area where Bill would soon excel. Likewise, partnering with Grubb brought in a friend Bill trusted who had expertise that he lacked.[38]

Shortly after the creation of Allied Development, Bill became involved in a deal with Don Benton, a builder who was in the midst of developing Karen Acres, a subdivision in Urbandale, north and west of downtown. By March 1960, his finances were tight, and while laying water mains and grading streets, he ran out of money. Benton approached Bill about buying some lots so he could finish the subdivision preparations. Bill saw an opportunity and jumped at the chance, buying twenty-three lots, most of which were along Benton Avenue. But unlike the Stuart Hills acquisition or the creation of Allied Development, which involved planning and holding of property, Bill turned around and sold these lots almost immediately. Three were bought by Jerry Grubb, John's brother, the following month, and in May, John Grubb bought the rest. The quick deal netted Bill a tidy profit.[39]

The two deals marked the end of an era and the beginning of a new one. From 1952 to the end of the decade, Bill's singular focus was expanding sales at Iowa Realty. In just seven years, he transformed the small real estate firm into an innovative operation that was arguably the city's largest. No one who knew Bill would have been surprised. Rival Realtor Joe Kirk, Sr. remembered Bill as "an aggressive businessman who saw opportunities others didn't and acted on them." Accountant Robert Timmins agreed but thought Bill's drive was the key: "He was the most ambitious guy I knew, and he kept pushing; he was never satisfied." Indeed, as the 1950s closed, Bill Knapp could look back over a decade of accomplishment, yet he was far from content. Successful though he was, the shadow of his hard life on the Depression-era farm still haunted him. "I wasn't comfortable back then," he recalled. "I still felt that I was one or two steps away from losing it all."[40]

With Iowa Realty running at full throttle, Bill moved into land development and then property management with the same intensity that had propelled him to build the brokerage business. His passion for work and his drive to make things happen only grew over time and, in fact, came to dominate his life. Even as he spent time away from the office with family and friends and even when he vacationed, business was constantly on his mind. He was always thinking about negotiating the next deal, buying the next property, or developing the next piece of land. He just could not turn it off; Bill Knapp was now the quintessential dealmaker, and there were always deals needing to be closed.

Chapter Four

A Piece of the American Dream

Journalist David Halberstam referred to the American dream as a "vast national phenomenon." From 1945 through the early 1960s, millions of Americans moved into the middle class. Postwar prosperity was transforming American society from one based on thrift and savings to one propelled by consumption, immediate gratification, and a "buy now, pay later" mentality. Economic abundance made the good life attainable, which, by the idealized standards of the 1950s, started with the single-family home. Here a breadwinning husband, a fulltime homemaker wife, and three children lived, surrounded by all the latest gadgets and conveniences in newly built subdivisions. These nuclear families reigned supreme in suburbia, touted in such popular television shows as *The Adventures of Ozzie and Harriet*, *Leave It to Beaver*, and *Father Knows Best*. Moreover, the promise of upward mobility meant the good life was destined to get even better as hard work led to higher paying jobs, greater disposable incomes, and more spacious homes in upscale neighborhoods. Although Hollywood depictions of the middle class families in all white neighborhoods glossed over reality and masked many problems of the period, much of its framework held true for central Iowa. It was here that Bill Knapp was ready to sell young couples their starter homes or help established families upgrade to stately houses in the upper-middle class areas of Des Moines. In essence, as he sold the centerpiece of the American dream to others, Bill Knapp carved out his own piece of the American dream.[1]

Indeed, the dream was alive and well at midcentury, when most Americans were enjoying a higher standard of living than ever before. Countless young adults who had experienced deprivation of the Great Depression and sacrifice during World War II were ready to enjoy the good life. Acquisitiveness, mass consumption, and then conspicuous consumption, fueled by the $100 billion Americans had saved during the war and newly available credit cards, ruled the day. This was an America that witnessed its gross national product climb from $285 billion in 1950 to $503 billion in 1960, while median family income rose to $5,620, a 70 percent increase over the period. It was an era when Americans marveled at the major advances in science and technology spawned by huge postwar expansion of research and development. Productivity increased and hours at work decreased, as most moved to the five-day work week.[2]

The economic boom coincided with the baby boom, which saw the nation's population jump from 154 million in 1950 to 183 million in 1960. Family life was celebrated, and much of the spending splurge focused on homes and appliances and furnishings to fill them, automobiles, baby products, toys, and vacations. Togetherness was emphasized, with stay-at-home mothers overseeing the brood and working fathers spending more time with their children. Religion grew in importance, and membership in churches and synagogues witnessed a surge over the course of the decade. When parents were not working or involved with the children, they were engaged in fraternal lodges, civic groups or service organizations, or sports leagues.[3]

A number of social critics bemoaned suburbia as bland and mindless. Writer John Cheever, for instance, referred to it as "a cesspool of conformity," but historian John Diggins noted simply, "Americans were falling in love with suburbia." Indeed, young couples and families flocked to these areas because of the sameness; they sought to surround themselves with neighbors from the same socioeconomic class in the same stage of life. By the end of the 1950s, one in four Americans lived in suburbia. So too did the Knapps.[4]

Much like many other young parents of the period, the Knapps soon realized that their one-bedroom home on Thirtieth Street was too small once their daughter Ginny, who had been born in 1950, became an active toddler. At the time, though, Bill had taken over the Hollis firm, and he was pouring all his extra money back into his nascent Iowa Realty operation. Still, it was clear a larger home was necessary, and in the spring of 1953, the couple bought a two-bedroom home at 3925 Clinton Avenue in the Beaverdale neighborhood, north and west of downtown Des Moines.[5]

It was a good move for several reasons. Besides the extra space, the home was situated in a much more family-friendly area. Ashby Park was just a couple of blocks away, and a number of other young couples with small children lived along Clinton Avenue. One family in particular stood out. Just down the street lived Kenny Grandquist, his wife Evelyn, and daughter Cindy. Grandquist would join Bill at Iowa Realty that July and become one of his closest friends and associates. The families saw a lot of each other and sometimes vacationed together. The other element that tied the two men together was the new office building on Beaver Avenue that Grandquist's father Olaf had built. In the summer of 1953, Iowa Realty moved into the structure, which was less than half a mile from their homes on Clinton.

Besides the Grandquist connection, the Knapps had the security of family on the block. Grace and Floyd Knapp, Bill's aunt and uncle, lived down the street. Shortly after Bill and Irene moved to the neighborhood, Ruth and Glen Gammell, Irene's aunt and uncle, moved in next door to them. The Gammells were childless and were especially attentive to Ginny and later Roger.[6]

The proximity of the office to the neighborhood was important as well. Real estate was a seven-day-a-week job, and not surprisingly, Bill was at the office every day. "Business came first," he recalled, and although the Knapps often enjoyed dinner at home together, Bill regularly returned to the office after the evening meal, where he and Grandquist frequently worked until 10 or 11 p.m. When he stayed home after dinner, the Knapps joined in what had become an American evening ritual—the family watched television together. Over the course of the 1950s, television had become a national phenomenon as the number of sets in the country climbed from 3 million in 1950 to 50 million by 1960. "But Bill was a lot like his father," Irene Knapp remembered, and "he wanted to be out working all the time." This drive, coupled with his impatience, made it nearly impossible for Bill to sit passively in front of the television. Instead, most of his evenings at home were spent on the telephone engaged in work. Here he scheduled meetings, cleaned up problems, or negotiated deals.[7]

In fact, once Bill was involved in real estate, he never truly separated his work life from his home life. The Knapps' home phone rang often, but most calls were for Bill and normally concerned business. His reaction to several telephone calls one afternoon in 1950 is illustrative of Bill's focus. He and Irene had recently purchased their one-bedroom home on Thirtieth Street, but it was definitely a fixer-upper. Among other things, it needed a coat of paint, and Bill dutifully began the project. While he was up on a ladder painting, several calls came in, all for Bill and all involving real estate deals. After climbing down the ladder to take each call, his patience wore thin and when yet another call came for him, Bill had had it. "Let's hire it [the painting] done," he shouted. This became his mantra; Bill hired others to do regular household chores and yard maintenance, which freed him to spend more time to Iowa Realty.[8]

His single-minded devotion to business had consequences for the Knapps' social life as well. In the early 1950s, the couple did not spend much time with friends. Bill was busy getting established in the real estate world, and Irene had her hands full caring for a toddler and maintaining the home. When the Knapps started socializing more in the mid-1950s, it was almost always with Bill's business associates, colleagues, builders, rivals, or customers. Bill and Irene especially enjoyed get-togethers with John and Zelda Grubb, Bill's brother Paul and wife Mary Lou, and Kenny and Evelyn Grandquist. More often than planned events, however, were impromptu dinners at the Knapp home. Bill regularly called Irene in the late afternoon and explained that he was bringing a group of businesspeople over for dinner that evening. Irene, of course, had to scramble around to prepare the dinner party, but after this happened several times, she kept food on hand in case Bill arranged one of his last-minute parties.[9]

This blurring of his business and private realms spread into all areas of Bill's life and soon affected Irene on a daily basis as well. Shortly after the Knapp family moved into 3925 Clinton, Irene became busier when she stepped out from the fulltime homemaker stereotype of the 1950s. Although she remained at home, she began handling all the paperwork for Iowa Realty's new insurance division out of the couple's basement. To help around the house, Irene and Bill hired Beatrice (Bea) Turner, a maid in her early thirties who was already cleaning several homes along Clinton. Initially, Turner cleaned the Knapp house every Thursday. When it became clear that Irene needed more uninterrupted time for the insurance venture, Turner began working full time for the Knapps. Besides cleaning, she also watched young Ginny. This allowed Irene to concentrate on the business, which she enjoyed. But by mid-decade, the operation had grown too much for Irene to handle on a part-time basis, and Bill moved it into Iowa Realty's office under the auspices of his closing manager.[10]

Nonetheless, Turner remained at the Knapps' full time, and Irene was soon back at work again; this time she stepped in for Iowa Realty bookkeeper Jo Ann Burman, who had been fired for embezzlement and starting the office fire. Conscientious and good with numbers, she capably filled the position for nearly two years before receptionist Marilyn Dailey took over the company books when Irene became pregnant. She gave birth to the couple's second child, Roger Bill, in September 1959. With the addition of Roger, the family was now complete, and the Knapps fell back into the rhythms long established over the course of the 1950s.[11]

In the meantime, the Knapps had moved twice. In 1957, Bill and Irene wanted more space. They found a new ranch home built by John Grubb located on Seventieth Street in the suburb of Windsor Heights. Irene loved the house, but it was not nearly as close to the Iowa Realty office as the Clinton home, which had been just a few short blocks away. Although the new house was only several miles from the office, it was now much less convenient for Bill to go home for dinner, so he started staying at the office through the evening and skipping family dinners altogether. This upset Irene, who enjoyed cooking big meals and having Bill home to share them. The couple soon settled the issue in dramatic fashion; after only a few months, the Knapps returned to the Clinton neighborhood and built a bigger home down the street from their former address. At the same time, Kenny Grandquist was considering a larger house as well. He and Bill started talking. The two decided to build homes adjacent to each other on Clinton. Grandquist's father built both split levels, which shared the same floor plan, and in 1958, the Knapps and Grandquists became next door neighbors.[12]

Once Roger was born, Irene asked Turner to move in and provide even more household assistance. Turner accepted and settled into a basement bedroom. She stayed with the Knapp family Monday through Friday but spent weekends with her mother. This routine continued over the next two years until Turner's mother's health declined, and although she remained full time with the Knapps, she moved back home with her mother. These live-in years were significant, as Turner became an essential part of the Knapp household. Over the period, she proved a great source of help and support for Irene, and the two became good friends. Equally important was the bond she had with the Knapp children. Childless herself, the protective Turner watched over Ginny and Roger as if they were her own. "Ginny was a good child," she recalled, "and didn't need much guidance. By the time I moved in, she was involved with her friends and lots of activities." Ginny attended local public schools, first Byron Rice Elementary and then Meredith Junior High, and as Turner suggested, she had a number of extracurricular interests. Although somewhat reserved like her mother, Ginny was active in Bluebirds—her mother served as the troop leader—and then Campfire Girls. She also played the violin, took dance classes with Evelynne Wheaton at the Beaverdale Dance School, and had piano lessons with Gloria Beneventi, a neighbor on Clinton Street. Bill attended Ginny's performances regularly, but he was never long on patience and had great difficulty sitting still for long periods. During a piano recital, in fact, when Ginny and a number of others performed at Critchett Piano Company, the recital dragged on, and Bill began experiencing chest pains. He thought he was having a heart attack and left early. The incident proved to be only heartburn, but it was another example of Bill's nervous energy and tightly wound personality.[13]

While Turner was close to both children, it was baby Roger, or Bubby as she nicknamed him, with whom she spent a lot of time and developed a special attachment. One of her favorite pastimes was taking young Roger for rides in his little red wagon down to Ashby Park, and Turner was there when the toddler took his first steps. A happy child, Roger was outgoing and became both competitive and athletic. He initially was interested in baseball and basketball, but tennis was the sport that ultimately became Roger's focus.[14]

Although employing a maid set the Knapps apart from most Americans of the period, the family reflected the white, middle class experience in many other ways. Church attendance on Sundays, for example, was a family practice. When Bill and Irene moved to Des Moines, they initially chose Highland Park Presbyterian Church because it was recommended by Bill's cousin Margaret and husband Herman Miller. They stayed there until Irene's sister Doris and husband Clair Niday moved to Des Moines in 1956. Niday had come to town to work for Bill at Iowa Realty, and he and his wife began attending St. Andrews Evangelical United Brethren Church. Not having particularly strong ties to Highland Park Presbyterian, the Knapps soon joined the Nidays at St. Andrews. Along with her sister Doris, Irene became very involved in this church and eventually taught confirmation classes. Ginny attended its Sunday school and was a regular in the church's Wednesday evening youth activities. When Roger was born, it was here he was baptized.[15]

Bill, however, was a different story. He attended services on Sunday, but he was not enthusiastic about organized religion. This may have gone back to his childhood when his parents emphasized prayer at home more than involvement in church. Then again, it may have come down to priorities: religious fellowship was just less important to him than other pursuits. When Bill attended church, he soon found a way to add a business component to the morning. Following the service, he often took Irene, Ginny, and eventually Roger on long drives throughout the city. These tours kept Bill up to date on the area's housing market and gave him ideas about ground to purchase and develop. The drives also became a special family event, a ritual that Ginny cherished as one of her favorite childhood memories.[16]

Toward the end of the decade, Bill's church attendance waned in favor of tennis, an activity he discovered and soon enjoyed. Joe Housman, an Iowa Realty agent, introduced Bill to the sport, which immediately appealed to him. Like boxing, it was an individual sport, which pitted one player against a single opponent. Even in doubles, a player had only to rely on one partner. At the same time, several sets of tennis did not require an inordinate amount of time and provided intense, competitive workouts. The exercise cleared his mind, helped keep him fit, and within a couple of hours, he could be cleaned up and back at work.

Bill became involved in a tennis group, which was made up of business associates that got together a couple of times a week to play. Besides Bill, regular players included Paul Knapp, Kenny Grandquist, Iowa Realty agents Roger Cleven and Housman, his brother Chuck Housman, and Don Watkins, an insurance agent. When the weather was warm, they played on public courts at Ashby Park or Birdland Park, and in the winter, Cleven made arrangements for the group to play inside at the Grandview College (now Grandview University) gymnasium, located north and east of downtown. Conditions there were less than ideal, however. Although the gym had nets for indoor play, it did not have the courts outlined on the floor, so Bill and the others had to walk off court dimensions and lay tape boundaries on the floor. Access to the gym allowed for year-round play, and from the end of the 1950s, tennis became an important part of Bill's life.[17]

Tennis was but one component of his growing interest in physical fitness. By the mid-1950s, Bill had installed a heavy punching bag and a speed bag in Iowa Realty's small basement, which was gradually turned into a workout room. Soon he added a ping pong table as well. Here he put together a daily exercise routine that involved push-ups, sit-ups, and time on each boxing bag. Weight lifting and jogging were eventually added to his regimen. Although he initially began these activities to relieve stress, he soon realized the physical benefits as well and became a dedicated fitness devotee. Once, for example, while Bill and Grandquist were out of town, Grandquist was awakened early one morning by a repetitive thumping coming from the next room. It was Bill jogging in place. "He just kept going and going and going," Grandquist recalled.[18]

His disciplined approach to exercise had immediate and long-term benefits. Working out burned off some of Bill's excess energy and helped him relax. It also kept him fit. Years later, someone noted that Bill "probably didn't weigh as much as a Chicago phonebook." Indeed, at 149 pounds, the five-foot-six real estate man maintained the solid, muscular build that harkened back to his boxing days in the navy. Bill, of course, explained his passion for exercise in business terms. "Staying fit pays big dividends," he noted. "If you lose your health, you don't amount to a damn."[19]

Toward the end of the decade, Bill added a massage table to the room and hired Harry "Flip" Flipping, a masseur/shoeshine man he had met at the local YMCA, to provide post-workout rubdowns. Flipping also did odd jobs around the building, including cooking chili for agents and staff on Saturdays. His warm and upbeat personality made him a favorite among Iowa Realty personnel. Young Roger Knapp was also drawn to him, and sometimes after going home for dinner, Bill brought his son back to the office workout room where Flipping enjoyed visiting with the youngster. Having his own massage table/masseur was an extravagance somewhat akin to Bill buying his first Cadillac: it was a little over the top; it was something that few others had; and it was something he enjoyed. And like the luxury automobile, it was a sign that Bill had made it.[20]

Two other sports captured Bill's attention as well. For a few years in the late 1950s and early 1960s, he took part in a bowling league with Grandquist, his brother John Grandquist, Paul Knapp, and several others from Iowa Realty. The group bowled at the Plaza Lanes on Euclid Avenue, north of downtown. But bowling never really held Bill's interest—it was not a strenuous workout, it ate up a lot of time, and league play was an organized group activity that cut against his grain—and he participated only sporadically over a couple of years before bowing out completely. Bowling, however, did not raise his ire as golf did.[21]

Bill detested golf. A round of golf was simply a waste of four to five hours. He believed the time could be much better spent working and making money. These strong feelings kept him from participating in the sport for years, but they also impacted Iowa Realty agents. "I used to hate golf," Bill recalled in 2000, "and I hated for my employees to play it." Instead, Bill wanted his agents making calls, showing homes, and closing deals. His position on golf was quite clear, but some at Iowa Realty played anyway, including Grandquist and Paul Knapp. Their outings sometimes caused friction with Bill, but they continued golfing. Others did not find it so simple, particularly those who needed cash advances. Bill usually handed out the advances, but in exchange he required the borrower to bring his golf clubs to the office, where they remained until the loan was repaid. Much later, Bill's views on golf would soften and he acknowledged, "Many deals are made on the golf course."[22]

For all Bill's interest in physical fitness and good health, he continued smoking cigarettes, a habit he had picked up in the navy in 1944. At the time, roughly 40 percent of adult Americans smoked, and although mounting evidence suggested it was harmful, most of the studies were circulated in medical journals and did not reach the public. This began to change in 1952, when journalist Roy Norr published an article linking cancer to cigarettes. It originally ran in the *Christian Herald,* but was soon reprinted under the title of "Cancer by the Carton" in *Reader's Digest,* the most widely circulated magazine of the period. Similar pieces in other popular magazines followed and raised public awareness, but few smokers felt compelled to quit. Certainly Bill Knapp did not.[23]

He was a self-described nervous smoker, going through a pack a day, lighting a cigarette, smoking about half of it, and then putting it out. Smoking gave Bill something to do when he was idle or in between projects and provided a sense of relaxation. But by the early 1960s, he reconsidered smoking because of his father's faltering health.

Actually, Bill's father's health began to decline in the late 1950s. He had been a long-time smoker who had increasing difficulty breathing, and he and his wife Anna had been considering trying something less strenuous than farming their land in Allerton. In 1957, son Bill stepped forward with an alternative. He had purchased a property with a gas station, small grocery, and motel in Albia, the county seat of Monroe County, fifty miles north and west of Allerton. He suggested his parents move there and run these businesses. They agreed. They rented out the farm for a year, and Bill's father, mother, and younger sister Carolyn relocated in Albia.[24]

However, it was readily apparent that his father's health was not improving. At the end of the year, Bill's parents and sister were homesick for Allerton and returned to their farm. His father was eventually sent to University Hospital in Iowa City for tests, which revealed that he had throat cancer. Bill knew that life on the farm was more and more difficult for his parents, and by the late 1950s, he had the financial wherewithal to help. After the Albia move failed, he decided to build his mother and father a home in town in Allerton. Since Irene's parents were also growing older, he built them a new Allerton home as well. His generosity did not stop here. When his father was scheduled for exploratory surgery at the famed Mayo Clinic in Rochester, Minnesota, Bill rented a plane, had his parents flown to the facility, and paid for all the medical expenses.[25]

The surgeons discovered that the cancer had spread, and so they removed Bill's father's larynx, which was filled with cancer. He recovered, although it took him a long time to learn to speak again. He and Anna eventually opened an antique store in town. Son Bill was certainly happy with the ultimate results, but his father's laryngectomy was a jarring experience. After the surgery, doctors showed family members the cancer-ridden organ. The image stuck with Bill. The reality that smoking probably caused his father's cancer made him consider giving up cigarettes.[26]

By 1964, Bill was planning to quit but had not taken the final step until one Friday evening when he was having drinks with Eldon Woltz, a friend and well known Des Moines photographer. Woltz was thinking of quitting as well, and the two decided to wager on who could quit first. The winner would receive $500 from the other. Although Bill had almost always shied away from gambling, he was confident he could win the contest. Sure enough, the following Monday, a determined Bill kicked his twenty-year habit cold turkey and won the bet.[27]

Such strong will and intensity served Bill well and, when combined with his independent streak, meant that he most often preferred operating on his own. This grew out of his long-held desire to control all aspects of his life. Consequently, he usually did not join clubs, service organizations, or even trade associations. Their goals might be worthy, but their meetings, the social gatherings, and camaraderie they entailed were not for him. Bill explained: "Other people enjoyed that kind of thing, but I saw it as a waste of my time." Nonetheless, he was pragmatic and understood that membership in some groups was important for business. If he joined, however, he kept his participation to a minimum.[28]

This was undoubtedly the case with the Masons. In the mid-1950s, builder Olaf Grandquist urged sons Kenny and John Grandquist as well as Bill and Paul Knapp to join the Scottish Rite Masons in Des Moines. Bill dreaded the rituals, pageantry, and the meetings but thought he might make valuable connections because, as he recalled, "a lot of people belonged [to the Masons] at the time." Indeed, people of the 1950s were joiners, and nearly all civic and fraternal organizations, including the Masons, saw spikes in membership during the decade. Bill went through all the steps, and eventually was granted thirty-third-degree status, the order's highest award conferred only to those who made important contributions to the fraternity or society. Besides taking part in organizational activities, Bill and Irene sometimes went to dances at the Scottish Rite Consistory in downtown Des Moines.[29]

Meanwhile, along with other area Masons, including John Grubb and builder Robert Underwood, Bill joined the Za-Ga-Zig Shrine. Here he participated in some of the Shriners' philanthropic activities, occasionally donning his red fez hat and driving a convertible as part of the Shriner motor corps in local parades. He was also briefly a member of Shriner motor scooter corps, which took part in parades as well. But Bill never really liked the miniature motorcycles, and after his daughter burned her leg on the scooter's hot engine while he was taking her for a ride, he gave up his spot in the unit. Actually, the event provided him an out, for riding in parades was certainly not something Bill wanted to do, and generally speaking, once ensconced in the Masons and Shriners, Bill attended their functions only when necessary.[30]

Bill's participation in the Greater Des Moines Board of Realtors was similar. As the central Iowa affiliate of the National Association of Realtors, the group looked out for the interests of local real estate agents. Bill was a member and saw value in the organization but left it to others to run. He rarely attended its meetings, never traveled to national conventions, and avoided serving as the organization's president until 1969, when he was elected to the position and evading the job was no longer possible.[31]

Political activity, on the other hand, was an entirely different matter and anything but a waste of time. Once a business owner, Bill immediately understood that connections with local politicians could prove valuable and building these bridges did not involve group activities. Just as he had carefully courted builders, bankers, and others in the real estate business, so too did he begin cultivating friendships with elected or appointed municipal leaders. John Grubb explained: "Bill made friends with people in parts of government that would do him the most good." Clearly, he surmised, these efforts could only help when matters involving Iowa Realty were under consideration. As more of his business issues were deliberated by public administrators, his schmoozing increased. But Bill did not always get what he wanted, and he freely expressed his dissatisfaction when he lost. In one instance, while John Grubb was serving on the Des Moines Plan and Zoning Commission, he voted with the majority against an Iowa Realty petition. Bill's temper flared and he flew into a rage outside the commission office. He eventually calmed down, however, and the two remained good friends. Soon after he suffered another loss, this time it was when the Urbandale City Council approved only single-family residential zoning on land Bill wanted to develop with apartments, townhomes, and commercial buildings. He was outspoken about the poor decision, referring to it as "probably the greatest misuse of that piece of land you can think of." On balance though, Grubb still believed Bill's political activities paid off, recalling that his friend almost "always got a favorable reception on the Plan and Zoning Commission and the City Council."[32]

These steps coincided with his initial moves into partisan politics. He had been introduced to the Democratic Party during the Depression by his father. "My father was a pretty good Democrat," Bill reminisced. "He liked its philosophy better than that of the Republican Party. It was pretty tough on the farm in those days, and I felt the Democrats had more feeling for farmers than some of the more conservative Republicans."[33] His party sentiments remained steadfast, and as he began seeking friendships with local political leaders, he took tentative steps into politics in the mid-1950s by providing a growing amount of financial support to his favorite candidates.

He became more seriously involved in politics in 1962. Bill had heard a lot of talk about gubernatorial candidate Harold Hughes and was eager for an introduction. He asked attorney Lex Hawkins, state chair of the Democratic Party, to arrange a meeting. Hawkins agreed, and brought Hughes to the Iowa Realty office on Beaver Avenue. Bill was impressed with the tall, ruggedly handsome Hughes. His magnetic personality and hardscrabble background appealed to Bill, who remembered instantly "liking him as a man." Shortly thereafter, he donated $1,000 to the candidate's campaign, which Hughes noted "was a generous contribution at the time." This was the beginning of a close friendship between businessman Bill Knapp and soon-to-be Governor Harold Hughes; it was also the beginning of Bill's move from a dabbler in politics to an important fundraiser for the party and a "must-see" for Democratic candidates seeking political office.[34]

Such a full and busy life did not leave much time for family vacations, which had become part and parcel of the American dream after World War II. A 1954 Gallup Poll found that nearly half those surveyed planned to take a summer vacation of at least a week. Initially, though, Bill's chasing the dream kept him from taking the family out of town. The real estate business was based on commissions, and Bill hated the idea of foregoing a sale here or an opportunity there for a respite from the office. Actually, work was not something he longed to avoid; on the contrary, he loved the business and explained, "Work was my pleasure." Moreover, summer was the busiest season for those in real estate, and even if Bill wanted a vacation he would have taken it during a different part of the year.[35]

As the family vacation became embedded in American culture, it eventually became part of the Knapp family routine as well. Initially, instead of taking full-fledged trips, Bill opted for a runabout he kept at Bird-land Marina, a small harbor on a bend of the Des Moines River just north and east of downtown. With a motorboat in the marina, the Knapps had access to the river, and this offered Bill, Irene, and Ginny and later Roger a quick and easy in-town getaway. Bill had great difficulty relaxing, and these afternoons on the water sometimes devolved into Bill motoring up and down the channel, returning the boat to the slip, and taking the family home.[36]

But being on or near the water was appealing, and when Bill and Irene considered actual vacations in the mid-1950s, they decided instead to buy a small cottage in Clear Lake, 115 miles north of Des Moines. Located on the south side of the lake, the two-bedroom A-frame sported a large deck, screened-in porch, and dock, where Bill kept a Chris-Craft motorboat. Here, Bill thought, the family could enjoy weekends of fishing, boating, picnicking, and swimming in the spring; longer stays could be arranged during the summer. The lake's proximity to Des Moines was especially attractive to him; he would only be a two-hour drive from his office and could easily get back and forth as needed.

Bill and Irene and family initially made the trip north relatively often. The cottage served as an escape for the Knapps and their children, but it was also a place they shared with friends and family. Most often, it was the Grandquists, the Grubbs, or the Nidays who joined them at the lake-front property. However, once the newness wore off, the Knapp retreats to Clear Lake gradually declined. Its short distance from Des Moines did not mitigate the fact that spring and summer were the busiest times of the real estate year, when Bill found it difficult to get away. This waning interest was compounded by a scare Bill had during a favorite pastime at Clear Lake: taking people out for boat rides. One afternoon when out of the lake with Irene and Ginny, Bill gunned the boat's engine, accelerated rapidly, and then made an abrupt turn. Water rushed across the stern, and for a moment, he thought they were in danger of sinking. Fortunately, the boat remained afloat, but Bill recalled that the incident "scared the hell out of me." Although the shock of the event soon wore off, he never forgot it, and boating soon lost much of its allure.[37]

Yet the couple was still drawn to the water, and late in the decade, the Knapps soon took their first family trip to Florida, flying down to Miami shortly after Christmas. The timing and the vacation proved ideal; it was during the slowest part of the real estate year, and the mild temperatures and warm water were welcomed respites from the bitter Iowa weather. The trip turned out so well, in fact, that the Florida excursion became a regular part of the Knapps' holiday season. Initially, they stayed at the Golden Strand Resort; later they switched to the more upscale Fontainebleau Resort.[38]

About 1958, a year before Roger was born, Bill, Irene, and Ginny headed to Miami with his brother Paul, wife Mary Lou, and their sons, Mike and Billy. Usually, though, it was with John and Zelda Grubb and their son Johnny that the Knapps most often shared their annual Florida vacation. By the mid-1960s, the destination had shifted from Miami to the state's gulf coast, first Naples, and later Siesta Key, a barrier island due east of Sarasota, where later in the early 1970s, the Grubbs, the Knapps, and the Grandquists all purchased condominiums in the same building.[39]

Of course, Bill and Irene also vacationed without the children as well. They went to Florida on their own or to more exotic locales, such as Jamaica, where in the winter of 1963, the Knapps traveled with Kenny and Evelyn Grandquist. Taken together, the cottage at Clear Lake, the annual family holiday treks to Florida, and the couple's getaways were emblematic of Bill's growing financial success and the family's rise through the middle class into it upper echelons of Des Moines society. As such, these indulgences announced his increasing socioeconomic standing. Historian Susan Rugh explained, "Spending money on vacation was like buying a car; it advertised that one could afford to spend time and money for leisure activities away from home."[40]

More than a vacation, however, the ultimate symbol of status was one's home. Societal position was often reflected in the size, location, and amenities of one's residence, and by 1965, Bill was ready for an upgrade more befitting of his hard-earned achievements in the business world. The Knapps did not make the uptown move alone; instead, just as they had done in 1958, Bill and his family and Kenny Grandquist and his family had new houses erected next door to each other. John Grubb built both homes, which had identical floor plans but different exterior styles, on land Grubb and Bill had purchased two years earlier. Bill's house was located on the southwest corner of Beaver and Aurora avenues; Grandquist's was immediately south on Beaver Avenue. With expansive front lawns, the elegant 3,000-square-foot homes featured four bedrooms and finished basements with an additional 2,000 square feet of living space. Each had identical swimming pools and bathhouses as well. Two elements, though, set Bill's property apart: at nearly an acre, his corner lot was larger than Grandquist's and on the additional land, he put in a luxury few others in Des Moines possessed—a private tennis court in his backyard.[41]

Still next door neighbors, but now in a swank new residential area, Bill and Grandquist continued their close friendship. Driven, ambitious, and competitive, the two men held the same vision of making money and building Iowa Realty. Their shared goals and compatible personalities meant the two were almost inseparable. Agent Roger Cleven explained, "If you saw Bill, you knew Kenny wasn't far behind."[42] As friends, neighbors, and business associates, Bill and Grandquist forged a complex relationship, which was yet another example of Bill's inability or indifference to separate his home and private life from his business life.

Paul Knapp fell into this complicated web as well. He and Bill had been close as children, and Paul remained Bill's closest confidant into adulthood. Somehow, Paul, Bill, and Grandquist developed and then maintained a seamless relationship with one another both inside and outside the world of Iowa Realty. The trio of friendships worked for years because of Paul's unassuming and laidback personality. Even though Grandquist ranked between the two brothers in the company's organizational chart, he did not feel threatened by Paul, and each man evidently understood his place in the firm's pecking order. As Grandquist put it, "I never had any trouble with Paul trying to edge in on me." Paul's place at the company was selling, and after ten years of being one of the firm's top salesmen, he was also ready to move into a larger home. Not surprisingly, given his relationship with his brother and boss, Paul and his family also relocated to Beaver Avenue, several houses down the block from Bill and Grandquist. It was 1966, and the three key figures at Iowa Realty who would take the company to even greater heights were now also neighbors.[43]

Like many others in the postwar landscape, Bill Knapp eagerly went after the American dream. Better at the game than most, the upwardly mobile real estate man rapidly breezed through middle class status, accumulating the trappings of those situated near the top of the socioeconomic ladder. Soon it was apparent that Bill and his family lived the good life. Hard work and long hours had paid off. Clearly Bill felt good about his achievements. He enjoyed the toys his money could buy, and he proudly displayed his mounting material wealth. But he took greatest pleasure in the pursuit. Never satisfied with his present position, Bill was constantly moving forward, looking for a new angle or negotiating another deal. Over the next few years, this drive would bring Bill an even bigger piece of the American dream.

Chapter Five

Properties, Plats, and Politics

Accountant Jack Wahlig recalled, "Bill was always open for business."[1] Wahlig was right on target; business was all consuming for Bill and dominated his life. By the 1960s, this singular focus took him down several paths. He realized what he did not know, and he worked to fill these gaps with smart and talented people. Iowa Realty's brokerage business remained essential to his success, and he oversaw its operations, battling new and existing rivals by adding more agents, new services, and new branch offices. Of course, Bill added value to the company by devoting more and more of his time to what he did best—spotting opportunities and negotiating deals.

Such transactions often involved Bill buying land, usually in areas others had not considered. He also developed commercial property and went into the apartment and motel business. These activities led him into construction and eventually condominium conversions. They also kept him involved in politics as did his growing friendship with Iowa's new governor, Harold Hughes. Although his fixation on business meant that

Bill often sacrificed time with his family, it did not mean that he neglected them completely.

The key figure to keeping Iowa Realty on track, Bill believed, was Kenny Grandquist. A bear of a man, Grandquist was the epitome of a people person, who, according to real estate man Gene Stanbrough, "could sell mittens to people in Florida." He had just the right touch with agents; he could nurture and hand-hold and he could educate and back-slap. Agents loved working for him. Shortly after arriving at Iowa Realty in 1953, Grandquist was named sales manager; the company grew rapidly under his leadership. By that time, he and Bill were also close friends and neighbors, but Bill still worried about the possibility of losing Grandquist to a competitor. So, to solidify Grandquist's ties to Iowa Realty, Bill began giving him company stock during the late 1950s and early 1960s. Part ownership, Bill reasoned, would be a powerful incentive for Grandquist to stay with the firm and work hard to expand the business. Initially, the plan worked well, and ultimately, Grandquist owned 30 percent of the company. Meanwhile, Bill did the same for his brother Paul, who held 10 percent of Iowa Realty stock.[2]

In another move that further cemented their business relationship, Bill and Grandquist established a partnership called United Investments. Separate and distinct from Iowa Realty, the company was designed to build and hold income properties. United was founded early in the 1960s and eventually bought or built several apartment buildings, including the first one the partnership constructed in 1962 at Sixty-third Street and Hickman Road, several miles north and west of downtown Des Moines. The actual building was undertaken by Alcon Construction, a joint venture Bill and John Grubb had started in 1959. As he had hoped, the partnership and the stock deal with Grandquist only tightened the bond between the two, and it seemed just a fact of life that the men remain the closest of business associates, friends, and neighbors.[3]

Grandquist was clearly his most significant associate, but Bill gathered several others around him who had the skills or knowledge he did not possess. All would prove important to his future business dealings. First was attorney Bill Wimer. Educated, suave, and sophisticated, Wimer was completely different than Bill Knapp, but once the two were introduced in 1956 by Roy Riley, a new agent at Iowa Realty, they immediately hit it off. Bill saw in Wimer a young attorney who knew real estate law and whose connections might open doors. Wimer saw in Bill an aggressive, rising star in the Des Moines real estate market. Iowa Realty could send a lot of legal work his way. That was exactly what happened, and by the late 1950s, Wimer and his firm, which by the early 1960s was called Stewart, Miller, Wimer, Brennan, & Joyce, was doing most of the company's legal work.[4]

Besides legal help, Bill also knew he needed a good accountant. For years, Iowa Realty had operated with only a bookkeeper, and the accounting work was handled by the McGladrey firm's Robert Timmins. Bill was very happy with the arrangement, but when Timmins left McGladrey for a position at Thermagas in 1962, the Iowa Realty account was taken over by McGladrey vice president, Jack Wahlig, who had been transferred to Des Moines from the firm's Dubuque office. Wahlig handled all of Iowa Realty's accounting needs as well as Bill's personal accounting. More importantly, though, Wahlig became a close financial advisor and confidant to Bill and remained so until he became McGladrey's chief executive officer (CEO) in 1982.[5]

Beyond top managers and advisors, Bill personally hired two agents with expertise Iowa Realty lacked. In the late 1950s when he began branching out into residential land development, Bill took tentative steps into apartment building ownership and considered commercial development as well, but had no experience in the areas. About the time he and Grandquist were erecting their apartment building at Sixty-third Street and Hickman Road, Bill mentioned to Ed Nahas, owner of the Commodore Hotel, that he was looking for someone with a background in apartment brokerage and management. Nahas introduced him to Marion Caldwell who was in the business, and Caldwell suggested Bill talk with his associate, George Benson. Impressed with Benson's background, Bill hired him to oversee Iowa Realty's new income property division, which, by the early 1960s, claimed it had "the largest selection of apartment buildings in Des Moines."[6]

Bill's other key recruit was Sid Bradley. The two met while Bradley served as the director of the Des Moines Industrial Bureau, the Des Moines Chamber of Commerce unit charged with bringing businesses into the city. Here Bradley became well acquainted with the directions of city growth and where developments were planned. Bill figured this was ideal training for a career in commercial real estate and hired him in 1962 to head up Knapp & Bradley, Iowa Realty's new commercial and industrial real estate division.[7]

But just as Bill was laying the groundwork for expansion into commercial properties, he faced new competition in the residential brokerage market. In 1960, Gene Stanbrough, a twenty-seven-year-old with several years of experience in the real estate business, opened his own agency. A native of Des Moines, Stanbrough graduated from East High School in 1951 and held several different jobs before finding a sales position at Crescent Chevrolet in 1953. Here he worked for three years, until one day a customer paid cash for a car. Stanbrough had never seen that before and asked the man what he did for a living. When he replied that he sold real estate, Stanbrough decided to give it a try. The following day, he went to see Arlan Banning, the man who had stunned him by paying cash for the car and was the owner of Highland Park Realty. They talked, and Banning gave him a job. Stanbrough stayed just long enough to get his real estate license, and then took a position at Central Realty, located on Beaver Avenue, down the street from Iowa Realty. Interestingly, this was the firm that Harold Knapp (Bill Knapp's cousin), Bob McCaughtry, Paul Manley, and Herman Miller (Bill Knapp's brother-in-law) bought when they left Iowa Realty in the mid-1950s.[8]

Stanbrough was doing fairly well at Central, but by 1958, he and Harold Knapp left to create Real Estate Sales, Incorporated. They set up shop at 2729 Douglas Avenue, about a mile north of Drake University. The partnership lasted only two years, however, because Stanbrough felt he was doing most of the selling but not reaping most of the benefits. He bought Harold Knapp's share of the company and on January 1, 1960, established Stanbrough Realty Company at the same Douglas Avenue location.[9]

Although Bill Knapp was unaware of it at the time, he now faced a young, aggressive real estate agent who would soon use unconventional and innovative methods to attract customers, sell homes, and grow his company. By the end of the decade, Stanbrough would be Bill's biggest rival in the brokerage business. Initially though, Stanbrough had modest goals: he wanted a relatively small operation with four agents and a secretary working for him. At a time when Iowa Realty had over twenty agents, this new startup was not a threat. However, within six months, the firm had four agents, and Stanbrough raised his sights, searching for new ways to increase his visibility and expand. He soon came up with a novel idea; in March 1961, Stanbrough started offering a television program that provided viewers with photographs and descriptions of the homes his company had for sale and highlighted open houses that would be held later that afternoon. Simply called "The Home Show," the fifteen-minute weekly broadcast aired on WHO-TV in Des Moines on Sunday mornings. It was hosted by Bob Williams, a well-known local television personality and was followed by Jim Zabel's popular "Let's Go Bowling" program. It cost $80 per week.[10]

As Stanbrough had hoped, television exposure led to more listings and eventually the need for more agents. At the same time, the program captured Bill's attention, and although Stanbrough Realty was only 20 percent the size of Iowa Realty, it eventually appeared as the firm on the move, while other large Des Moines realtors such as Chamberlain, Kirk & Cline and Neal Adamson were either stagnant or declining. Continued growth at Stanbrough led to a budding rivalry with the much larger Iowa Realty. Each company worked to differentiate itself from the competition, recruit and retain talented agents, and spread its brand throughout the city.

Stanbrough Realty began advertising itself as "the TV Realtor," playing up its use of the relatively new medium to sell homes. Iowa Realty stuck with its familiar "Iowa's Largest Realtor" slogan, relying on the notion that bigger was better. By the beginning of 1965, however, Iowa Realty developed its own Sunday broadcast, a fifteen-minute television program called "Open House," which presented homes it was showing that afternoon in the Des Moines area and aired from 12:15–12:30 p.m. on KRNT (now KCCI). The program was originally hosted by Mary Jane Chinn, but when she left the station for a job in Chicago in 1967, it was taken over by Bill Riley, a long-time KRNT broadcaster. Currently called "The Home Show," the program has continued to the present. It now airs on WOI, Des Moines's ABC affiliate, and is hosted by local television personality Mike Pace.[11]

Both companies grew over the next few years, adding agents and working to retain talented ones, especially because it was relatively easy to move between companies and "poaching," or stealing agents from rival firms was a common practice among Realtors in Des Moines. Bill understood the value of keeping skilled, experienced agents in the fold, but sometimes he proved unwilling to give agents what they wanted to stay. A case in point was Jim Cooper. Cooper headed Iowa Realty's branch office

on the south side of Des Moines and had done so since Bill took over the
building's lease in late 1956. By 1963, there were three agents in the office:
Cooper, Ed Mitchell, and Bob Dennett. Together, they sold a lot of south
side homes, and eventually Cooper decided he deserved a percentage of
the business for managing the operation. Bill stalled when presented with
Cooper's demand; he did not want to lose the agent, but he was tight with
company money and not prepared to share profits. Once it was clear that
Bill would not negotiate on the issue, Cooper, along with Dennett and
Mitchell, chose to leave Iowa Realty and establish their own company.
They went over to the Beaver office in January 1964 to tell Bill of their
decision, but he was not in the office, so they talked with Grandquist and
returned to their south side branch. Bill's temper rose when he heard the
news. He and Grandquist raced over to the branch office, where an angry
Bill confronted the three agents and told them in an expletive-laced rage to
pack up and get out immediately. Cooler heads eventually prevailed, and
they were not forced out that day. But the exodus proved costly. Not only
did Bill lose three good salesmen, he lacked any other agents with experience on the south side and was forced to shut the branch office.[12]

Although Iowa Realty had been one of the first Des Moines real estate companies to establish a second office, after the south side office was
closed, it was Stanbrough, not Bill, who opened the next branch office—in
Ankeny, a suburb north and east of downtown—in November 1964. Iowa
Realty would not respond in kind until the spring of 1967, and it was
motivated by more than just a desire to add another office. By this time,
women had begun to break into the area's real estate business and enjoy
success. Bill and Grandquist took notice, but given the widespread sex-
ism of the time, they decided to introduce female agents to Iowa Realty
by setting up a branch office staffed exclusively by women. Before doing
so, they needed an established real estate woman to manage the branch.
Bill found her in Eleanor Leachman, who had been a top salesperson at
Neal Adamson's firm on Ingersoll Avenue, about a mile west of downtown. Leachman started at Iowa Realty in January 1967, and the branch
office at 115 Grand Avenue in West Des Moines, just west of Sixty-third
Street in Des Moines, opened for business in April 1967. Besides Leachman, who recruited other top female agents, Bill hired a rising real estate
star named Dee Sullivan away from Chamberlain, Kirk & Cline in 1967.
Initially, male agents at Iowa Realty derisively referred to the new office

as the "henhouse," but attitudes gradually changed as a number of the female agents became leading salespeople for Iowa Realty. In 1972, for example, two of Iowa Realty's six million-dollar producers were women, Dee Sullivan and Marie Shadur, and by this time, women were beginning to be integrated into the other Iowa Realty offices.[13]

There were other reasons why 1967 was significant. Stanbrough and Iowa Realty introduced new programs to distinguish themselves from each other as well as the rest of the competition.

Stanbrough was now staffed with fifteen agents; the rapid growth was pushed by its continuing presence on television and its new Colorful Photo Listing Gallery available at its office—the Ankeny branch had been shut down because of slower than expected growth in the area. Designed to save home buyers time, the album provided extensive photos and detailed information of all available homes in the area, allowing customers to preselect homes to visit. The following year, Stanbrough added another convenience that made viewing these homes even easier. It laid out a play area called the Kiddie Korner, which gave parents the luxury of leaving their children under adult supervision in a safe play area at the real estate office while they looked at homes. These photo galleries and play areas were also available at Stanbrough's two new branch offices, which also opened in 1968—a south side office on Southwest Ninth Street and an east side office on Hubbell Avenue.[14]

With forty agents by 1967, Iowa Realty remained significantly larger than Stanbrough, but Bill was paying close attention to his growing rival. However, before the company could launch its answer to Stanbrough's photo galleries, Iowa Realty's main office was destroyed by fire. On Saturday evening, June 24, 1967, a blaze started in the building at 3617 Beaver Avenue, shortly after Iowa Realty had closed for the day. No salespeople were inside when an automatic fire alarm went off at 6:24 p.m. The fire was probably started by a gas leak and was brought under control within thirty minutes, but Bill estimated the total damage to the building and office equipment at $75,000. "Records were somewhat damaged," he noted. Fortunately, temporary office space was found almost immediately. When John Fitzgibbon, vice president of Iowa-Des Moines National Bank, heard of the fire, he called Bill and offered him use of the basement in the bank's branch building just up the street at the corner of Beaver and Douglas avenues. Bill readily accepted, and Iowa Realty kept its operation running without interruption. Good fortune continued in finding permanent space as well. Several years earlier, Bill had built a building a block south of Iowa Realty and leased it to an insurance company, which serendipitously needed more space and vacated the office that July. The timing could not have been better, and after several weeks of renovating the building, Iowa Realty relocated in its new headquarters at 3521 Beaver Avenue.[15]

With the fire behind them, Iowa Realty personnel planned a program to simplify home buying and counter Stanbrough's latest volley. That fall, the company rolled out a computerized system designed to select certain homes from more than 1,500 listings based on customers' specific requirements. Dubbed Electronic Home Selection, the IBM-installed computer picked homes "suited for the home buyer's tastes" based on criteria input by the customer. Originally available only at the Beaver office, the service was added to the West Des Moines branch the following year.[16]

Bill would not add any other branches until 1972, when Iowa Realty established a new office on the south side of the city on Fleur Avenue and an east side office at East Euclid and Twenty-fifth Street. That year the company also set up a small information center at the Des Moines Municipal Airport. Still, growth continued, and by the end of 1970, Iowa Realty boasted fifty-two residential agents, compared to forty salespeople at Stanbrough. Its residential sales stood at $26 million, up from $11 million in 1958.[17]

But for Bill, the residential brokerage operation was just one piece of the pie. Unlike most of his competitors, he was active in land acquisition and commercial and residential development; indeed, it was here that he could deal. Certainly, many other successful businesspeople possessed a drive and work ethic similar to Bill's, but few had his instinct for the deal. This was his special talent. Gene Stanbrough explained: "He had a nose for a deal and wasn't afraid to move on it. He could smell a good one, and he could smell a bad one. This gave him a huge edge. Not only was he involved in areas the rest of us weren't, he was really good at making great deals."[18]

Bill's first two big deals of the 1960s involved Hy-Vee Food Stores. Then based in Chariton, a small town fifty miles south of Des Moines, Hy-Vee had been looking to enter the Des Moines area. In 1959, company CEO Dwight Vredenburg opened a store in the northern suburb of Johnston, and the following year he bought a market in the northeastern suburb of Altoona. He then sent Harold Trumbull, a vice president in charge or real estate, to scout out potential store sites in Des Moines. In the midst of his investigations, Trumbull came across Bill Knapp, and the two began talking. Eventually, Bill had ironed out two deals between Allied Development, his partnership with John Grubb, and Hy-Vee. Allied Development would build Hy-Vee stores to the grocer's specifications on its properties and then lease the facilities to Hy-Vee. One was constructed at 2537 East Euclid Street, north and east of downtown, and the other at 6501 Douglas Avenue, just west of the new Merle Hay Plaza and immediately south of the Stuart farm, land that the Knapp-Grubb partnership was still developing. Alcon Construction, another Knapp-Grubb venture, erected the buildings. Alcon also constructed other buildings for Allied Development, including two structures adjacent to the Hy-Vee grocery on Douglas. It built an office building immediately east of Hy-Vee (Grubb located his headquarters there) and a Kentucky Fried Chicken franchise just across Sixty-fourth Street on Douglas.[19]

The long-term lease deals with Hy-Vee proved lucrative for Bill, and they led to additional agreements with the food store chain, but they also highlighted differences between his money-making philosophy and that of John Grubb. These discrepancies ultimately resulted in the dissolution of their Allied Development/Alcon partnerships. Grubb had always been interested in making a quick profit. He bought land, developed it, and sold it. Bill, meanwhile, was much more patient and took the long approach, buying and holding properties. He was willing to wait, according to Grubb, for "later money." The Hy-Vee leases aligned much more closely with Bill's approach than Grubb's, and their differences soon led to disagreements on how and when to sell and develop land. In 1964, the Allied Development partnership came to an end with Bill buying Grubb's share of the company as well as his portion of Alcon Construction. Still, the two remained good friends and continued working together on other joint development projects. Their biggest was the Meredith estate.[20]

The estate was actually a dairy farm established in 1919 by Edwin T. Meredith, founder of the Meredith Corporation and publisher of such magazines as *Successful Farming* and later *Better Homes and Gardens*. Approximately 370 acres, the property was located north and west of downtown, with a large portion of it lying outside the city limits. Meredith died in 1928, but his widow continued to use the farm, building a mansion on the property to entertain her guests. When she died in 1961, there was little family interest in the acreage, and the Meredith Publishing Company, which held title to the land, began considering various options. Attorney Bill Wimer heard rumors that the land might be put on the market. He alerted Bill, who went to look at the land. He liked what he saw, imagining a new suburban development.[21]

This was where Bill's special talent kicked in. As Grubb put it, "Bill has great vision about the future value of land. He has always bought land in advance of the city's expansion. Bill has the uncanny ability to look at a piece of vacant land and immediately visualize what it will be good for. His insight allows him to pay farmland prices and sell the land for development prices." Bill believed the Meredith land was perfectly situated, just north of the thriving neighborhood of Beaverdale and primed for subdivision. He convinced Grubb to partner with him and began talking with Meredith representatives. In July 1963, he hammered out a deal: he and Grubb bought the lion's share of the estate, 275 acres, for a reported $1 million. The land was essentially bounded by Meredith Drive to the north, Madison Avenue to the south, Beaver Avenue to the east, and about Fifty-fourth Street to the west. Many at the time thought the purchase had been a mistake, remembered Les Calvert, a real estate competitor of Bill's. The two businessmen had doled out a lot of money for a big piece of rural land abutting a mature neighborhood. Despite the naysayers, the purchase proved hugely successful for Bill and partner Grubb. The first subdivisions were laid out and homebuilding commenced in 1964 and 1965. It was here that Bill, Grandquist, and shortly thereafter Paul Knapp built their own gracious homes in the area's first plat—Westchester Manor One—along Beaver Avenue between Aurora and Madison avenues.[22]

However, the development did not proceed as rapidly as Bill and Grubb had hoped. Problems loomed for the acres of the Meredith estate outside the corporate limits of Des Moines. Wimer went to work immediately, siding with the Des Moines city officials, who wanted to annex the land. This, Bill and Grubb argued, would mean the availability of better municipal services, such as police and fire protection, for homeowners in the area. Although Des Moines was finally successful in annexing most of the land, Johnston and Urbandale schools fought the extension of the Des Moines Community School District, and Aurora Avenue remained the northern boundary of the city's schools. This created the unfortunate situation for would-be residents along Aurora Avenue: those on the south side of the street were in the Des Moines district, and their children would attend the new neighborhood schools of Meredith Junior High and Hoover High schools, located respectively on Madison and Aurora avenues. But youngsters of the north side of the street were in the Johnston Community School District. At the time, most felt Des Moines schools had much more to offer than the smaller district, and this meant that lots north of Aurora Avenue, where much of the old Meredith estate was located, were more difficult to sell.[23]

Eventually, all the land was developed, but it was not until the early 1980s that all the lots were finally sold. Regardless, skeptics had changed their minds by the mid-1970s, and as Les Calvert suggested, the consensus became that Bill had driven a shrewd bargain and gotten a great deal on the Meredith acreage. Of course, no one else had visualized the farmland as bustling residential neighborhoods of tree-lined streets and blocks of new homes. This magic was not lost on John R. Grubb's son, John W. Grubb, who explained Bill's penchant for seeing undeveloped land differently than most, saying, "He had a better crystal ball than the rest of us."[24]

Another key example of Bill seeing possibilities where others did not was next to an interchange of the newly constructed interstate highways northwest of downtown Des Moines. Sometime after sections of the east-west Interstate 80 and north-south Interstate 35 systems were completed through Des Moines in 1960, Bill realized Des Moines could become an important highway nexus, making it an ideal location of warehouses and distribution centers. In particular, he began looking at several farms adjacent to the intestate elbow created in Urbandale where the interstates met: northbound I-35 turned into eastbound I-80 for several miles before I-35 turned north again just short of Ankeny. Here there was an interstate entrance/exit at Douglas Avenue and roughly a mile to the east was a rail line: the Chicago, Milwaukee, St. Paul and Pacific Railroad, generally known as the Milwaukee Road. Parker Brothers, the board-game maker, was the first to act on this potential. In 1962, it opened a distribution center just east of the farmland Bill was considering, on the northwest corner of Douglas Avenue and 100th Street, now the site of the Homemakers Furniture store. Parker Brothers took advantage of this transportation hub, and "freight car loads of game parts could now be shipped from Salem [its headquarters in Massachusetts] to Des

Moines, assembled, and then trucked to accounts in the Midwest, especially the lucrative Chicago market."[25]

That same year, Bill and Sid Bradley, his newly hired manager of commercial real estate, spent a lot of time driving around the metro area looking at land to purchase and eventually develop. But most of their time was focused on ground just east of the I-35/I-80 hub. In October 1962, they bought 77.7 acres on Douglas Avenue from Dalo, Incorporated, for $80,000. At about $1,000 per acre, this was roughly four times the average price of an acre of Iowa farmland, quite a bit more than Grubb suggested Bill paid for ground, but a lot less than developed land would bring. Five years later, they acquired 200 acres northeast of the Dalo land from the Edith Noble estate, again paying roughly $1,000 per acre. Two hundred more acres were eventually purchased, making Iowa Realty's total holdings 500 acres, bounded by Douglas Avenue to the south, Interstate 35 to the west, Meredith Drive to the north, and the Milwaukee Road and 104th Street to the east.[26]

Several years after the purchase, Iowa Realty began planning an industrial park for the area. William McCarty, director of the Greater Des Moines Chamber of Commerce's industrial bureau, had suggested the idea after hearing how pleased Parker Brothers was with its site, just east of Bill's land. In the spring of 1966, Governor Harold Hughes was on hand for the opening of Interstate Acres, Iowa Realty's major new industrial park, which was expected to include $11 million worth of new commercial and industrial construction over the next five years. The first building to go up was a 57,000-square-foot warehouse for Sears, Roebuck and Company, built by Iowa Realty and leased to the retailer. Bigger facilities were added to the park over the next two years: a Pepsi-Cola warehouse was constructed immediately north of the Sears facility and a large SuperValu food distribution center went in just to the west. Other companies soon came into Interstate Acres as well, including Continental Western Insurance, Western Electric, and Northwestern Bell, which established a training center there.[27]

As the telephone company's facility was going up, Bill saw another opportunity. He and Jack MacAllister, Northwestern Bell's CEO, played tennis together, and as was typical of Bill, he often talked business before, during, or after the sets. This relationship most likely led to the training center being built in Interstate Acres. While the two continued talking about the industrial park and the center, it became clear that Bell employees brought to Des Moines for training would require a place to stay, and at the time, there were not many options in this northwestern part of the metro area. Discussions went forward, and the two reached a broad agreement: Iowa Realty would build a motel and restaurant, and Northwestern Bell agreed to rent a certain amount of rooms during the week. Others worked out the details, which called for Northwestern Bell to take 60 percent of the motel's rooms at an agreed-upon rate, which would rise annually with the consumer price index, for a ten-year period. With such a guarantee, Bill built the 120-unit Peppertree Motel and Restaurant in 1972 and 1973 at almost no risk. The motel proved profitable, but the restaurant less so, as many motel patrons had cars and often chose to eat elsewhere.[28]

Actually, Bill had already gotten into the motel business when he became aware of the shortage of affordable living space downtown. It was Governor Hughes who introduced Bill to the situation, but once he began looking downtown, he saw opportunity for profit as well. Beginning in 1965, he started buying property south of Iowa Methodist Hospital in an area between Twelfth and Fourteenth streets and High Street and Woodland Avenue. Bill eventually pieced together a building site by purchasing fifteen parcels from individuals and the City of Des Moines for a total of about $250,000. As he was buying, he initiated talks with hospital officials about their housing/motel needs for staff and patients' families. Plans called for two buildings; the Inntowner One would have eighty-seven efficiency apartments, while the Inntowner Two would have fifty-two efficiency apartments and thirty-five one-bedroom units. Bill and Don Cordes, the hospital's CEO, arranged a deal: the hospital agreed to rent a number of apartments for staff, nurses, and interns, while Iowa Realty could rent the remaining rooms to outpatients, people visiting hospital patients, or others who sought the convenience of living close to their downtown jobs. The Inntowner opened in 1970, and the contract with Iowa Methodist, which continued to take more and more rooms, made it a profitable venture.[29]

Bill's interest in apartments continued. Over the years, he had been buying them for rentals and as investments for future sale. He also became involved in converting such buildings to condominiums. This began with his 1972 purchase of the elegant 3660 Grand Avenue apartment building from Arthur Sanford and his partner Joe Rosenfield. A prominent

Des Moines business figure, Rosenfield had practiced law, served as president and then chairman of Younkers Department Stores, was a director of General Growth Properties, and one of the state's leading Democrats. It was through the Democratic Party and Harold Hughes that Bill and Rosenfield became acquainted in the early 1960s. During that time, the two became good friends, and Bill expressed interest in buying 3660 Grand. Rosenfield always refused, but promised Bill first crack at it when he was ready to sell. Eventually, he contacted Bill and offered him the apartment building. As Bill considered the deal, others heard about it and made Rosenfield offers—some were considerably more than the amount he had floated to Bill—but he turned them all down saying, "The apartments are not for sale until Bill Knapp tells me he doesn't want them." Bill did want them, and in March 1972 he bought the building.[30]

Shortly thereafter, Bill decided to convert the apartments to condominiums, but Rosenfield, who lived in the building and was in his late sixties, did not want to buy his unit because, he said, "He was not going to live that long." Bill accommodated his close friend by renting him the apartment as long as Rosenfield chose to stay there. "Joe lived until 2000, but I never raised his rent," Bill remembered. "I liked to joke that I subsidized a millionaire. Of course, I didn't expect him to live that long!"[31]

All along, Bill understood that business was based on connections, and knowing the right people often created opportunities or greased the skids for making deals. This understanding originally led him into politics, and over the years, he developed relationships with local officials. Such activity did not always guarantee he got what he wanted, but it did grant him access and allowed him to "get an ear" with almost any local official.[32] More often than not, his work with city officials, school board members, planning and zoning commissioners, and the like moved his projects forward. Of course, it was this interest in politics and his penchant for the Democratic Party that led him to become acquainted with gubernatorial candidate Harold Hughes in 1962. A truck driver who had overcome alcoholism, Hughes had gone on to head a trucking association and was elected to the Iowa Commerce Commission in 1958. From this job, Hughes launched his run for governor. Bill liked the charismatic politician immediately and became a major supporter. Out of this working relationship, a warm and close friendship developed.

For Hughes, Bill became a key fundraiser over his next few campaigns, but maybe more importantly, he became a confidant of the governor's, one of the few people with whom Hughes said he could "let his hair down." The two spent quite a bit of time together, occasionally hunting and fishing, pastimes enjoyed by the governor but only tolerated by the businessman. Bill said, "I remember sitting in duck blinds by the hours, freezing to death, while he [Hughes] loved every minute of it." When Hughes needed to get away to think or just relax, Bill made his Sugar Creek retreat west of Des Moines available to the governor.[33]

For Bill, Hughes opened his eyes to the wider world, pointing out inequities in society and encouraging him to help the less fortunate. Over the years the Allerton native had had little contact with minority groups such as African Americans, but two experiences early in life had left an impression. When Bill's father had taken the family to Florida in the late 1930s, the children encountered the harsh reality of Jim Crow racism for the first time. While in Miami, Bill's mother and father operated a small restaurant. Local law and convention at the time dictated that African Americans could not enter the café; if they wanted food, they could only place and pick up an order at the back door. Although Bill did not completely understand the situation, the injustice did not seem right and stuck with him. Several years later in the navy, he again saw African Americans treated differently than whites: they were allowed only the lowliest of jobs aboard ship. Again, he was struck by the unfairness of the system.[34]

Once in the real estate business, Bill saw residential segregation in Des Moines, based on both deed restrictions and economic realities: most of the area's African American population lived in the older and poorer sections of the city. But he was a salesman trying to make a living and build a business, and he focused on selling homes within the current system. As Hughes became better acquainted with Bill, he saw compassion beneath the aggressive, business exterior. He tapped into this by taking the real estate man to see the most blighted areas of Des Moines and introduced him to those in greatest need. Bill acknowledged Hughes's role: "Harold broadened my outlook. He made me more focused. He helped me in caring more for people who don't have much because early in his governorship we worked with the inner city....Harold got me interested in that arena."[35]

As part of this effort, Hughes appointed Bill, John Grubb, and several others in the real estate and construction industries to a state committee on low-income housing. By 1967, there was serious push to build such housing as part of an urban renewal project sponsored by the Des Moines Area Council of Churches in the city's Oakridge neighborhood, northwest of downtown. The plan faced several stumbling blocks, however, one of which was that the Federal Housing Administration (FHA) was dragging its feet in providing low-interest loans necessary for construction to begin. That fall, Hughes led a delegation that included Bill, Grubb, Les Calvert, Eldon Woltz, and Dick Bryan of Des Moines Savings and Loan on a two-day trip to Washington, D.C., to address the issues of urban renewal in Iowa and break the logjam for FHA funding. The group had a roundtable discussion with Housing and Urban Development (HUD) officials and lunch with its undersecretary Robert Wood, but the highlight of the stay was the ten-minute private meeting scheduled with President Lyndon Johnson, which turned into a memorable forty-five-minute conversation with the president.[36]

The trip was successful, and the group won assurances that the FHA would ensure the necessary loans for the Oakridge development. The initial housing units of the Homes of Oakridge, which was the city's first and largest low-income housing project, were opened in 1969, and a second, bigger complex was built the following year. This would be the small beginning of Bill's interest in downtown Des Moines and in helping the less fortunate, which would blossom over the next few decades. In the meantime, he became the key fundraiser for the governor, helping Hughes get reelected to a second term in 1964 and again in 1966. According to historian Joe Wall, Hughes "gave the state its most exciting and progressive administration." But by 1967, Hughes was contemplating retirement at the end of his term. Late that year, Senator Robert Kennedy called him, encouraging him to run for the United States Senate. The two had become acquainted in 1962, and Hughes's later anti-Vietnam War stand strengthened the bond between the two men. Bill was pleased when Hughes finally decided to run. He won the 1968 election, and when he headed to Washington, D.C., Bill went with him to help the senator-elect and his staff members find homes.[37]

While Hughes was governor, it was alleged that he leaked information to Bill about interstate routes through the state and locations of planned entrances and exits. At several of these sites, Iowa Realty did indeed purchase land, sometimes ahead of development, but Hughes flatly denied any wrongdoing, explaining that Bill "never asked me for a thing in a political way," and he added, "I've never asked him for anything." Hughes aide Ed Campbell also denied any impropriety and noted that planned highway routes were not secret and such information was available to the public. Furthermore, while Bill readily admitted that he had purchased land at several entrances and exits along Interstate 80 and Interstate 35, he explained that he did so based on public information. No firm evidence ever surfaced to confirm the rumors. Moreover, in all cases but one, the interstates were already built through the areas when Bill bought the land at or near the interchange sites. In the one exception, he purchased land at the Roland exit forty-five miles north of Des Moines on the I-35 route three months before that section of highway was completed. These acquisitions actually looked quite similar to Bill's purchase of land at the Douglas exit off of I-80/35, which became Interstate Acres, another example of Bill thinking ahead and buying land that would appreciate in value.[38]

Although these rumors continued to surface from time to time, they did not affect Hughes's political career, which by 1969 had taken him to Washington, D.C., as a freshman senator. Once there, his commanding presence and spellbinding oratory soon impressed a number of people. In December 1969, the *Des Moines Register* reported that Hughes had "acquired somewhat of a national reputation and is often mentioned as a dark horse candidate for president in 1972." Such attention proved flattering, and Hughes began thinking about a run for the presidency. In late 1970, Hughes set up a Washington, D.C., office for a small group tasked to determine his presidential chances. Bill was thrilled. "The sky was the limit for Harold," he recalled. "He was a natural born leader." But this operation was expensive, costing $5,000 a month. Initially, it was bankrolled by Bill, Joe Rosenfield, and New York philanthropist R. Brinkley Smithers. Soon though, it was decided broader based funding was required, and in early 1971, Bill set up the Hughes for President office in the Hubbell Building in downtown Des Moines.[39]

He looked to Connie Wimer to manage the office. He came to know her because she was the wife of attorney Bill Wimer. Actually, the Knapps and the Wimers had been friends for several years. The Wimers knew a lot of people in Des Moines, and Connie frequently threw dinner parties where she often mixed people who would not normally encounter one another. Early on, she invited the Knapps, who initially declined, with

Bill ostensibly explaining that he was too busy. In truth, he and Irene were both shy in social settings, especially with groups of people they did not know. By the late 1960s, though, Bill and Irene started attending some of these parties. Bill found he enjoyed them; Irene less so. Still, the Knapps went out with Bill and Connie Wimer on a regular basis, and the couples even vacationed together in Florida. Bill thought Connie was a perfect fit to head the Hughes office. Savvy, bright, and engaging, she had experience as a secretary and office manager and was interested in Democratic politics. Bill first asked Bill Wimer if it was all right for him to offer Connie the job. Wimer agreed, and so too did Connie, who readily took the position.[40]

Fundraising was the office's primary purpose, and Bill employed two unique approaches to raising money for Hughes. First, to make giving to the campaign as easy as possible, he established an installment plan, allowing donors to meet their pledge obligations over an extended period of time. Then, because he felt there were more wealthy Republicans in the area than Democrats, he along with several others organized the Republicans for Hughes campaign to target this specific demographic. The strategies worked, and by early spring, $20,000 a month was pouring into the office.[41]

Then, much to Bill's dismay, Hughes's interest in pursuing the presidency waned. He did everything he could to keep the senator in the race because he believed Hughes "had the ability to be a great politician because he could communicate with people." A man of deep convictions and principles, Hughes became increasingly uncomfortable with what he thought was compromising his ideals to win people's support. Sometimes, he went out of his way to express his opinions even when he was certain they would not be well received. This occurred, for instance, when Hughes was visiting with a small group of Jewish business leaders in New York, who were interested in funding his campaign. When the topic of Israel came up in the conversation, Hughes's response was immediate: "Well, I'll tell you what, gentleman, if you think for one minute I'm going to give a blank check to Israel, you have the wrong candidate." The room turned deadly quiet, and as Bill recalled, "You could have heard a pin drop." This "take it or leave it" attitude suggested Hughes's heart was no longer in the race, and it did not win Hughes any friends. His problems only increased when some of his extreme views on the afterlife surfaced.[42]

Hughes and his family were devout Methodists, but the senator was also associated with Spiritual Frontiers Fellowship, an interfaith group dedicated to investigating altered states of consciousness, mystical experiences, and psychic phenomena such as mental telepathy, extra-sensory perception, and clairvoyance. He took ideas of eternal life as described in the Bible literally and occasionally attended séances to connect with those who had died. Bill once accompanied Hughes to an Arthur Ford séance in Chicago; Bill thought it nonsense, but Hughes was a believer. In fact, Hughes attended séances where he communicated with his dead brother, who spoke to him "through the vocal cords of a medium." The *Des Moines Register* reported this oddity when it ran an interview with the senator in early July. Bill knew Hughes would make no effort to spin his beliefs, and when they came out, "the ball game was over." The senator withdrew from the race on July 15. But Bill was still angry and disappointed: "He had a special ability to be great, and I don't think he utilized himself to the point that he could have." Two years later, Bill was again disheartened by Hughes's decision not to seek reelection to the senate. Instead, Hughes would devote himself to lay religious work and then the development of alcohol treatment centers. The two remained good friends, however, and their paths would cross again in the 1980s.[43]

Besides opening Bill's eyes to social issues, the senator introduced him to or better acquainted him with a number of important Iowa Democrats including Joe Rosenfield, John Chrystal, Neal Smith, and John Culver. It was his relationship with Hughes and his work on the politician's behalf that put Bill on the Iowa Democratic map. By the end of the senator's political career in 1975, Bill had become the key power broker within the state's Democratic Party.

Just as connections were essential in politics, so too did Bill realize they were vital in business. This understanding led him into the Breakfast Club. The group was the brainchild of Pete Choconas, an insurance agent with Connecticut Mutual Life, who wanted to bring together decision makers from different Des Moines businesses to exchange ideas, do business with one another, and socialize. Founded in 1962, the Breakfast Club's five original members were Choconas, Bob Bunce of KCBC Radio, David Miller of West Des Moines State Bank, Rex Roupe, an attorney, and Gary Staples of Polk County Federal Savings and Loan. The group met weekly on Tuesday mornings, initially at the downtown Hotel Savery. It grew relatively quickly, and by the end of the following year, the Breakfast Club boasted twenty members. Miller recruited his old friend, accountant Jack Wahlig, into the Breakfast Club in 1963, shortly after Wahlig had been transferred to the McGladrey firm's Des Moines office. Wahlig had recently taken over the accounting work for Iowa Realty and was so impressed with the club and the potential networking it provided, he told Bill it was something to consider. Shortly after that, Bill was recruited into the club by Bob Maddox of Allied Construction Services. He joined in late 1963.[44]

As Wahlig had suggested, the Breakfast Club proved valuable for Bill. Members became acquainted with businessmen in other fields, information was traded, and often, deals were struck. A relationship made here with David Miller, for instance, led to Bill's 1983 partnership with him in the purchase of the Blue Horizon Motel in Clear Lake. The following year, Miller brought Bill into a small group that purchased West Des Moines State Bank from the Chase family. And although not motivated by business, this connection with Miller also led Bill into a prayer group. Never really interested in organized religion, Bill had gradually stopped attending Sunday services with his family at Westminster Presbyterian Church in favor of tennis, but a number of conversations with Harold Hughes about faith and religion had returned Bill to prayer. In the late 1970s, he joined a small prayer group that included David Miller and Dwight Swanson, president of Iowa Power and Light Company. The group generally met Thursday mornings for breakfast; it eventually settled in at the downtown Howard Johnson's and ultimately comprised other prominent businessmen including John R. Grubb, Weitz Company head Fred Weitz, attorney Tom Flynn, and broadcasting executive Tom Stoner. It was intentionally kept small to allow for serious conversations about biblical passages, religious issues, and current topics. When in town, Harold Hughes sometimes joined in the meetings, but he had a habit of lecturing, and Bill sometimes had to tell him back off a bit and allow for group discussion.[45]

Of course, not everything related to the Breakfast Club involved networking, business deals, or serious issues. There was plenty of socializing. In addition to its weekly morning meetings, the club held seasonal parties throughout the year. Some were stag, some involved spouses, and some were mini-vacations, in which members and their wives often went on boating excursions on the Mississippi or other area rivers. Bill was a regular at the stag gatherings, and he and Irene sometimes attended the couples parties, but they rarely went on the boat trips.[46]

Nonetheless, one Breakfast Club event was memorable for the Knapps. Most club parties were held at restaurants or country clubs, followed by what the group called "afterglow" gatherings. These were held at the members' homes, which allowed the festivities to continue late into the night. Much to Bill and Irene's surprise, the afterglow following the January 1965 dinner dance was scheduled at their home without their knowledge. This was especially uncomfortable because Irene did not generally allow liquor in the house—this dated back to her strict religious upbringing—and there would be a lot brought in for the afterglow. When the afterglow location was announced at the end of the dinner dance, Bill was furious. He let a string of obscenities fly as he and Irene rushed to their Clinton home before others arrived. When they pulled into their driveway, they saw a donkey tied to the garage door, a jab at Bill for being the club's only Democrat. Not thinking, Bill pushed his garage door remote, and the donkey rose in the air as the door opened. Fortunately, he lowered the door and untied the animal without incident. But once he secured the donkey to a tree, it brayed long into the night. The joke was not over, however. In the midst of the afterglow, a police officer knocked at the door and asked to speak to the owner. Bill came barreling over. The officer explained that party and donkey were too noisy and in violation of city code. Bill's temper rose until the officer finally said he was off duty and playing a prank as instructed by a Breakfast Club member. Eventually, Bill laughed about the practical joke, but he was not amused that night.[47]

Such parties, though, were not regular events for the Knapps. While they did entertain occasionally, it was usually with family or small groups of close friends. Besides being somewhat bashful, Irene was also hesitant about socializing because she still had a young child at home, and her world revolved around her family. Shortly after the Knapps moved into their new home on Beaver Avenue in 1965, Ginny turned fifteen and Roger was just six. Ginny, of course, was becoming more and more independent; in three years she graduated from Roosevelt High School. She headed south to William Woods College in Fulton, Missouri, in 1968, but after three years, she had had enough of the women's college. Ginny was homesick for Des Moines and her boyfriend, Mark Haviland, whom she had dated since junior high school. She returned home and attended Drake University, where she studied art education before marrying Haviland in 1972. Irene was thrilled Ginny was back in Des Moines. She saw her often, but her life was soon dominated by Roger and his burgeoning interest in tennis.[48]

When the Knapps were planning their new home, Bill decided to build a backyard tennis court for himself but also for Ginny, who intended to take lessons. After moving in, he contacted Lloyd Stokstad, the Wakonda Country Club tennis pro, about giving Ginny lessons. Stokstad could not do it, but he recommended his son Arden, who assisted him at the club and had been the number one player on the University of Iowa's tennis team. Arden Stokstad took the job, and he started giving Ginny lessons on the Knapp court the following spring. A couple of weeks into the lessons, Roger came out to watch, picked up a racket, and started hitting tennis balls. "He was a natural," remembered Stokstad. "Roger had amazing hand-eye coordination, and was very mature for a six-year-old." Before long, Roger was taking lessons as well, but Ginny did not like her younger brother tagging along and decided to squelch his interest. "I thought if I beat him badly, he would quit, and I bet him he couldn't beat me," Ginny recalled. "So we played. He was no bigger than the racket, but he won, and I decided tennis was for him, not for me." Soon, Ginny quit taking lessons; Roger continued.[49]

If defeating Ginny was his first big victory, Roger's second came that August 1966, when the small six-year-old southpaw stunned a number of the older players and won the boys' ten-and-under division in the Des Moines city tennis tournament. From then on, Roger was hooked, but tennis was far from his only interest. Although he began to spend a growing number of hours on the court, the competitive youngster was a talented all-round athlete and played both Little League baseball and interscholastic basketball. Like his sister before him, Roger also became involved in the youth group at Westminster Presbyterian Church. Irene, at this time, much like millions of other suburban mothers, kept busy taking her son from event to event.[50]

But it was tennis—lessons twice a week with Stokstad, hours of practice, and a growing number of tournaments—that gradually became the focus of Roger's life, and by extension, the family's focus as well. After Roger started winning consistently in local Des Moines tournaments, his parents sought stronger competition for him beyond the city. This meant entering junior tournaments of the United States Tennis Association (USTA) Missouri Valley division. These summer matches were held in regional locales such as Kansas City, St. Louis, Oklahoma City, Wichita, and Omaha. Irene always escorted her son to these events, and just as Bill had made a point of being present at Ginny's various childhood recitals and performances, so too did he arrange his schedule to see Roger play tennis. Jean Stauffer, the mother of John Stauffer, another top junior tennis player from Des Moines remembered, "Bill stood out at the tournaments. Fathers weren't usually there because most couldn't get off work, but Bill had flexibility; he owned the company." When she was able, Ginny went as well. The Knapps were all there, for instance, when Roger notched his first big regional victory in 1972, defeating number-one seed Mark Johnson in Oklahoma City to win the twelve-year-old division championship. As the *Des Moines Register* reported, the success garnered Roger his fifty-sixth tennis trophy. More importantly, it suggested that the talented youngster was something special and that he could compete and win against the best regional players in his age bracket.[51]

If 1972 appeared a turning point for young Roger, it was clearly one for Bill and Iowa Realty. Up to this point, the company had been running smoothly. Bill's investments in land and his ventures in commercial development and property management were paying off, and the brokerage business was thriving. He and Grandquist still seemed the perfect team. They were close friends, neighbors, and partners who enjoyed each other's company and worked closely together. When both were at the Beaver office at midday, for instance, they almost always went across the street with Bill's brother Paul to the Mandarin restaurant for lunch. But company growth began to create strains between Paul and Grandquist, and this put Bill in the middle.[52]

Before the addition of branch offices, Iowa Realty's agents had been divided into two teams: one reporting to sales manager Clair Niday, and the other reporting to sales manager Roger Cleven. After the West Des Moines office began to grow, Cleven was transferred to oversee its operation, which by the early 1970s had begun to include men as well. But no one replaced him at the Beaver office, and Niday was overwhelmed. Paul Knapp, the company assistant manager, picked up a lot of the slack, but he became increasingly disgruntled with Grandquist, whom he felt was not pulling his weight at the understaffed office. Others agreed. Daryl Neumann, who joined Iowa Realty as the controller in early 1972, felt that Grandquist seemed to be slowing down, and "just slacking off a little bit. He was playing more golf and not paying attention to details." John Grubb believed that "Kenny [Grandquist] was satisfied" and had lost some of his energy and drive.[53]

Paul's dissatisfaction grew when Grandquist opposed his idea of doubling Iowa Realty's sales force. He thought the move necessary to counter rival Stanbrough's rapid growth. Paul remembered: "I had been going to a lot of national conventions, and I could see that there were a lot of things we should be doing. We should have a training school and we should hire more agents. Ken's idea was that it was better to have 40 'good' agents than 100 'average' agents. I thought it was better to have 100 who were 'good'." This difference of opinion was compounded by Paul's mounting ambition and the fact that as long as Grandquist was vice president and general manager, Paul could not advance in the company.[54]

His frustration finally bubbled over in December 1972. Late one night, Paul called Bill and arranged an immediate meeting with him at the office. He was going to quit. The two brothers had a lengthy and heated exchange. The heart-to-heart discussion focused on Grandquist, Paul's future, and the direction of the company. Bill was stuck. He was dead set on keeping Paul, but he had a long, close, and successful relationship with Grandquist and wanted him with Iowa Realty as well. Ultimately, he sided with Paul. Grandquist was promoted to president, Bill took the title of chairman, and Paul became vice president and general sales manager. More important than titles, however, Paul was now in charge of the residential brokerage business, Grandquist oversaw the property management division, and Bill continued devoting himself to "new acquisitions, investments, and properties currently under development."[55]

Bill hoped the reorganization would work, but that remained to be seen. Nonetheless, the event closed a hugely successful decade for Bill and Iowa Realty. The company had become a residential and commercial development powerhouse, and it now dominated Des Moines's real estate brokerage business. From this strong foundation, Bill began moving in new directions. For most of his career, he had operated on the periphery of the city, but this changed in the mid-1970s, when he began working in the downtown core. One thing did not change, however. Bill would continue to deal, and it was here that he found continued success.

Chapter Six

Uptown and Downtown

For much of the 1970s, Bill's career followed a recognizable path. Iowa Realty remained the engine of his expanding empire, growing in the city's residential neighborhoods and its suburbs. Here the firm's familiar blue and white "For Sale" signs were constant reminders that Bill's real estate agents dominated the market, and here Bill bought and sold land and developed and managed properties.

But a shakeup in Iowa Realty's top management created rifts and ultimately took the firm in a new direction, while a second generation of Knapp family members joined the company. Significant though these changes were, they did not affect Bill's business dealings. He remained the consummate broker, who, according to James Hubbell III, loved nothing better than "get [ting] in there and making deals." Over the decade, more and more of his transactions took place in Des Moines's downtown, especially after his purchase of the rundown Hotel Savery in 1977. This move coincided with the beginnings of downtown's renaissance, and Bill became a key figure, constantly pushing the rebuilding of the city's core. "He was a driver," businessman Fred Weitz recalled. "Bill understood people, he understood deals, and he got things done." The *Des Moines Register* noted his influence and wrote in 1985, "Knapp is recognized as the godfather of downtown housing, both apartments and condominiums as well as one of the earliest adherents of the philosophy that what's good for downtown was good for all of Des Moines."[1]

Before he became involved in downtown, he was forced to choose who would lead Iowa Realty's residential real estate division: his brother Paul or his close friend Kenny Grandquist. As noted earlier, Paul had become frustrated by what he viewed as Grandquist's decreasing interest in the company and its growth. He went to Bill in December 1972 and argued that his brother should elevate him to head the residential real estate operation. Bill agreed; Paul was advanced to vice president and general manager of Iowa Realty, while Grandquist became president and put in charge of the company's commercial operation. Not surprisingly, Grandquist was both angered and hurt by the decision. He vacated his office, which was next to Bill's, and moved to the other side of the building; a year later, he relocated in the Iowa Realty's commercial real estate office on Ingersoll Avenue. After the realignment, Bill and Grandquist successfully avoided each other at work, but the situation remained especially awkward because the two lived next door to each other in their Beaver Avenue homes. Grandquist remedied this in 1974, when he moved into a new home about a half mile south and west of Bill's. The move suggested the depth of the breach: the two had been next door neighbors since the late 1950s. Still, Bill, Paul, and Grandquist all thought the new structure might work, but according to journalist Walt Shotwell, most in the local real estate industry "regarded this as a demotion" for Grandquist. There were also hopes that the management shuffle might "wreck Iowa Realty."[2]

Grandquist accused Bill of making the move simply because of familial ties. It was true that he wanted to move his brother up in the company hierarchy, but Bill would not have endangered Iowa Realty's success to advance Paul's career. Rather, he trusted his brother, and when Paul suggested he had a better plan for the company's future, Bill gave him the opportunity. It proved a good move; although Paul's management style and vision were different than Grandquist's, the company grew even more rapidly under his leadership.[3]

With his big personality and charisma, Grandquist had managed through charm and, when necessary, intimidation. Paul was not such a magnetic figure. Congenial, but quieter and more serious than Grandquist, he was much happier in the background than in the limelight and could rely on his broad knowledge of the brokerage business. He was more interested in organizational structure than Grandquist, and according to controller Daryl Neumann, "was much more likely to work closely with agents on the nitty-gritty details." Likewise, while Grandquist operated in the moment and reacted to situations, Paul was thoughtful and future oriented. It was his idea of growing the business that ultimately appealed to Bill.[4]

Paul jumped right into his new job, immediately taking over the one-hour daily sales meetings. These meetings assured that all agents knew of the homes sold the previous day, the availability of new listings, and they allowed time for questions and discussion. Held each morning at the Beaver office, agents at the branch offices participated via teleconference. The daily meetings provided continuity for the Iowa Realty sales force and except for the absence of Grandquist's commanding presence, the transfer of power in the residential brokerage business appeared seamless. But real change was on the horizon; Paul was interested in implementing ideas he had garnered at regional and national real estate conventions. Regular attendance at these conferences had convinced him that more agents meant more sales, and once he had operational control, he rapidly added branch offices throughout the metropolitan Des Moines area. When Grandquist was moved aside, Iowa Realty had five offices and roughly sixty-five agents in the city. To this core, Paul began adding branches, and by 1975 the company had eight offices, with new ones located west of downtown on Ingersoll Avenue, in the suburb of Urbandale, and in Indianola, the Warren County seat, twelve miles south of the city. A farm office had also been established in the town of Winterset, thirty-seven miles south and west of Des Moines. Growth continued, and by the end of 1977, Iowa Realty had fourteen residential real estate offices blanketing greater Des Moines as well as its commercial office and seven farm offices that handled acreage transactions.[5]

One of these new offices fell well beyond metropolitan Des Moines; it was located 100 miles to the north and west in Fort Dodge, the county seat of Webster County. Its opening represented the beginning of Paul's strategy of expanding beyond central Iowa. To do so, he looked to Jack McWilliams, an Iowa Realty sales agent since 1971. McWilliams began scouting for appropriate towns and sites for new Iowa Realty operations, and in 1978, eight more offices were opened including branches in Guthrie

Center, Perry, Boone, Ames, and Nevada—towns to the west, northwest, and north of the metro area. Expansion continued, and by the end of 1980, Iowa Realty had thirty-three offices in Iowa, 268 residential sales agents, and sales of $121 million, up from $26 million ten years earlier.[6]

The expansion significantly increased revenues but it also led to new problems. Rapid growth required recruiting a large number of new agents, many of whom had little to no experience in real estate. Paul addressed this issue in 1978 by introducing an in-house formal training program for his agents. The idea was relatively new. He had come across it at a trade association meeting. Tim Meline, a young Iowa Realty sales agent with an undergraduate degree in education, persuaded Paul to give him a shot at leading the operation. Meline was first sent to Atlanta, Georgia, where he attended a one-week seminar with Steve Brown, the foremost figure in real estate training at the time. He then went to Edina Realty in suburban Minneapolis to examine its training program, one of the few in the region. Back in Des Moines, Meline began piecing together his own curriculum, the first real estate training program in the city. Initially, he created a three-day introductory course for new Iowa Realty agents covering the industry in general and company procedures in particular. Then he developed a pre-licensing class, which was open to anyone preparing for an Iowa real estate license and became a moneymaker for the company. Eventually he put together continuing education courses for current Iowa Realty agents, teaching them about "using a calculator, financing, tips on selling and getting clients, and advertising."[7]

Meline understood that education was part content and part entertainment, and he quickly became well known for including humor in his presentations, especially at the two or three annual meetings Iowa Realty held for all its agents. Here he kept everyone's attention with his over-the-top impersonations of famous figures including General George Patton, Walt Disney's Aladdin, and Forrest Gump. Such antics made Iowa Realty's training enjoyable and as the only such program in the area, it gave the company a competitive advantage over its rivals by not only bringing in recruits but also assuring they were well prepared for the business.[8]

The training program was also useful when Paul and Bill decided on the strategy of selling franchises. The idea had been bandied about for several years, but it became more pressing due to problems of operating distant branches and a changing real estate market. Shortly after Iowa Realty set up offices outside the Des Moines area in places like Guthrie Center or Ames, for example, it became clear that running these branches was difficult and expensive. Instead, Paul decided that linking with proven real estate professionals, who already had local contacts and experience, might be a better way to expand. At the same time, national real estate franchising operations such as Century 21 and Electronic Realty Associates (ERA) were establishing beachheads in Des Moines. The field became more crowded in 1978, when the Meredith publishing company leveraged its flagship magazine's brand name by starting Better Homes and Gardens Real Estate Service to sell franchises. It scored a coup in Des Moines by immediately signing on Stanbrough Realtors, Iowa Realty's biggest rival. The following year, Cedar Rapids realtor Fred Gibson and several others created Partners, another franchise that threatened to cover the state.[9]

In response, Paul had Jack McWilliams—his point man in branch office operations—and Des Moines advertising man Joe Pundzak put together a slide presentation about selling Iowa Realty franchises. Bill and top management gathered to hear the pitch early one morning in late fall 1979. The program did not start well. The slide projector had been in the trunk of a car overnight, and its lens had frozen, causing a delay in the presentation. This aggravated Bill, who was not known for his patience. The equipment was soon fixed and the slide show began, only to be interrupted shortly by Bill, who was yelling, "Wait a goddamn minute; slowdown the show, slowdown the show. Stop the thing." McWilliams did so but told Bill that the Traveler projector system was automatic and its speed could not be adjusted. He then explained that the slide show presented franchising as a revolutionary force in Iowa real estate market and restarted the projector. The last slide featured locally renowned blue and white Iowa Realty "For Sale" sign with the name of an independent Marshalltown real estate agent-owner who had already expressed interest in an affiliation with the firm. The voiceover proclaimed, "Iowa Realty works for you." Bill's response was typical. He had the ability to assess ideas and situations quickly and act immediately. "I like it," he said. "Let's do it."[10]

With that, Iowa Realty was in the franchise business, but unlike others who sold franchises nationally, it planned to stay within Iowa where it knew the market. McWilliams was named head of the new division in March 1980. For a $4,500 upfront fee and 5 percent of annual sales, agent-owners throughout Iowa could become franchisees. In return, they received Iowa Realty signage and promotional materials; and access to Iowa Realty's training program, legal department, and closing department; as well as its valuable relocation service and referral network. As expected, Marshalltown real estate agent Kim Kimberlin became the first Iowa Realty franchisee that April. Seven more franchises were added that year, and it appeared that Iowa Realty had found a cost-effective way to expand across the state.[11]

As Iowa Realty was growing, it was also becoming more of a family firm. In addition to Bill, his brother Paul, and brother-in-law Clair Niday, two more Knapps joined the company in the 1970s. First to come into the fold was Mike Knapp, Paul's oldest son. An Eagle Scout and fine athlete, Mike had been raised around the business but had not expressed any interest in going into real estate. Yet, while studying marketing at the University of Iowa, Mike took and passed the real estate exam, and when he graduated in 1972, he asked his father for a job. Paul hired him immediately, and Mike began working as a residential agent out of the Beaver office. His younger brother Billy took a more circuitous route to Iowa Realty.[12]

Billy also attended the University of Iowa but was not sure what he wanted to do and not very motivated. He joined a fraternity, often cut classes, and received mediocre grades. Eventually, Paul pulled the plug and told Billy to come home. In 1971, he spent some time volunteering at the Hughes for President office in the Hubbell Building in downtown Des Moines, and when that closed, he took a job at the SuperValu warehouse. It was then two people intervened; both Bill Wimer and Ed Campbell, at the time a Hughes political aide, suggested that Billy return to school, finish his degree, and give Drake Law School a try. Billy decided to follow the advice. He went to his father and guaranteed he would become a lawyer if Paul paid for the rest of his education. Paul agreed. Billy graduated from the University of Iowa in 1974, enrolled in Drake Law School, and began clerking for the Wimer law firm in 1975, where he largely worked on the Iowa Realty account. He stayed with Wimer after he finished law school in 1977 and continued focusing on Iowa Realty work. Eighteen months later, Billy joined Iowa Realty as its corporate counsel. Shortly after taking the job, however, it became clear that having two Bill Knapps at the same office created a lot of confusion, so Billy legally changed his name to lessen misunderstandings; from that point on, he was William Clare Knapp II, or Bill II.[13]

Shortly before Bill II became part of the company, however, a major change took place; Kenny Grandquist resigned. Ever since 1972, when Bill moved him over to the commercial operation to make way for Paul on the residential side, tension among the three had been high. Grandquist's ego was bruised, and he began to see himself in a dead-end position. Sometime in 1976, he started thinking about establishing his own real estate company. He talked about it with Larry Cedarstrom, a commercial agent who had been with Iowa Realty since 1964. Cedarstrom thought highly of Grandquist and when he decided to go out on his own, Cedarstrom went with him. With their plans in place, Grandquist and Cedarstrom left Iowa Realty in January 1977. In a telephone interview with the *Des Moines Tribune,* Grandquist explained that disagreements with Bill led him to resign. But it was more than that; Grandquist had ambitions of running his own firm, and given his strained relations with the Knapp brothers, he felt it was time to leave.[14]

Universal Realty was founded later that month; Grandquist became president and owned two-thirds of the business, while Cedarstrom served as vice president and general manager, owning one-third. They initially set up shop north and west of downtown at 2175 Northwest Eighty-sixth Street, and signed on their first agent, Dick Andrew, who had also worked at Iowa Realty. A couple of months later, they began construction of their own building a block away at 8400 Hickman. Well known and well liked in the industry, Grandquist had no trouble getting listings and recruiting agents. The company moved into its new office in June, opened a south side office on Army Post Road that fall, and by the end of the year, it had opened another branch west of downtown on Ingersoll Avenue. By then, the upstart company had thirty agents.[15]

Grandquist's founding of Universal Realty rankled Bill and only worsened their relationship, which was already complicated by the Iowa Realty stock Grandquist owned and the money he had in the company's profit-sharing plan. He wanted to cash out, but Bill did not want to fund a competitor, and the two could not agree on a valuation of the stock. In the spring of 1978, Grandquist and Cedarstrom sued Iowa Realty for their portion of the profit-sharing plan. Meanwhile, Universal Realty continued growing, and by early 1979 it boasted nearly 100 sales agents.[16]

Over the next several months, lawyers and accountants for both sides scrambled behind the scenes to find a settlement and avoid a court case.

Iowa Realty's longtime accountant and financial advisor, Jack Wahlig, believed the feud was hurting everyone and suggested Bill "give more than you must to settle." The nudge was apt, and an agreement satisfactory to all was finally reached in early 1979. First, Grandquist had to sell his interest in Universal Realty and sign a non-compete clause stipulating that he would stay out of the central Iowa real estate business for five years. One exception to this allowed him to participate in a small real estate brokerage firm, which would employ no more than six brokers (including Grandquist). In return, he received a payment of $95,000. He also received the $248,000 that he had accumulated in Iowa Realty's profit-sharing plan. Then for turning over his 30 percent stake in Iowa Realty, he received five properties—the West Hampton Village Apartments in Iowa City; the Eastview Circle Apartments and the Silhouette Apartments in Des Moines; the 200-acre Eilers farm in Warren County; and the 99-acre Dalcon farm in Dallas County—valued at $3.9 million.[17]

Universal Realty continued, but without Grandquist and given the increasingly poor economy, its rapid rise ended and it was no longer viewed as a potential threat to Iowa Realty. Grandquist, meanwhile, established Ken Grandquist and Associates, a small brokerage business allowed under the agreement, but he soon focused on minor league baseball. In 1981, he was part of a group of local investors who purchased the Iowa Oaks, a Des Moines-based minor league baseball team. The following year, the club became the triple-A affiliate of the Chicago Cubs and changed its name to the Iowa Cubs. In 1985, Grandquist moved out of the real estate business altogether when he sold Ken Grandquist and Associates to Gene Stanbrough, and twelve years later, he became the Iowa Cubs' majority shareholder.[18]

Despite his changing relationship with Kenny Grandquist, Bill continued his rise in the Des Moines business community by expanding on what he had been doing. This meant operating on the outskirts of the city, where Bill bought, sold, and developed land, built and managed motels and apartments, converted apartments to condominiums, and tried getting into the shopping mall business. While involved in these familiar activities, he gradually gravitated toward downtown Des Moines, where he would become a major player in its redevelopment.

Several of these themes came together in 1971. Bill had been eyeing some federal land that made up part of the old Fort Des Moines, located several miles south of downtown. Eventually, he began talking with General Services Administration (GSA) officials about buying the fifty-eight-acre tract. The GSA, meanwhile, wanted a piece of land in Huron, South Dakota, where it planned to construct a federal building. So GSA officials and Bill struck a deal: he was to buy the Huron land and exchange it with the GSA for the Fort Des Moines parcel. He followed through, paying just over $200,000 for the South Dakota land; but then, the GSA abruptly changed its mind and wanted to back out. Bill's temper erupted. He had always lived by his father's folksy adage: "You go through with a deal once you've made a commitment, whether it takes hide, hair, or what all," and he expected others to do the same. At a Kansas City meeting, Bill told GSA officials in no uncertain terms, "It's fine with me if you want out, but you buy back the land in South Dakota, because you're not going to stick me with it." Then, for emphasis, he threatened to take them to "the highest court in this land" if they did not pay him for the ground in Huron.[19]

The GSA ultimately backed down, abided by its original agreement, and the deal went through. As often happened, Bill got what he wanted. But then he did not. Bill thought the Fort Des Moines site perfect for a south side shopping center, and after obtaining the land, he began talking with mall developers. At the same time, Des Moines-based General Growth Properties (GGP) was considering erecting a south side shopping center as well. Bill tried working with General Growth, but in the end the company decided on another piece of land several blocks east at the juncture of Army Post Road and Southeast Fourteenth Street/Highway 65-69. In March 1972, GGP announced its plans to build Army Post Plaza. The center's name would be changed to Southridge Mall shortly before it opened in 1975.[20]

Stymied, Bill reconsidered how his land should best be used and eventually devoted most of it to housing. Here he built the Landmark South Apartments, a 360-unit apartment complex (now called Willow Park Apartments), on what originally had been part of the fort's old parade ground. The units were erected by Midland Builders, Iowa Realty's construction arm, created in 1968 to replace Alcon Construction, its former building unit. Kenny's brother, John Grandquist, was hired to manage it.[21]

Building or buying apartments and then managing them was nothing new to Bill, but at that time he stepped up past efforts. Over the course of the 1970s, he added a number of new properties to the Iowa Realty fold.

Besides Landmark South, Midland Builders erected the Green Valley Apartments in West Des Moines, Horizons East, City View, Westchester Village, Watrous and Wedgewood apartments in Des Moines, and the Ambassador West Apartments in Urbandale. In addition to those he built, he bought the Embassy Apartments and the apartments at 4323 Grand in Des Moines and the Plaza Gardens and Jensen Manor in Urbandale. The latter three complexes were purchased to be converted into condominiums, which Iowa Realty completed by 1980.[22]

Other suburban projects grew from groundwork he had laid earlier. Of continuing importance was his relationship with Hy-Vee, which, by the early 1970s, had leased another building from Bill and was operating a grocery store on his property on Twenty-second Street in West Des Moines. Soon, however, the space proved too small, and he cut another deal with Hy-Vee. He put up a much larger facility built to Hy-Vee's specifications on Iowa Realty land across Thirty-fifth Street (now Valley West Drive) from the recently opened Valley West Mall. He leased the property to the grocer in 1979. That deal led to two more: Bill made an agreement with Service Merchandise to construct and then lease the discount retailer a building directly south of the Hy-Vee structure, and he sold his remaining land immediately north of Hy-Vee to Target, where it erected a large store.[23]

By the end of the decade, Bill was also opening up more land in Interstate Acres, his commercial parcel north and west in Urbandale. In September 1980, Iowa Realty and Bankers Life (now Principal Financial Group) announced a $56 million joint venture to develop "more than 2 million square feet of warehouse or light industrial space for lease or sale." Iowa Realty sold a 160-acre piece of land, which was north of Bill's original Interstate Acres development, to the partnership. That December, Jacobson Warehouse Company agreed to lease the first of the partnership's 100,000-square-foot warehouse, which was completed the following month. At the same time, Jacobson-Larson Investment Company—a subsidiary of Jacobson Warehouse—joined the Iowa Realty and Bankers Life partnership as an investor.[24]

Building on past successes carried over to his interest in motels and hotels as well. Already operating the Peppertree and the Inntowner, Bill increased Iowa Realty's investment in such properties by building the Saveway Motel on Merle Hay Road in 1973 and the Hickman Motor Lodge in

1978. He also bought the Howard Johnson's on Grand Avenue in 1976 and the downtown National Motor Inn in 1977, which became Howard Johnson's later that year. But it was his purchase of the dilapidated downtown Hotel Savery in 1977 that marked another major transition in Bill's life.[25]

Over the years, Bill had only dabbled in downtown Des Moines properties, but this started to change in 1973 when John Ruan, a leading Des Moines business figure who had made his fortune in trucking, asked Bill to serve on the board of Bankers Trust, his downtown-based bank. Like many, Ruan had followed Bill's career and must have been seen some of himself in the real estate man; both were self made, both were known as determined and hard charging, and both had risen rapidly. They also had Joe Rosenfield in common. He was a close friend and mentor to both, and it was most likely Rosenfield who introduced the two.[26]

Bill took the spot on the Bankers Trust board. The following year, after Ruan was named president of the Greater Des Moines Committee (GDMC), he invited Bill to join this select group. Originally incorporated in 1907 by past presidents of the chamber of commerce, it was intended to "promote, develop, and protect commercial, manufacturing, and other business interests of the city of Des Moines and the state of Iowa." Composed of wealthy and powerful business leaders, the GDMC met weekly for lunch to discuss current business issues. Ruan saw the group as "pretty much an advisory committee" that could "make things happen." For Ruan, this meant continuing the fledgling revitalization of downtown.[27]

Service in these two positions reacquainted Bill with prominent businesspeople and connected him with others he did not know. Besides providing networking opportunities, it gave him a front row seat to the business district's rebirth. By the late 1960s, Bill recalled, "Downtown was really kind of a disaster." Retailers had pulled up stakes following the population flight to the suburbs, and business offices began to follow, leaving a growing number of old, decaying, and empty buildings in their wake. Many began referring to the once vibrant downtown as "Dead Moines." There had been some glimmers of renewal, however: a new federal office building as well as the United Central Bank tower opened in 1967. Other downtown projects followed. Four years later, Employers Mutual completed its new home office, and a new J. C. Penny store opened. City officials and business leaders, most of whom were GDMC members, realized downtown's health was vital to the wider metro area and hoped to build on these pockets of renewal. In 1972, redevelopment got a boost from the announcement of two major downtown buildings: Iowa-Des Moines National Bank's twenty-five-story Financial Center, and John Ruan's thirty-six-story Ruan Center. These two structures, completed in 1974 and 1975, dramatically changed the city's skyline and its outlook for the future.[28]

Bill watched the renewal with great interest but was not yet actively involved. That would come shortly, as the second stage of the revitalization began, set off by the closing of the once grand, but now decrepit KRNT Theater—downtown's 3,000-seat auditorium—because of a badly leaking roof. Under the leadership of James W. Hubbell, Jr., chairman of the Equitable of Iowa Insurance Companies, the Greater Des Moines Committee asked New York architects Charles Luckman Associates to develop plans for a theater–hotel–convention center complex on land between Grand Avenue and Walnut Street and Second Avenue and Fourth Street. Their proposal called for a 300-room hotel, a 2,500-seat performing arts center, a convention center, and an open-air plaza.[29]

The $22 million project was to be funded with urban renewal bonds, but the city council required that a referendum on the bond issue be held before approving the project. Des Moines Mayor Dick Olson and Hubbell campaigned for its passage, but in September 1973, the vote fell short of the required 60 percent majority. Over the next couple of years, the project was rethought and scaled back to only a theater and plaza. Olson persuaded city officials to donate the land if private financing could be found. John Fitzgibbon, president of Iowa-Des Moines National Bank, and David Kruidenier, chief executive officer (CEO) of the Des Moines Register and Tribune Company, led the fundraising effort with great urgency, and in just three months of 1975, they collected more than $9.5 million in donations.[30]

With the needed funds pledged, the civic center and plaza went forward and both were completed in 1979. In the meantime, Bill, Joe Rosenfield, and John Ruan took a brief break from downtown activities and attempted to buy the city's first shopping center. The idea originated with Rosenfield who, as the CEO of Younkers department stores in the late 1950s, had helped a group of Chicago investors choose a site for building Merle Hay Plaza. Younkers became one of center's major anchor stores. At some point, Rosenfield had a falling out with these investors, and in the spring of 1976, he talked Bill and Ruan into joining him in a bid to take over the shopping complex, which had been renamed Merle Hay Mall when it was enclosed in 1972. The three Des Moines businessmen offered $1.75 million for a 35 percent stake in Merle Hay Plaza, Inc., the company that owned the mall. If successful, the Rosenfield group had an agreement to combine its shares with Leonard Lamensdorf, a Los Angeles attorney who owned 15 percent of Merle Hay stock. Together, the four men could control the company. The partners, Bill explained, had no interest in making significant changes to the mall. "I'm in the real estate business," he noted, "and I'm always interested in a good investment at a reasonable price. This is that kind of investment."[31]

Rosenfield and company were not interested in a minority stake in Merle Hay; if they fell short of the 35 percent share, they intended to drop the offer altogether. Unfortunately, that was what happened, and the three walked away defeated. More often than not though, these men won, and their many successful careers were recognized by the *Des Moines Register* later that year.[32]

In October 1976, the *Register* ran "The Powers That Be," a three-part series examining the most powerful figures in the city. It developed the list by questioning a panel of the city's foremost business and community leaders. John Ruan was named Des Moines's most powerful; Rosenfield was eighth. The rest of the top ten, save Governor Robert Ray, who was fourth, had played important roles in downtown's redevelopment (and included, for example, Kruidenier, Fitzgibbon, Olson, and Hubbell). Bill, clearly an up-and-coming figure, was ranked fifteenth. Of his position, the paper noted: "Because Iowa Realty... has emerged as the preeminent force in real estate sales and development in Des Moines, Knapp, who heads and built the company, holds a key position in the community." And then, as if predicting Bill's impending role downtown, it wrote: "The many civic and economic development projects so near and dear to the hearts of the powerful people in Des Moines are keyed to the control of real estate."[33]

Making this 1976 list was quite an achievement and suggested how far Bill had come, but it captured him just as he was on the cusp of major involvement downtown. This work solidified his position as a powerful business figure. Shortly after the money for the civic center had been raised in 1975, business and city leaders split over where the new downtown hotel (originally part of the civic center plans) should be built. John Ruan opened the discussion the following fall with plans for construction of a luxury hotel at Seventh and Locust streets, immediately west of his recently completed Ruan Center. He created City Center Corporation, which would own the hotel, and lined up investors for the project, such as Younkers, F. M. Hubbell, Son and Co, Iowa Power and Light, and Bill's Iowa Realty. Others, led by Kruidenier and Fitzgibbon, and supported by editorials of the *Des Moines Register*, called for the new downtown hotel to be located near the civic center, as was initially proposed. While the debate raged on, the well-connected Bill Wimer heard that Ed Boss was interested in selling his downtown Hotel Savery. He passed this information on to Bill.[34]

Boss wanted out of the hotel business, likely because of future competition from either the Ruan-sponsored hotel or the Kruidenier-Fitzgibbon project. He had sold the Hotel Fort Des Moines in June and now looked to unload the Savery. Bill saw the downtown situation differently. A new hotel, he reasoned, would be good for all downtown and thus help the Savery. In addition, the civic center would be located across the street and a couple of blocks to the east; and the land on which the hotel sat would certainly appreciate in value. He contacted Boss and made an offer. The two dickered, and three days later, the deal was done. Bill bought the Hotel Savery in October 1977 for $700,000. He paid cash and was now fully vested in downtown redevelopment.[35]

Many, including his brother Paul, thought the purchase of the hotel had been a mistake. "There were people who said I'd met my Waterloo," Bill remembered. But he knew property and felt it was a good risk. He believed the business district's ongoing renaissance would continue, pulling downtown property values up with it. After deciding against demolition, he poured $7 million into the building's restoration. The effort was headed by Iowa Realty's in-house architect and designer, Don Bemis, and carried out by remodeling specialists, Bloodgood and Associates and Bill's own Midland Builders. Refurbishing began in early 1978, but quickened after the Ruan hotel project broke ground that fall. Upstairs was tackled first; guestrooms were decreased in number (from 350 to 250) as they were expanded in size and updated, the luxurious presidential suite was modernized, and a honeymoon suite and plush penthouse were added. The following year, Bill hired experienced hotel and food manager Gene Moore to run the Savery and brought in Guido Fenu, a chef who had worked for years at Johnny & Kay's restaurant on Des Moines's south side before opening his own eatery. Once this team was in place, the lobby was remodeled; and the coffee shop, restaurant, and bar area were redone and opened as the Sidewalk Café, Guido's Restaurant, and Guido's Savery Lounge.[36]

Before long, it was clear that Bill had made good decisions. Guido's was soon regarded as the area's leading restaurant, and the lounge became the place to see and be seen. Manager Moore remembered that after initially losing money, the Savery "always made money, starting in 1980." Improvements continued over the next few years, with Bill adding a health spa and pool to the establishment.[37]

It was also clear that although Bill bought the hotel as an investment, he soon relished the place. He kept his main office at Iowa Realty's headquarters on Beaver but also had an office in the hotel and increasingly was found there. He enjoyed the buzz and excitement of people coming and going, he loved visiting with dignitaries in the lounge and restaurant, and he delighted in showing off the building. It was here he met people to discuss downtown development and here he entertained. One of his get-togethers in October 1979 captured the attention of the *Des Moines Tribune*. As part of the city's redevelopment, the old twelve-story Paramount Theater Building, a block north and west of the hotel, was scheduled for demolition. The day of the structure's demise, Bill threw an elegant party at the Savery's rooftop penthouse where guests could get an unobstructed view of the Paramount implosion.[38]

Actually, this downtown environment of old buildings coming down and new developments going up was tailor made for Bill's skill set. He understood that keeping the redevelopment going would improve the value of his own holdings. To that end, he acted as a broker. He brought people together, planted ideas, kept deals on track, and pushed both city leaders and businesspeople to work in concert and to see projects to completion. He could cajole and charm, but he could also threaten, often using rough language to make his points. Des Moines city councilman George Nahas explained that Bill was "the type who will stir sugar in your coffee, but he's not averse to arm-twisting if charm won't work."[39]

Over the course of the next few years, Bill used all these techniques, negotiating a number of deals that maintained downtown's momentum. Much of this activity was undertaken as a member of the reinvigorated Des Moines Development Corporation (DMDC). Established in 1961 as the financial arm of the city's chamber of commerce, the group did not become a significant force until it was reconfigured in 1978. When reorganized, the DMDC became a nonprofit affiliate of the Greater Des Moines Chamber dedicated to the "economic development of greater Des Moines with primary emphasis on the downtown Des Moines area." It stressed that it was a catalyst for development, not a developer. Membership was reserved to company CEOs so decisions could be made quickly, and annual dues were high—initially ranging from $10,000 to $50,000 depending on size of the company—which provided the group with operating funds. There was no paid staff, and the group relied heavily on the leadership of its president, Robert Houser, president and CEO of Bankers Life. Seventeen others rounded out the original membership, including heavy hitters such as Ruan, Hubbell, Kruidenier, Fitzgibbon, Robert Burnett, president of the Meredith Corporation, and Bill.[40]

Bill became one of the DMDC's most active members, pushing for downtown projects, finding new recruits for the group, and spending hours putting together deals on behalf of DMDC. Its early focus was the so-called Ward Block, which was immediately west of the planned civic center plaza (currently known as Nollen Plaza but soon to be rechristened Cowles Commons) located between Locust and Walnut streets and Fourth and Fifth streets. On the north side of this ground sat the empty Montgomery Ward Building, the Manhattan Hotel, and an abandoned parking garage; the south half of the block included the Ginsberg Furniture Store and the old Valley National Bank. The property was also located on the south side of Locust Street, directly across from Hotel Savery, which gave Bill a real interest in seeing its redevelopment take place rapidly.

Kruidenier and Fitzgibbon had originally considered the Ward Block for a hotel–retail–convention center complex, but the idea had not received much traction, and Ruan was moving ahead with his plans for a hotel several blocks to the west. In the meantime, the DMDC entered the fray, hoping to get the development ball rolling on the Ward Block by acquiring the land. Its plan was to buy the land and sell it at cost to the city, which in turn would sell it to the eventual developer. Bill was the group's point man. It took him just over a month, but in the summer of 1978, he bought the north half of the Ward Block on the DMDC's behalf for $863,500, $66,000 under the properties appraised value.[41]

Then the progress stalled because of the Valley National Bank Building. As Bill recalled, "The Iowa government owned the building, and we couldn't get them out of it." At issue was the roughly 400 state workers housed in the structure's eight upper floors. While the state understood that the city wanted the land for redevelopment and was willing to sell it, it had to find office space for all its employees in the building. By December 1979, the state finally put the building up for sale, and the City of Des Moines, as the only bidder, bought it. State officials agreed to vacate the building in eighteen months. However, when potential developers said that getting the land in January instead of June 1981 meant that they would gain an entire construction season, which could save $6 million in building costs, Bill worked behind the scenes to speed up the process. At the time, Governor Robert Ray explained, "The state's problem, of course, is availability of space and the cost of moving our people." Indeed, the state director for general services, Stanley McCausland, remembered: "The state wanted to cooperate, but we couldn't just throw them [the state employees] out. It was a hellish problem, but Knapp never herded or pushed anyone around." His persistence did pay off. In the spring of 1980, the state agreed to turn the building over to the city in January 1981, six months ahead of schedule. The compressed timeline was not without headaches, though, and Bill was quite unpopular with a number of people in state government. In the rush to meet the deadline, for example, the Iowa Commerce Commission, one of the state agencies operating out of the bank building, was initially relocated into an unfinished floor of the Lucas State Office Building, which was in the process of being remodeled to handle the additional workers.[42]

Nonetheless, with this delay alleviated, the city moved forward by acquiring the Ginsberg Building, also to be vacated by January 1981. In the meantime, officials put up the Ward Block for bid and asked developers to submit proposals for a complex to include office, retail, and possibly residential space. Two groups did so. Fourth Street Partners—a local consortium made up of F. M. Hubbell, Son and Co., United Federal Savings and Loan, and Iowa Resources (the owner of Des Moines's gas and electric utility, Iowa Power and Light)—pitched "a $30 million, 12-story structure oriented around a glass-enclosed 'atrium' running the height of the structure" with three floors for retail, three floors of office space, and six floors of apartments. The other bid came from Chicago developer, Draper and Kramer, which proposed "a $40 million eight-story building with an open atrium in the center running the entire eight floors." The first and second floors would be reserved for retailers, with office space filling the remaining six floors.[43]

City officials mulled over both plans, and in June they gave the nod to Draper and Kramer. Although they realized the decision might cause some resentment for not selecting the local group, the staff of city manager Richard Wilkey believed the Chicago developer's greater experience at such projects gave it the edge. It was not a yet a done deal, however. Before Draper and Kramer could secure the necessary financing, it needed to line up major tenants; its initial efforts yielded nothing. Some speculated that "resistance arose from the firm being an outsider in Des Moines's tight-knit business community."[44]

Bill stepped in, bringing in tenants. First was UFS. The bank planned to lease 60,000 square feet of space in the Fourth Street Partners' building if the group won the Ward Block bid. When it did not, the bank started looking elsewhere. Bill inserted himself in the process, massaged UFS chairman and CEO Joe Strasser's bruised ego, and convinced him to consider leasing space in the same location it had originally intended, albeit in the Draper and Kramer structure. By November 1980, the bank announced it would locate its headquarters on three floors of the Ward Block project—then called The Square—leasing a total of 60,000 square feet. The *Des Moines Tribune* noted this was considered "a significant boost" for The Square, but the developer needed a commitment of 65,000 additional square feet before it could line up lenders.[45]

Next, Bill went after Kirke-Van Orsdel Insurance Services (KVI). After wooing the insurer for a while, Bill arranged a meeting early the following year at the Savery for company co-founders and top executives Gary Kirke and Bill Van Orsdel, Des Moines city manager Wilkey, Draper and Kramer vice president Eamonn Collopy, and his assistant, Tim Cardamon, who was in charge of leasing space at The Square. In short order, Bill brokered a deal, and KVI became The Square's second anchor tenant, leasing 60,000 square feet atop the planned building. Other tenants, including Pioneer Hi-Bred and Brenton Bank, had signed leases early that spring and by April, construction of Capital Square, as the development was finally named, began. When it opened in the spring of 1983, Bill could look out of his Hotel Savery to the south and take pride in the gleaming "downtown showplace" which replaced the "drab and dreary" buildings of only a few years before.[46]

If he paused for a moment to do so, no one noticed, for he had been wrapped up in a number of other deals while pursuing the Capital Square project, and they were in various stages of completion. For Bill, the greatest pleasure was in the negotiation anyway. Once a transaction was done, he was on to the next, pausing very little to reflect on done deals. When given the opportunity, he usually closed them much more rapidly than the Capital Square deal. Such was the case with a badly needed parking garage. Amid all the downtown changes, a lack of parking was becoming a serious issue. The city considered several options, and one involved building a ramp on the south side of Grand Avenue spanning Fourth Street. Part of the garage would be located on Bill's land directly north of the Savery. Bids were solicited but came in higher than the city could afford, so in the spring 1979, city manager Wilkey and his right-of-way manager, Jim Duff, went to discuss the issue with Bill. They sat on folding chairs in the middle of construction in what would soon be Guido's Restaurant on the Savery's first floor. Wilkey explained the situation and asked if Bill might consider discounting the price of his land, which would make erecting the ramp feasible. Bill knew the garage would benefit his hotel, and he also knew it was badly needed by downtown in general. After thinking a bit, he asked, "What if I give you the land?" A moment later, he added, "I'll talk with Joe (Joe Strasser of United Federal Savings, located across Fourth Street, directly to the east of the Savery), and I bet I can get him to donate the bank's land you need as well." Wilkey was stunned. Bill followed through immediately, and he and the bank donated their lots. The savings the city enjoyed meant the project went forward at once, and the parking ramp was finished by the following fall of 1980.[47]

By the late 1970s, downtown's redevelopment was fully under way, with new office towers, the civic center, and parking structures studding the once stagnant core. The Ruan-backed Marriott Hotel would be finished in 1981, and new retail space was in the works as well. Progress was clear, but Bill understood that without more to pull and hold people downtown, the derisive "Dead Moines" image would remain a reality. "When all you've got is banks and savings and loans and insurance companies," he explained, "you've got a ghost town after 5 o'clock." Housing, Bill and others agreed, was the missing element. Over the next several years, it was Bill who became the key figure in shepherding three important downtown housing projects from inception to completion.[48]

In 1978, the First Baptist Elderly Housing Foundation, a group affiliated with Des Moines's First Baptist Church, proposed downtown construction of a high-rise apartment complex for the elderly and disabled. Business and community leaders were thrilled and saw this as a huge first step in bringing badly needed housing downtown. Designed to provide federally subsidized housing, the seventeen-story building was to be financed by a $4.7 million Housing and Urban Development (HUD) loan. Initially, the foundation looked to erect the structure a couple of blocks north of the rising civic center, but business leaders, especially the DMDC, thought that land might be better suited for commercial uses. Another site was sought.[49]

Relocation delayed the project and brought Bill into the picture. All involved agreed a good compromise spot for the church-sponsored housing was the southeast corner of Fifth and Grand avenues. The land was kitty-corner (northwest) from the Hotel Savery, and Bill owned it. He had originally bought the parcel from Central National Bank, but by the time the Baptist foundation considered it, the bank had decided it wanted to put a drive-in facility there. Complex negotiations ensued, with Bill working out a deal. He explained, "We're selling the land to Central National Bank for $500,000, and they have agreed to sell the air rights to the Baptists for $200,000." The bank would own the land and erect a single-story drive-up bank, and the Baptist foundation would purchase the authority to build its apartments atop the bank. It seemed a win-win: the bank obtained its desired location and by selling its air rights, it cut the ground's purchase price by 40 percent, while the Baptists acquired a building site for well under market value.[50]

But HUD threw a wrench into the mix. Its valuation of the quarter block was only $115,000, which was $85,000 less than the $200,000 air rights fee. Worse, however, HUD did not have a policy regarding air rights, so it refused to loan any funds for the building site. Joe Jongewaard, president of the First Baptist Elderly Housing Foundation, appealed the decision, but was turned down. Nearly two years had passed since the inception of the idea and Des Moines had nothing to show for it. Bill and others on the Des Moines Development Committee thought the project too important to be stymied by HUD. Committee members discussed options and took action. Early in the summer of 1980, Robert Houser announced that the DMDC had purchased the air rights from Central

National Bank and donated them to the Baptist foundation. This proved the needed catalyst. HUD gave final approval for the financing, which had risen to $6.9 million, and construction began that October. Called the "crown jewel of downtown Des Moines development," by Mayor Pete Crivaro, the apartment building opened two months ahead of schedule in December 1981. It was named Elsie Mason Manor, after a longtime pastoral assistant at First Baptist Church.[51]

While Elsie Mason Manor was under construction, Bill was already working on more housing. In the summer of 1981, he used his perfect salesman pitch to go after local investors for a downtown apartment complex. Three weeks later, he had pieced together a consortium, which read like a who's who of Des Moines leading businesses. Made up of twenty-six local companies, the group proposed Civic Center Court—a $3.8 million facility designed for people who worked downtown—to be located on the block of land north of the completed Civic Center of Greater Des Moines, bounded by Second Avenue and Third Street. Plans called for 141 medium-priced apartments in four, three-story buildings surrounding a courtyard. The garden-apartment concept garnered widespread support, but there were concerns, such as the lack of parking. This came up in September during the city council meeting to approve the project. Councilman Tim Urban grilled Bill on the issue and then said, "These people need parking. No one has come forward…saying where these people are going to park." Bill responded curtly to questions about parking and then began lecturing angrily: "I'm not here with my hat in my hand to plead with you to accept this project….Everybody says we need housing downtown. The business community has come forward with $3.8 million to build it. I want to see a parking problem downtown at night." He ended with a warning that if the council rejected the plan, "Don't ever come to me and ask for housing downtown."[52]

Bill's outburst notwithstanding, the council voted unanimously to give tentative approval for the Civic Center Court, but per Iowa law, it provided thirty days for others to submit proposals. In early October, Des Moines developer Sidney Epstein offered a rival, informal plan of two seven-story towers, with residential apartments as well as office and retail space, and 120 parking spaces. Besides addressing the parking question, Epstein's preliminary concept was more in line with the Architecture Review Committee—a group that reported to the Urban Renewal Committee—which believed the Civic Center Court's three-story design "belonged in the suburbs." Instead, it suggested "any building on that site should be at least five stories tall to complement the Civic Center."[53]

But Epstein needed more time to finalize his plans and arrange financing, and on the last day of the thirty-day period for submitting bids, he asked for a ninety-day extension. Bill was irate, recalling, "We worked with the city every step of the way and we covered all our bases." Now he applied pressure to the council by threatening to withdraw his group's proposal if Epstein's requested extension were granted. "I don't even feel like pitching our project anymore," he snapped. The council responded by calling a special meeting on October 15, 1980, to decide the issue. It would either give Civic Center Court final approval or grant Epstein's extension. Although most council members felt there were positives to the Epstein proposal, they could not support giving an extension and risk losing the ready-to-go apartment project; thus, the council voted 5–1 (Tim Urban was the lone dissenter) in favor of Bill's plan. With the green light, construction on the garden apartments started almost immediately; the units opened the following spring.[54]

Well before Civic Center Court was completed, Bill had envisioned developing high-end housing in downtown Des Moines. He dropped hints of the idea as early as September 1980. Soon thereafter, while on a tour of the Minneapolis–St. Paul skywalk system, Bill made an important connection that ultimately resulted in such a downtown project.

By the late 1970s, Des Moines's business and civic leaders had begun seriously considering a skywalk system for downtown. Initial figures pushing the concept were the mayor, Dick Olson, the city manager, Richard Wilkey, and business leaders Houser, Ruan, and Hubbell. Bill became involved a little later but was soon a major advocate because he noted, "Six months out of the year we live in a bad environment." Part of the planning involved visiting cities that already had skywalks in place, and one of the key destinations was Minneapolis–St. Paul. Bill, Wilkey, and Joe Strasser, were among those on this trip and were being given a tour of the skywalks by Minneapolis developer Ted Glasrud. During the stroll, Glasrud led the three down a skywalk and into a high-rise condominium he had under construction. They went up an elevator and into an unfinished unit. Out of nowhere, Bill asked Strasser, "Joe, do you have your checkbook? Let me borrow it, I forgot mine." Puzzled, Strasser handed him the checkbook, and Bill, with a flamboyant flourish, asked Glasrud: "How much for this unit? I want to buy it." Glasrud was caught off guard, but named a price. Bill filled in the amount, Strasser signed the check, and just like that, Bill bought a soon-to-be-completed condominium at the Crossings Building in Minneapolis. More significantly, he had made a big impression on Glasrud. Somewhere down the road, Bill believed, this might pay off.[55]

Meanwhile, Bill had plunged ahead with plans for luxury condominiums called Civic Plaza Towers, the nineteen-story project was slated to go in just west of the Hotel Savery on the northeast corner of Fifth and Locust streets. He suggested the proposed building and the skywalk system promised "an exciting new lifestyle...for people to shop and to go to work" in enclosed, climate-controlled walkways. "The plans are definitely in a 'go' position," he had said in January 1981, "but the timing is not." Although officials greeted the scheme warmly, historically high interest rates kept the project from moving beyond the drawing board.[56]

Discussions about Civic Plaza Towers continued, but it was Bill's connection with Ted Glasrud that ultimately led to downtown's first luxury condominiums. Shortly after their first meeting, developer Glasrud contacted Bill. He would soon be returning to Minnesota from Florida and wanted to stop by for a visit. Bill agreed and invited city manager Wilkey to the meeting. This began a series of regular conversations, usually at the Hotel Savery—always involving Bill and Glasrud, usually Wilkey, and sometimes Glasrud's son, Ted, Jr.—about luxury condominium developments, the difficult market, and eventually the possibility of Glasrud erecting such a building in downtown Des Moines. It looked like these discussions were bearing fruit: as early as September 1981, the *Des Moines Tribune* reported that Glasrud was "preparing plans" for high-rise condominiums on the so-called Kurtz block, just south and west of the Civic Center. Bill had acted as an intermediary and negotiated a six-month working commitment with Kurtz Realty for Glasrud and turned it over to the Des Moines Development Corporation. Although the project would be competition for his own Civic Plaza Towers (if ever erected), Bill was "anxious to see it [Glasrud's condominium complex] built." He explained, "If interest rates come down, his building would actually give me more encouragement. The more housing downtown the better, especially when they can be tied in to the skywalks."[57]

It was not smooth sailing; other developers considered the block and Glasrud kept tinkering with his plans, waiting for interest rates to fall. The meetings at the Savery continued. Bill remembered, "Glasrud required a lot of handholding," while Wilkey recalled, "He [Glasrud] came to Des Moines every other week; I ate so many lunches at the Savery I got sick even of Guido's steak sandwiches." But finally there was a big pay-off. By December 1982, Glasrud's latest plans had been approved and he went ahead, presenting Wilkey with a check for $500,000 as a deposit for the project. Groundbreaking for the $25 million twenty-five-story condominium, called The Plaza, took place the following August. Iowa Realty acted as the exclusive sales agent for the tower, which opened amid much fanfare in November 1985.[58]

The Plaza's completion represented another coup for Bill and capped nearly a decade of activity focused on downtown. Many hailed his work, but there were detractors. Some derided him for his apparent eagerness to level old structures in the name of progress. The party Bill held at the Savery for guests to witness the demolition of the Paramount Theater Building was often used as an example of his disregard for preservation and glee in bringing down old structures rather than retrofitting and restoring them.[59]

Others pointed to his temper and the steamrolling tactics he occasionally employed to get what he wanted. In an odd twist, one example involved Bill's desire to restore an aging building, which he considered "blighted" and in desperate need of renovation. In the spring of 1983, he invited Joseph Coppola, owner of the Hotel Kirkwood and other downtown properties, and Richard Wilkey to a meeting at the Savery and explained that he wanted to buy the Kirkwood and convert it to apartments. Coppola refused to sell, and the exchange between the two quickly turned nasty. The meeting ended with Bill pointing toward Wilkey and threatening Coppola: "I'm going to have the city condemn you if you don't sell." But Coppola remained resolute and promised to resist "completely and absolutely." Bill lost; it was one of the rare deals he did not close, and the Kirkwood remained in Coppola's hands. In the grand scheme of Des Moines redevelopment, it was a minor incident, but it did instill an image of Bill running roughshod over the city.[60]

The critiques bothered him but did not alter the way he did business. He played hardball when he thought necessary and no doubt ruffled feathers from time to time. But that was Bill. He was a doer and a pusher who made things happen. And much of his work downtown—negotiating land deals, bringing in developers, securing tenants—was done without benefit of commissions, a detail lost on all but a few people. Of course, Bill's actions were not entirely benevolent. In October 1978, the *Des Moines Tribune* reported that Bill, James Hubbell, Jr., and John Graham, founder of the Graham Group, a local real estate and development company, had become the largest land owners in the city's downtown core. Thus, while most agreed the revitalized downtown was good for Des Moines generally, the accompanying increase in property values made it especially good for Bill Knapp. But he would make no bones about it, recounting some wisdom in his straightforward, unvarnished way: "You have to do good by doing good." Indeed he had.[61]

The Plaza Condominiums in downtown Des Moines. Courtesy of Bill Knapp.

Longtime competitor Gene Stanbrough presents Bill with the community service award from the Greater Des Moines Board of Realtors, 1986. Courtesy of Iowa Realty.

The Drake Diner was symbolic of the turnaround of the Drake University neighborhood in the 1980s. Courtesy of Steve Vilmain.

Napa Valley, 1990. Photo by Gary Fandel. Copyright 1990, The Des Moines Register and Tribune Company. Reprinted with permission.

Bill with his mother and siblings. Bill and Paul are standing; seated left to right are Carolyn Doggett, Anna Knapp, and Mary Louise Cawthorn, ca. 1993. Courtesy of Susan Knapp.

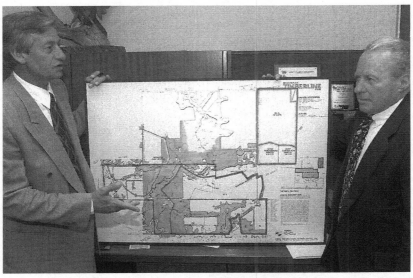

Mike Knapp and Bill discuss a residential development in Urbandale, 1996. Photo by Bob Modersohn. Copyright 1996, The Des Moines Register and Tribune Company. Reprinted with permission.

Roger Brooks and Bill Knapp after announcement that AmerUs was selling Iowa Realty to MidAmerican Energy, 1998. Bill was recovering from shoulder surgery. Photo by Bob Nandell. Copyright 1998, The Des Moines Register and Tribune Company. Reprinted with permission.

Bill Knapp and David Kruidenier in Egypt, 1998. Courtesy of Susan Knapp.

At an Iowa State Fair Blue Ribbon Foundation golf outing, 2008. From left to right are Jim Cownie, John Putney, Bill Knapp, and Denny Elwell. Courtesy of Bill Knapp.

Bill and Susan (Terry) Knapp on gondola in Venice the evening he proposed, 1998. Courtesy of Susan Knapp.

Ribbon-cutting ceremony at the dedication of William C. Knapp Varied Industries Building at the Iowa State Fair, 2001. From left to right are Speaker of the Iowa House Brent Siegrist, Governor Tom Vilsack, and Bill Knapp. Courtesy of the Iowa State Fair Blue Ribbon Foundation.

Susan Knapp, Willie Nelson, and Bill Knapp at the party for Bill's seventy-fifth and David Kruidenier's eightieth birthdays, 2001. Courtesy of Susan Knapp.

"Groundbreaking", the oversized spade sculpture Bill's family gave him for his seventy-fifth birthday adorns the grounds of the Knapp Properties headquarters in West Des Moines, 2001. Courtesy of Susan Knapp.

The Knapp home in Siesta Key, Florida. Courtesy of Susan Knapp.

The Knapp ranch home in Van Meter, Iowa. Courtesy of Susan Knapp.

Bill and Arnold Palmer look over land being developed into the Tournament Club golf course in Polk City, Iowa, 2001. Courtesy of Bill Knapp.

Knapp family at Bill's Iowa State Fair campsite, 2003. Standing from left to right: Sable and Montana Knapp, Anna and Sara Terry, Brooke and Cole Graznow, Kendy and Tyler Granzow, and Mark Haviland. Seated left to right: Roger Knapp, Susan and Bill Knapp, Ginny Haviland, and Bells, the Labrador Retriever. Courtesy of Susan Knapp.

Susan Knapp on Heavenly Mac in the Arizona Sun Circuit, a western riding competition, 2011. Courtesy of Susan Knapp.

Bill with his two trusted associates, Gerry Neugent, left, and Bill Knapp II, 2008. Photo by Christopher Gannon. Copyright 2008, The Des Moines Register and Tribune Company. Reprinted with permission.

Veterans from the Bill Knapp Honor Flight tour the World War II Memorial in Washington, D.C., 2010. Courtesy of Bill Knapp.

Bill and World War II shipmate, James Penney served together on the USS Catron during World War II. They were reunited after sixty-six years in March 2012. Courtesy of Susan Knapp.

Bill being congratulated after receiving the Iowa Award. Susan Knapp is to the right. Photo by Bill Neibergall. Copyright 2011, The Des Moines Register and Tribune Company. Reprinted with permission.

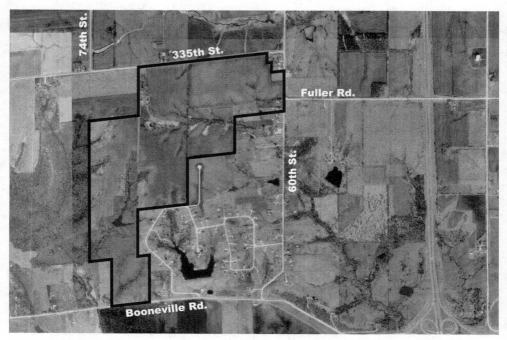

Aerial photo of undeveloped area in and around Staples farm (marked by black border), several years after Bill purchased it in 1987. Courtesy of Knapp Properties.

A 2011 aerial photo showing same land after development, which included the Wells
Fargo campus and Galleria shopping area. Courtesy of Knapp Properties.

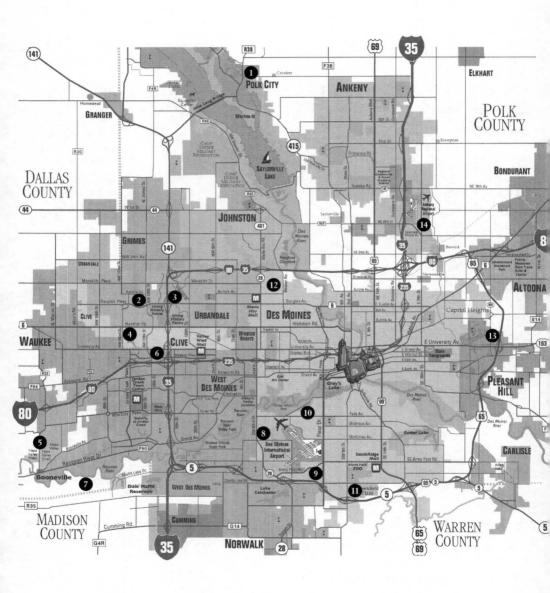

MapArt courtesy of Steve Peglow.

SIGNIFICANT KNAPP DEVELOPMENTS

	Development Name	City	Acres
1	Tournament Club of Iowa	Polk City	500
2	Timberline Village	Urbandale	460
3	Interstate Acres	Urbandale	450
4	Country Club	Clive	720
5	Napa Valley	Booneville	350
6	West Lakes	West Des Moines	400
7	Raccoon River	West Des Moines	2000
8	Airport Commerce Park West	Des Moines	240
9	Airport Commerce Park South	Des Moines	100
10	Southern Woods	Des Moines	80
11	Southern Ridge	Des Moines	330
12	Westchester	Des Moines	200
13	Metro East	Pleasant Hill	40
14	Corporate Woods	Ankeny	80

(includes Iowa Department of Transportation driver's license station)

These Des Moines metro area projects have been developed by Bill Knapp and his management team at Knapp properties and Iowa Realty. Courtesy of Knapp Properties.

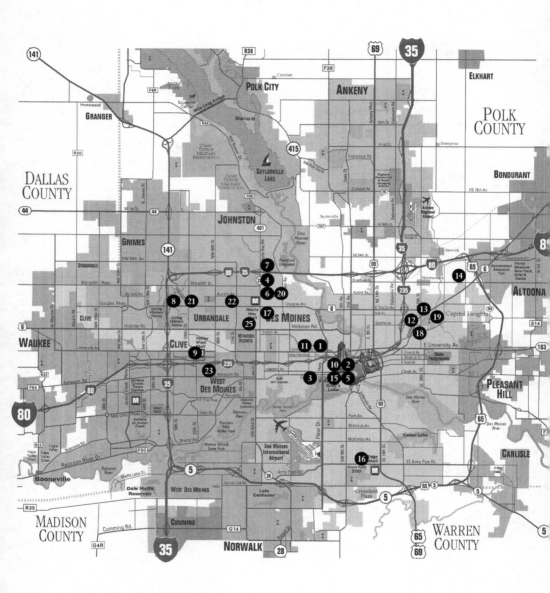

MapArt courtesy of Steve Peglow.

SIGNIFICANT KNAPP HOTELS, MOTELS AND APARTMENTS

	Project Name	City	Units
1	Drake Inn	Des Moines	52
2	Howard Johnson - 6th Avenue	Des Moines	150
3	Howard Johnson - Grand Avenue	Des Moines	54
4	Rodeway Inn	Des Moines	123
5	Hotel Savery	Des Moines	240
6	Saveway Motel	Des Moines	80
7	Merle Hay Inn	Johnston	140
8	Peppertree Inn	Urbandale	120
9	Valley West Inn	West Des Moines	140
10	City View	Des Moines	144
11	Drake Area Apartments	Des Moines	297
12	East View Circle	Des Moines	96
13	Embassy	Des Moines	32
14	Horizons East	Des Moines	378
15	Inntowner	Des Moines	180
16	Landmark South	Des Moines	360
17	Silhouette	Des Moines	48
18	Watrous	Des Moines	54
19	Wedgewood	Des Moines	72
20	Westchester	Des Moines	244
21	Peppertree	Urbandale	90
22	Plaza Manor	Urbandale	140
23	Green Valley	West Des Moines	96
24	Civic Center Court Apartments	Des Moines	141
25	Hickman Motor Lodge	Windsor Heights	40

These Des Moines metro area projects have been developed by Bill Knapp and his management team at Knapp properties and Iowa Realty. Courtesy of Knapp Properties.

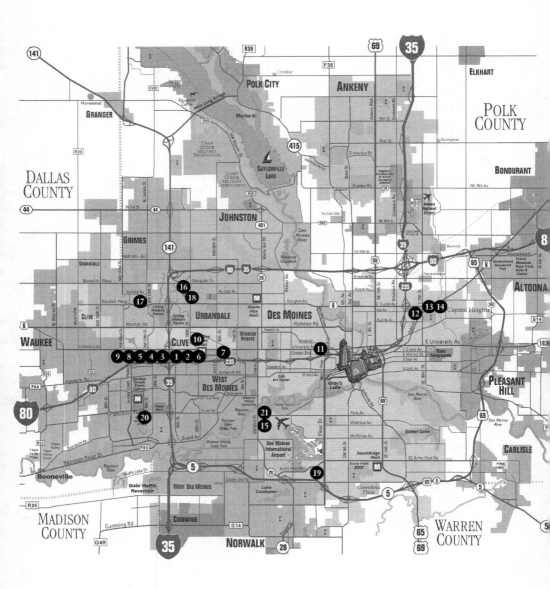

MapArt courtesy of Steve Peglow.

SIGNIFICANT KNAPP COMMERCIAL BUILDINGS

	Project Name	City	Square Feet
1	5000 Westown Parkway	West Des Moines	65,000
2	4949 Westown Parkway	West Des Moines	65,000
3	5500 Westown Parkway	West Des Moines	55,000
4	6000 Westown Parkway	West Des Moines	120,000
5	6800 Lake	West Des Moines	80,000
6	Hy Vee 35th Street	West Des Moines	60,000
7	Hy Vee 22nd Street	West Des Moines	34,000
8	KVI Campus	West Des Moines	275,000
9	Sears Credit Card Building	West Des Moines	55,000
10	Service Merchandise	West Des Moines	60,000
11	Drake Diner	Des Moines	10,000
12	Fairmount Office Building	Des Moines	20,800
13	Hy Vee East Euclid	Des Moines	26,000
14	Walgreens Euclid	Des Moines	34,000
15	Walnut Woods Buildings	Des Moines	96,000
16	Interstate Acres Warehouses	Urbandale	700,000
17	Timberline Tennis Facility	Urbandale	30,000
18	Urbandale Business Center	Urbandale	112,000
19	2200 Rittenhouse	Des Moines	60,000
20	Galleria	West Des Moines	150,000
21	6200 Park Avenue	Des Moines	140,000

These Des Moines metro area projects have been developed by Bill Knapp and his management team at Knapp properties and Iowa Realty. Courtesy of Knapp Properties.

Chapter Seven

It's Complicated

As Bill became more prominent in business and politics, socializing became a bigger part of his life. He enjoyed the evenings out, the hubbub, and the schmoozing. If nothing else, the gatherings provided additional places for him to make deals, but they also accentuated the differences between Bill and his wife Irene. While he loved being around people, she much preferred a quiet life, being at home with the family or a few close friends. Gradually, the two began leading increasingly separate lives. At the same time, the Knapp household was going through other transitions. Ginny had moved out and married in the early 1970s, and Roger, a rising star in local prep tennis, began dreaming of someday playing on the professional circuit. To do so, Roger needed topnotch coaching and year-round tennis, and by mid-decade, Bill and Irene agreed with their son that he needed to relocate in southern California.

It was during this time of flux that Bill began a long-term affair with Connie Wimer. The affair and the eventual fallout would dominate his private life for two decades. He and Connie (the wife of Bill's attorney, Bill Wimer) had known each other for years. Bill and Irene began socializing with Bill and Connie Wimer sometime in the late 1960s. Conversations at their get-togethers usually focused on business, a subject Irene found tiresome. She soon begged off these gatherings, but Bill delighted in the evenings out, and he and the Wimers continued going to dinner on a regular basis. This seemed the case of opposites attracting; Bill Wimer was polished and well read, a raconteur who was the life of the party. Connie was quick-witted, inquisitive, and beautiful. Although from modest, small town beginnings, she had grown into a sophisticated woman. Together, Bill and Connie Wimer made a striking couple. Bill Knapp, on the other hand, was smart, probably the smartest person in a room at any given time, but he was rough around the edges. He understood people and the business world as well as anyone, but his education was rudimentary, his grammar poor, and his interests provincial. Still, the Wimers saw something special in Bill and were intrigued by his raw intelligence and business savvy. Bill was drawn to the Wimers' style and wide-ranging interests; and they all shared a love of politics.[1]

Connie's strong personality and ambition especially appealed to Bill. Most were cowed by his aggressiveness and success, but not Connie; she was one of the few to question and challenge him. He liked her willingness to stand up to him. Connie was captivated with Bill's shrewdness and tenacity. The two became much better acquainted in 1971, when they worked closely together at the (Harold) Hughes for President office, which Bill had asked Connie to manage. Shortly after Hughes decided he would not pursue the presidency and the office closed later that year, Bill hired Connie to design, set up, and then run the Iowa Realty kiosk at the Des Moines Municipal Airport. They grew close during these two projects, and their friendship soon became more intimate, slipping into an affair.[2]

Initially, the couple worried about hurting family members and so they were diligent to keep the liaison under wraps. Bill continued going to dinner with the Wimers, but this did not raise suspicions because they had been a threesome in public for a while. Since the three spent so much time together, Bill Wimer likely suspected the affair, but he never said anything to his wife or Bill. Irene, meanwhile, was not initially aware of the liaison.[3]

Always independent, Connie began worrying about her lack of any retirement funds and began investigating moneymaking opportunities. She knew many lawyers, bankers, and real estate people, so she considered going into the abstract business. Bill thought it a great idea and promised to send initial business her way. He loaned her $75,000 for the purchase of

Iowa Title, the smallest of Des Moines's title companies. She bought the firm in November 1976 and learned the job on the fly. Actually, Connie claimed her lack of background proved a plus because she had no pre-conceived notions about the business. In 1978, she computerized the title company, which decreased the turnaround time of an abstract from two weeks to two days. This gave Iowa Title a huge competitive advantage, and it soon became the biggest such company in town, with one-third of its business coming from Iowa Realty. Three years later, Wimer bought the *Daily Record,* a local newspaper, which printed legal notices. Over time, Connie renamed it the *Business Record* and expanded the publication's coverage of local business news. She diversified in 1984 by starting the *Skywalker,* a biweekly publication focused on area entertainment. The alternative newspaper was eventually renamed *Cityview.*[4]

While Connie was getting started with Iowa Title, both Bill and Irene were adjusting to Roger's move to southern California, a major step in his effort to make it in professional tennis. Roger had shown aptitude for the game almost immediately, but it was after the youngster won a regional twelve-and-under tournament in 1972 that many began to take notice. The next summer, thirteen-year-old Roger won three titles, the fourteen- and sixteen-and-under singles titles and the sixteen-and-under doubles title at the Missouri Valley tournament in Decatur, Illinois. At fourteen, Roger entered three age divisions in the Iowa junior boys' tournament; he won his own division, won the sixteen-and-under division, and was leading in the eighteen-and-under division before leg cramps after two sets (and four other matches earlier that day) cost him the match. That same year, he and Hoover High School junior Cindy Clason won the mixed doubles tournament at the statewide Hawkeye Open.[5]

The following year, Roger was a fifteen-year-old freshman at Des Moines's Meredith Junior High, but he was the number one player on Hoover High School's varsity boys' tennis team, even though he only took one class at the school. At five foot ten, he was already four inches taller than his father, and using a steel Wilson T-2000 racquet like his idol Jimmy Connors, Roger became known for his big, left-handed serve and powerful forehand. He went 17–0 in singles matches, which did not surprise Mike Schaumburg, Hoover's tennis coach. Schaumburg explained, "On a given day, there is no adult or junior in Des Moines that Roger can't beat." Then Roger capped it off by sweeping through the Iowa high school tennis tournament in Iowa City, becoming the first freshman to win the title. He had not lost a set that entire season.[6]

Roger's personality was perfectly suited for the game. He had the calm demeanor of his mother and the fierce, competitive determination of his father. He also had incredible support from both parents. Irene attended all of Roger's matches and soon developed a scoring system, in which she tracked her son's serve, shots, and plays throughout the matches. "It was a sophisticated tool," prep rival John Stauffer remembered. "Any coach would have been proud." Bill, likewise, went to many of Roger's tournaments and was, in Stauffer's words "a good tennis father," who provided "constructive criticism" to his son.[7]

The teen's mounting success, combined with his maturity, athleticism, and natural talent, convinced tennis instructor Arden Stokstad that Roger had great potential but needed access to year-round outdoor tennis and top-flight instruction. He talked with Bill and Irene and then Roger about the youngster's future. By this time, he noted, the fifteen-year-old "had his heart set on being a tennis professional." The Knapps now considered what was best for their son. Initially, Roger wanted to go to Sarasota, Florida, where the family had a condominium and where he could play year-round tennis. In the meantime, Roger had played a mixed doubles match with Nancy Chaffee Kiner, once the world's fourth-ranked women's tennis player, who was in town for the Younkers-Kodel tennis tournament. Kiner thought Roger had real ability but like Stokstad, she believed he needed professional coaching. She called Pancho Segura, a top men's tennis player in the late 1940s and 1950s, who had become a leading teaching professional, first at the Beverly Hills Tennis Club, and then at La Costa Resort in Carlsbad, thirty miles north of San Diego. He was well known at the time for coaching tennis stars Jimmy Connors and Stan Smith, and she told him about Roger. Segura invited Roger to La Costa for a week of evaluation. The young Iowan went to see Segura between tournaments in July 1975.[8]

Segura was impressed with Roger, and although the teen remained in Des Moines for his sophomore year, he made regular trips to the resort for lessons with Segura. When there, he and Irene, who always accompanied him, stayed at a La Costa home Bill had purchased for that very purpose. By the following April 1976, Segura believed, "Roger has the determination to be a good one. He just needs some exposure to some good, outside talent. He's got the strength and he's got a big plus in the fact that his family is behind him 100 percent." Segura was ready to mentor Roger, and that cinched it; Bill and Irene decided their son should relocate in southern California.[9]

Before the move, Bill sent attorney Bill Wimer to investigate the area and schools. Wimer reported that if Roger lived in the family's La Costa home, he would attend school in the Carlsbad district, but if the Knapps resided in La Jolla—a wealthy seaside village twenty miles south of La Costa and ten miles north of San Diego—Roger would go La Jolla High School, with more rigorous academics and a top tennis program. That convinced Bill and Irene, who sold their place in La Costa and bought a home in La Jolla. They would drive Roger north to La Costa several times a week for lessons with Segura. Meanwhile in May, Roger finished his high school career in Des Moines by defeating his cross-town rival, Roosevelt High School junior John Stauffer for his second straight state title. "This is the way I want to go [out]," Roger explained, "as the Iowa champion."[10]

In the fall of 1976, Roger and Irene moved out to the tony beach community. Irene and Bea Turner, the family maid who had known Roger since he was born, arranged a rotation to look after Roger. Irene stayed six to eight weeks at a time, and when she shuttled back to Des Moines, Turner replaced her in La Jolla, where she would remain for several weeks until Irene returned. Bill usually flew out a couple of weekends a month, and their daughter Ginny, who had given birth to the Knapps' first grandchild in 1974, often visited with her young daughter Kendy Sue in tow. Roger found leaving home difficult, but he was happy he had made the move, and his tennis game flourished. In 1977 he won the southern California boys' eighteen-and-under championship, and the following year, he accepted a full tennis scholarship to the University of Southern California (USC), which boasted one of the best tennis programs in the country.

It was also during these years in La Jolla that Turner and Irene, as well as Ginny and Roger, became suspicious that Bill and Connie were having an affair. Meek by nature and not a confrontational person, Irene was slow to question Bill about the relationship. When she did, he responded that it was just business. After raising the matter several more times and receiving the same answer, Irene dropped the issue, although she was eventually certain of the affair. Instead, she went about her life hoping the infidelity would end on its own. It did not.[11]

As the relationship persisted, Bill and Connie began to be spotted together in public more often, and by the end of the decade, rumors of the affair were widespread. Prior to that time, the couple had kept a low profile, seeing only a very few people. Most often, the two got together with Ed Campbell—who had become good friends with Bill during his long service as an aide to Governor and then Senator Harold Hughes—and his wife Bonnie. The couples usually met at Timberline, Bill's acreage in Grimes that he often used for entertaining. At the same time, Irene was spending a lot of time in southern California to be near Roger, and Bill still flew west relatively often for short visits. By now though, the Knapp family was situated near Palm Springs. Bill loved the sun, and shortly after Roger moved on to USC, the Knapps sold their La Jolla home, replacing it with two condominiums in Rancho Mirage, a well-heeled enclave 120 miles east and south of Los Angeles.[12]

It was as if Bill were leading dual lives. He wanted to keep his family intact, but he also wanted to continue seeing Connie. Bill was clearly torn and uncharacteristically struggled with what to do. He usually made decisions quickly and effortlessly, but in this case, he could not. He told friends he was unhappy in his marriage but did not believe in divorce, once attributing this conviction to his mother's Catholic background. His indecision and Irene's inability to stand up to Bill meant that the situation festered.[13]

In the meantime, Roger was thriving. A two-time All American, he won the United States Tennis Association (USTA) Amateur Indoor title in 1980 and for a while was number one in the nation in the twenty-one-and-under amateur division. He played the Grand Prix circuit (a professional men's tennis tour from 1970 to 1989) in the summer of 1981. But the following year, after graduating from USC with a degree in public administration, he lost interest in competing. He had become a devout Christian and was worried about his parents' troubled relationship. Roger quit tennis, returned to Des Moines, and sought solace and direction in religion. He enrolled in Faith Baptist Bible College in Ankeny, a suburb just north and east of Des Moines. By that time, Bill and Irene had sold their home on Beaver and moved to the Timberline property, a change they both thought might provide a fresh start. Roger moved into a cabin on the acreage.[14]

Bill was happy Roger was home and especially happy when he began working part time at Iowa Realty the following year. Although Bill had not pushed him into the business, he had always hoped his son would join the company. But Roger had no desire for a career in his father's firm; he wanted to do something on his own, and Irene believed that Roger intentionally failed the real estate exams several times because of his complete lack of interest in the field.[15]

After being back in Des Moines for a little over a year, Roger began thinking of returning to the world of competitive tennis. Shortly after winning the city's Hilltop Open tennis tournament for the second year in a row, he called his father about the prospect of professional tennis, and the two met at Racket Club West to talk it over and hit some tennis balls. Roger was soon convinced to try tennis again. Much like his father, he had a need to prove himself. He wanted to see if he had "the talent to play with the big boys." With the backing of both Bill and Irene, Roger packed his bags and flew to southern California. He was joined by Chuck Hull—a friend of Roger's since junior high school and a tennis player while at Drake University—and they took up residence at one of the Knapp family's condominiums in Rancho Mirage. Hull served as Roger's hitting partner and coach, and the two began training.[16]

Following several tune-up tournaments, Roger headed overseas that next spring, logging thousands of miles and playing on three different circuits of the Association of Tennis Professionals (ATP) tour. "In 1984," he noted, "I played more weeks of tennis than any other professional." The hard work started paying dividends. By March of 1985, he had competed in Australia, Singapore, Finland, Greece, Italy, and India and moved up to 212th in the world rankings. His climb continued, peaking that June, when Roger upset top-seeded Herni Leconte—ranked sixth in the world at the time—in the quarter finals of the West of England tennis championship in Bristol, England. Although he lost in the next round, his world ranking shot up to 142. But the tour had worn him down. "[Professional] tennis is not something that has all the glory people think. You live out of a suitcase, rely on rides. It's a tough life," remembered Roger. His parents' crumbling marriage was the other factor that eventually pulled him away from tennis. Bill had moved out a couple of times in the mid-1980s, but always returned. Irene was increasingly upset, and Roger felt he should be there to support her.[17]

That fall, he decided to hang up his racket and come home. Roger had proven he could compete at the game's top level, and recalled, "I met my two goals: I made the top 150 and I beat a player in the top 10. I didn't want to travel anymore. I wanted to have a solid and stable life." In November 1985, he played what he termed as his "last hurrah": an exhibition at Veterans Auditorium in Des Moines. Unfortunately, Roger lost his match, which preceded the evening's main attraction, a match between Bjorn Borg and John McEnroe.[18]

Also lost was his parents' marriage. Bill moved out for good at the beginning of 1986, eventually settling downtown in his penthouse in The Plaza condominium tower. Roger recalled that his mother was "all broken up" and "needed me." He remained in town for several months consoling her before returning to Los Angeles. That spring, he accepted a position as the assistant men's tennis coach at USC.[19]

While both Ginny and Roger were disturbed by their parents' failed marriage, it had a greater impact on Roger, who blamed the problems on Connie. This put stress on his relationship with his father, and he was more than happy to dodge the difficult situation by remaining in southern California. In fact, he was thrilled to be back at the university, and after his first season coaching, he told a reporter, "This is the only place I would ever want to be. I will always be a Trojan, and I can't see myself anywhere else."[20]

The Knapps' divorce settlement was brokered by Bill Knapp II and was finalized in April 1987. Irene received 20 percent of Bill's estate immediately, which included the Timberline property, the condominiums in Rancho Mirage, a lake home in Panora, a small town forty-five miles west of Des Moines and was assured another 20 percent when Bill died if she had not remarried. Irene would receive this latter 20 percent immediately if Bill remarried without a prenuptial agreement disclosing the details of this settlement. Ginny and Roger, meanwhile, were each guaranteed 20 percent of their father's estate. Not surprisingly, although Irene was provided with a very comfortable lifestyle, she remained hurt and angry. "Why," she asked, " didn't he leave several years ago so I could start a new life? I wouldn't think of it at this late stage in life. It would add nothing but confusion. You can't help but be bitter when you went through those years and struggled to get ahead. You didn't have anything at all, and you raised the kids. Then, about the time when you can do something, they go off with someone else. Such men aren't only hurting the women; they hurt the kids to no end." Clearly, Irene felt abandoned, but she was also responding to what she saw as a developing pattern. Her marriage ended on the heels of Paul Knapp's, who divorced Mary Lou in 1986 and Kenny Grandquist's, which he ended in 1983.[21]

Bill, meanwhile, pressed forward. Although he worried about his relationship with his children, he continued seeing Connie. The two were now together much more frequently, and the *Des Moines Register* noted that many considered them *"the* [original italics] power couple in Des Moines." Still, he regretted the way his marriage had ended and years later admitted he had handled the situation badly. "I should have asked for a divorce much earlier rather than letting the marriage limp along."[22]

Once divorced, Irene and Bill did their best to avoid seeing each other, but the two were thrown together a year later in Palm Desert, California, when Roger married girlfriend Amy Shultz in September 1988. The young couple was soon expecting a baby, and Roger began to have second thoughts about staying at USC and raising a child in the area. "All of a sudden, Los Angeles didn't appeal to me as much as it did before. The traffic was unbearable. Crime was terrible. And from my standpoint, what hasn't been accomplished at USC? If you don't win a national championship, it's an off year." Bill knew of his son's feelings and hoped to bring him back to Des Moines. While talking with Michael Ferrari, the president of Drake University in early 1989, Bill mentioned that Roger was intent on leaving Los Angeles. At the time, Bill served on the university's board of trustees and was aware that Drake was interested in beefing up its tennis program.[23]

Ferrari saw a great opportunity. Hiring the former pro would add a certain cachet to Drake's tennis team. Plus Roger had coached at one of the nation's top collegiate programs and would undoubtedly attract talented players. Of course, there was another factor to Ferrari's thinking: landing Roger as the tennis coach could very well tie Bill more closely to the university, something the president indeed desired. Curt Blake, Drake's athletic director, fully supported the idea, and Ferrari called Roger in February 1989, asking him to come home and build Drake into a tennis power. Several weeks later in April, Roger was named Drake's men's tennis coach. "I want to make the Drake program the best it can be," Roger said. "Drake definitely wants a national-caliber program, to win the Missouri Valley Conference, and compete in the NCAA tournament. Those are my goals. I wouldn't have taken the job if Drake hadn't made a strong commitment."[24]

Roger stepped back into life in Des Moines, where he remained close to his mother, but his continuing anger at Connie complicated his relationship with his father. At a party at Bill's Napa Valley home, for instance, Roger walked out when he realized that Connie was there. Ed Campbell was also at the event and saw that Roger was upset. Campbell caught him on the way out. He tried to ease the situation and keep him at the party. Roger would have none of it and responded quickly, "I'm not going to go anyplace where she is." Campbell pleaded, "Well, it's your dad." But Roger was already on his way out the door. "I'm not going to do it," he said.[25]

Still, like many other fathers and sons, Bill and Roger connected through sports. In their case, it was tennis. Bill was immensely proud of Roger's tennis game and what he had accomplished on the tour and as a coach at USC. Now he was looking forward to following his son and what he hoped would be the rise of the Drake tennis team. To that end, shortly after Roger returned to town, the two decided an indoor tennis facility was needed. Bill built the Timberline Tennis Ranch on Douglas Avenue, just west of the property where Irene lived. "We wanted it for the Drake program and for the grassroots programs in Iowa. We want to run camps here and teach lessons," Roger explained. The $700,000 facility opened in October 1989, featuring indoor courts "in beautiful Drake Bulldog Blue," noted *Des Moines Register* sports columnist Marc Hansen. The courts were surfaced with Deco Turf II, the same material used at the U.S. Open. Timberline Tennis Ranch was open to the public (at $20 per hour), but most importantly, it would serve as the home of Drake's tennis teams. Roger and his assistant coach, Jonas Wallgard, acted as the facility's resident pros.[26]

While Bill worked with Roger on the tennis courts, Connie Wimer, who had been separated from Bill Wimer for several years, finally filed for divorce. Odd though it may seem, Bill and Bill Wimer maintained a friendship during the affair, and Wimer and his law partners continued doing the vast majority of Iowa Realty's legal work. As the divorce process moved forward, attorneys for both sides jockeyed for position, and nasty accusations began flying. Bill became irate at the way Connie was being treated by her husband's attorney and partner, Roger Hudson, until he finally exploded and told Bill II to pull all the Iowa Realty business from Wimer, Hudson, Flynn and Neugent.[27]

147

It was an agonizing task for Bill II; he was one of Bill Wimer's good friends and had interned and then worked for him before taking the position at Iowa Realty. "Telling Bill Wimer we were moving our business was one of the hardest things I've ever had to do," he remembered. The immediate beneficiaries were attorneys at the Davis, Hockenberg, Wine, Brown, Koehn & Shors (now called the Davis Brown Law Firm) who initially took over the account. Iowa Realty's business would not be there long, however. Sometime after Bill pulled his account, Tom Flynn, also a partner at the Wimer firm, was recruited by Belin, Harris Helmick, Tesdell, Lamson, & McCormick (now called Belin McCormick), a larger Des Moines law firm. Flynn was interested in moving but suggested Belin hire his partner Gerry Neugent as well. Neugent, a specialist in real estate law, had handled most of the Iowa Realty work for Wimer. Flynn and Neugent saw growth opportunities at the bigger group and along with Bonnie Campbell, who was then at the Wimer firm, all decided to join the Belin group in September 1989. Once the deal was signed, Neugent regained the Iowa Realty account, when Bill and Bill II moved the company's business to the Belin firm.[28]

Bill's break with Connie's soon-to-be ex-husband was significant. He had known Wimer since the late 1950s, and the attorney had done Iowa Realty's legal work for at least thirty years. Although he rarely let personal feelings influence business decisions, Bill did have a temper and was action oriented; he could not sit by idly while Connie was being attacked. Indeed, Bill was a doer by nature who very much lived in the moment. "I do things and move on," he noted. "I don't dwell on the past; if you do, you lose focus on the present." This laser-sharp focus on the present served him well, especially when the deep recession in the late 1970s and early 1980s engulfed the business world. Bill and his Iowa Realty team would have to navigate the most difficult period they had ever encountered.[29]

Chapter Eight

Steering Through Tough Times

The recession that began in the 1970s hit real estate agencies especially hard. Rising unemployment and interest rates devastated the housing market across the country. Many real estate companies downsized or merged; others closed. In central Iowa, Bill and others in the industry employed a number of strategies to get through the difficult period. Consolidations mounted, and between 1983 and 1985, the number of real estate firms in greater Des Moines decreased by more than a third, which only increased competition between Iowa Realty and rival Gene Stanbrough and his Better Homes and Gardens Realty franchise. The changing market led Stanbrough to expand through acquisition but eventually falter, while Bill surprised many by shifting course and selling a majority stake in Iowa Realty to Central Life Assurance (now Aviva). He remained chairman, however, and given free rein, stepped up development activity, often on the metro's western fringes. This fueled Iowa Realty's growth and led to its rapidly expanding brokerage business, making it even more profitable before Bill cashed out completely in 1989.

With no end in sight to the economic troubles, many wondered if the American dream was over. From 1978 through 1981, people throughout the nation watched in disbelief as the annual inflation rate moved from single to double digits and stayed there for three years. At the same time, home mortgage interest rates soared from 9.6 percent to 16.6 percent, and unemployment increased from 6.1 percent to 7.6 percent. Single-family housing starts fell by half during the period, and the real estate market waned. The malaise made Bill gloomy. "These are as tough times as I've ever seen," he said in 1980.[1]

But he was better prepared for the downturn than most. By the early 1970s, he had proven he could make money. His incomparable deal making all but guaranteed that the cash kept rolling in. What he did not know, necessarily, was how best to preserve that capital and protect his company in case of a serious market downturn. Despite great success, Bill was still haunted by the fear that he might be "a step or two away from losing it all." This concern came up during a meeting with Dick Bryan, president of Des Moines Savings and Loan, in the summer of 1972. Bill had borrowed a lot of money from this bank over the years, and Bryan knew his financial situation well. During their conversation, Bryan pointed out, "The real estate business has its ups and downs, and I'm not sure you are prepared for the downs." To help Bill develop a strategy for dealing with recessions, Bryan made him an appointment with James Downs, Jr., a real estate consultant in Chicago.[2]

An economist, Downs was the highly regarded founder of Real Estate Research Corporation, one of the first firms to specialize in real estate research and analysis. Bill and Jack Wahlig went to Chicago to talk with Downs that fall. The meeting was "eye opening" for Bill. Downs reiterated the point Bryan had made, that the real estate industry was cyclical and told his visitors that Iowa Realty should have enough cash on hand to cover two years of loan payments and all other expenses. "This was a shock," Bill remembered. "We didn't keep a hell of a lot of cash in the bank because it was all invested in real estate." "We left shaking our heads," Wahlig, recalled, but Bill followed the advice. He set aside money for a rainy day fund and "stuck with the formula." These reserves gave Bill and Iowa Realty a cushion when the economy soured late in the decade.[3]

By 1980, the slowdown had hit the Des Moines real estate market hard. Home buying slowed, reaching a seven-year low in 1981, and new home construction slumped. The tough economy also hit the apartment rental business because a growing number of people chose to share living space, and vacancy rates rose. Local realtors fought to stay in business by reducing expenses. Some, such as Joe Bell, owner of Bell Realty, moved to smaller office space "to cut down on overhead." But downsizing was not enough, and later that year he closed his agency and went to work for Iowa Realty. Others, like Kamber-Van Dorn Partners and Homestead Realty, sought economies through merger. Although Iowa Realty's reserve fund could sustain the company for some time, business was off, and Bill was worried. Company sales volume had peaked at $149.5 million in 1979 and fell to $121.1 million the following year. It was at that point, company trainer Tim Meline remembered, that Bill started "tightening the belt." Corporate staff was cut and subsidiary Midland Builders let people go. Planned projects were shelved, in the hope of revisiting them in better times. One example was the purchase and conversion of Camelot West Apartments in West Des Moines to a condominium complex. Iowa Realty had been involved in a number of condominium conversions earlier in the decade and took out an option on the property in 1979. Midland Builders went ahead with painting and carpeting the common areas before it was clear that rising interest rates dried up the market for such units. The company halted the project, chose not to exercise its option to buy the apartments, and walked away. Four years later in 1983, however, interest rates were down from historic highs; and Iowa Realty dusted off the plans, bought Camelot West, and went forward with the conversion.[4]

Amidst these difficult times, Knapp family members made their way up the corporate hierarchy. In 1980, Clair Niday, Bill's brother-in-law, was promoted from manager of the Beaver office to general sales manager of the company. Until then, vice president Paul Knapp had served as general manager as well, and the move was designed to free him from the day-to-day responsibilities of running the company. Mike Knapp, Paul's oldest son and a leading Iowa Realty salesman since starting with the company in 1972, replaced Niday as manager of the Beaver office. Four years later, Niday became director of operations, a new position created for him as he headed toward retirement, and Mike Knapp was named general manager. As Mike was moving up on the brokerage side, his brother, Bill Knapp II, remained corporate counsel and became more and more involved with Bill in development. Since Bill was not at all interested in detail work, it was left to Bill II to follow through with the paperwork and tie up all the loose ends. "Bill makes deals on napkins," Bill II once explained. "You don't see him carrying…a briefcase or a lot of stuff around. I was the one lugging the briefcase around." Since Bill was involved in so many real estate transactions, Bill II remembered, "I was thrown into the fire right away. My job was to document the agreements. I wrote things down, and I kept the files. But it was amazing to see him work. He was the best deal closer I've ever seen."[5]

Meanwhile, Mark Haviland, Bill's son-in-law, became the manager of the property division and Midland Builders. Then in what were essentially cosmetic changes, Paul took over the company presidency in late 1980, but Bill remained chief executive officer (CEO), and he continued focusing on the firm's direction, land developments, and investments. Daryl Neumann, Iowa Realty's chief financial officer (CFO), was named corporate vice president.[6]

Even as Bill and his management team were working through the slump, he made two additional significant hires; both involved friendship and politics. First was Ed Campbell, who over the years had become one of Bill's closest friends. As Harold Hughes prepared to leave politics, Campbell ran John Culver's successful 1974 effort to succeed Hughes in the Senate, and he then worked for him for two years as a field coordinator in Iowa. He made a bid for a state senate seat in 1976, and although he lost the campaign, he was soon elected chairman of the Iowa Democratic Party. At that point, Campbell joined Iowa Realty, selling real estate for three years before becoming Bill's assistant in March of 1979. Bill saw Campbell as his right-hand man, handling a job that involved both politics and real estate. His duties ranged from the mundane, such as opening mail, to the critical, such as navigating state or federal bureaucracies for Bill or lobbying on behalf of Iowa Realty.[7]

In December 1980, Bill announced another hire; after several years of trying, he had finally convinced Harold Hughes to return to Iowa. Hughes was to provide personal and professional counseling for Iowa Realty personnel, but he would also be given plenty of leeway to continue his lay ministry work. In April 1981, Hughes bought a home on five acres several miles south and east of Norwalk, a small town just south of Des Moines. The following month, he left Maryland for Iowa, where he began at Iowa Realty as the new director of community and public affairs. Well before

Hughes even arrived in the state, there was speculation that he would run for governor. Although he initially claimed he was not interested, he left the door open in an August 1981 interview: "I didn't return to Iowa with any thought in my head of running for public office, but I do want to be open-minded about what way I can serve with my life, whatever that may be."[8]

Bill Knapp and Ed Campbell had been working quietly behind the scenes for months encouraging Hughes to run and laying the groundwork for his campaign. Although Hughes did not return to Iowa to reenter public office, it is clear that he and Bill had discussed the topic and that he was considering it. By October, it looked like Hughes would enter the race. The following month he announced his intention to run for governor, but attorney John Law, head of the Hughes exploratory committee and then campaign manager, discovered a possible problem—the Iowa residency requirement. For a gubernatorial candidate to be eligible, he or she had to reside in Iowa for two years prior to the election.[9]

Hughes officials asked the secretary of state, Mary Jane Odell, Iowa's top election official, to rule on whether Hughes met the residency requirement. A Republican, Odell sought legal counsel from the state's attorney general, Tom Miller, who was a Democrat. Because Miller had been a supporter of Hughes's candidacy, however, he believed a conflict of interest kept him from offering an opinion. Instead, attorney David Belin was hired by the state to advise Odell, and by the end of December 1981, she ruled against Hughes, saying he did not meet the Iowa residency requirement to run for governor. Hughes decided against contesting the decision, and a week later in January 1982, he told a group of supporters at his campaign headquarters—located in Bill's Howard Johnson's downtown Des Moines motel—that he was withdrawing from the race. Bill was upset that Hughes bowed out and upset with Miller for not fighting for Hughes. During the announcement, the *Des Moines Register* reported, Bill "sulked in a chair in the corner" and said, "I'm not too happy today."[10]

Bill was not morose very long. Ed Campbell had considered a run for governor before Hughes became interested, and when Hughes withdrew, he and Bill encouraged Campbell to enter the race. He did, and all the campaign apparatus that had been created for Hughes was geared up for Campbell. Bill was the campaign's chief fundraiser and went after contributions in his typical aggressive manner. In March, Hughes threw his public support behind Campbell and joined the team in a job the *Des*

Moines Tribune characterized as "somewhere between a 'figurehead' and a day-to-day manager." By this time, two others had also entered the race for the Democratic nomination: Roxanne Conlin of Des Moines, a former United States attorney for the Southern District of Iowa, and Jerome Fitzgerald of Fort Dodge, a former Iowa house majority leader and Democratic candidate for governor in 1978.[11]

The Campbell campaign was hobbled from the start. While some believed Campbell's long service as an aide to Hughes and his years in the private sector with Bill at Iowa Realty gave him the perfect background to be governor, others saw his association with these two powerful Democrats as a problem. *Des Moines Tribune* reporter David Elbert explained, "Many Democrats find it difficult to see him as anything other than a 'substitute candidate for Hughes,' or, worse yet, 'Bill Knapp's candidate for governor.'" The issue was compounded by Bill's overzealous fundraising efforts. It was immediately clear at Iowa Realty that Bill was pushing Campbell's campaign. The March 1982 edition of the *Iowa Newsletter*, the firm's internal monthly publication, featured a full-page cover story about Campbell's candidacy and made suggestions of how employees could help. It was noted that the piece was paid for by the Campbell for Governor Committee. A couple of months later in the May issue of the newsletter, a headline, "The Government Needs You," pleaded for help. "The 'Campbell for Governor' campaign needs you," the story explained. "Telephoning, addressing envelopes, mailings, etc. all need to be done to keep Ed's name out in front of the public." It concluded, "Ed is our friend and co-worker. Let's give him our total support."[12]

Several weeks earlier, Bill had been even more direct with employees, sending out a letter soliciting their campaign donations. After noting the benefits of a Campbell victory, he wrote, "Remember, Ed is one of us. He needs our support and I am asking for your help to raise the necessary capital to get the job done....Please bring your contributions to your Office Manager." The move was vintage Bill, exploiting an advantage to attain a goal. But some at Iowa Realty did not appreciate the pressure, and one sent a copy of the letter to the *Des Moines Register*. On April 29, 1982, the paper published the letter with a piece chiding Bill for such "arm-twisting" tactics. Then it explained, "The letter to Iowa Realty employees magnifies one of Campbell's biggest problems: escaping from the shadows of Knapp and Harold Hughes."[13]

The editorial highlighted the concern, but it had been clear for weeks that Campbell faced a serious uphill challenge. Although he announced his candidacy first, Conlin had been campaigning for a year, and by March, a *Des Moines Register*'s Iowa Poll showed her leading Campbell by 20 percentage points and Fitzgerald by 8. Campbell never closed the gap, and Conlin went on to win the June primary taking 48 percent of the vote; Campbell came in a disappointing third with 21 percent. Conlin's big primary win notwithstanding, she lost the general election to Republican Terry Branstad.[14]

While his candidates, Hughes and then Campbell, both fell short of the mark, Bill was committed to Democratic politics and remained a principal power in the state party. Over the years, he had been a steadfast supporter of Congressman Neal Smith as well as congressmen and then senators John Culver and Tom Harkin. In 1986, he was a major supporter of Lowell Junkins's failed gubernatorial campaign. But in 1990 he tasted victory, when Campbell's wife, attorney Bonnie Campbell—who had been a staffer for senators Hughes and Culver and later worked as an agent for Iowa Realty—was elected Iowa's attorney general. He was disappointed when Bonnie Campbell lost the governor's race to incumbent Branstad in 1994, but more political successes soon followed. Bill became an important supporter and later good friend of Governor Tom Vilsack (1999–2007), and he served as co-chair of the election committee for Chester (Chet) Culver, John Culver's son, who succeeded Vilsack as governor. In fact, from the 1970s on, Bill "contributed more money to Iowa Democratic candidates and causes than anyone in the state." Involvement in politics, he understood, was about gaining and maintaining access, important to anyone in the business world. But more pressing in 1982 was the continued sluggishness of the economy.[15]

Bill found that saving money with cost-cutting measures and canceling projects was not enough. On Paul's suggestion and in an effort to jumpstart the brokerage business, Iowa Realty made it easier for customers to obtain home loans by establishing an in-house mortgage banking option. In October 1980, the company became the first real estate firm in Iowa to make such a move, creating Iowa Mortgage Corporation. The subsidiary originated loans, initially only offering FHA and VA mortgages. It gradually expanded into other products, and by 1983, nearly one in four home mortgages in Des Moines went through Iowa Mortgage.[16]

In addition, Bill worked to retain important managers by expanding the incentive package. In the early 1970s, he had created a profit-sharing plan for corporate staff. Now he sweetened the pot for key company figures by developing a stock ownership plan. Those who received stock included CFO Daryl Neumann, general manager Clair Niday, general counsel Bill Knapp II, Beaver office manager Mike Knapp, as well as managers Roger Cleven, Howard Stacey, and top salesman Ken Whitehead. The stock was in addition to the profit-sharing program. Several years later in 1984, Paul extended profit-sharing to sales agents as well.[17]

Even so, company sales volume continued to drop, falling to $105.6 million in 1982. CFO Neumann recalled, "Bill was very, very nervous. He had never been like that in all the years I'd known him [since 1972]. He was concerned about the possibility of losing everything he had accumulated because we were at risk on loans and houses weren't selling." Neumann did not believe the situation that dire, but it clearly impacted Bill who was increasingly apprehensive and started thinking about ways to protect the company from future economic trouble.[18]

He moved to shore up his liquidity by unloading some properties. Bill and the company attorney, nephew Bill Knapp II, realized that even though the market was still soft, they could find ready buyers for particular holdings because they had been purchased or built in the early 1970s at favorable interest rates and the mortgages did not carry a "due on sale" clause. This meant that Bill could sell the properties and buyers could assume the low-interest mortgage. It also meant that the lenders who held these mortgages were motivated to buy them and get these low-interest rate loans off their books. In 1983, for instance, Bill sold the Peppertree Motel and Restaurant, the Saveway Motel, and the Westchester Village Apartments to United Federal Savings, which held the mortgages on all three. The following year, he sold a Beaverdale strip mall to the note holder, Midland Financial (formerly Des Moines Saving and Loan, and today, Bank of the West), and in a deal that did not involve the due on sale clause, he sold the ninety-six-unit Green Valley Apartments in West Des Moines to the Al Icheson-led Merit Holding Corporation.[19]

More importantly, he had come to a significant decision: "If things ever turned around," he considered, "I would move to become involved with someone with a lot of staying power, someone with a lot of capital." When the economic recovery did begin in 1983, Bill started looking for a well-heeled partner. Actually, over the past few years he had turned down a couple of proposals to combine Iowa Realty with other real estate firms. In the late 1970s, American Invsco (AI), a Chicago real estate development company, was expanding beyond Chicago by buying local real estate operations. Mark Kline, an AI vice president, was overseeing some condominium conversion projects in Des Moines and initiated talks with Bill about AI acquiring a stake in Iowa Realty. Several discussions ensued, but Bill finally rebuffed the offer, which he believed was too low and would not add to Iowa Realty's profitability. Later, after an effort to make Mel Foster Company—a large real estate agency located in the Quad Cities on the Iowa-Illinois border—an Iowa Realty franchise fell through, management of the eastern Iowa firm suggested merging. But again, Bill did not see that merging provided any advantages for Iowa Realty, and talks went nowhere.[20]

While Bill began looking for potential partners, rival Gene Stanbrough, owner of Stanbrough/Better Homes and Gardens Real Estate, saw that change was necessary as well. But he decided the answer was growth through acquisition. Stanbrough envisioned a real estate and banking operation designed to provide homebuyers "one-stop shopping for their financial needs." He established a holding company called First Group in 1983, and with $3.4 million in assistance from the Federal Savings and Loan Insurance Corporation, he bought two troubled savings and loans: First Financial Savings and Loan Association of Knoxville and later Scandia Savings of Des Moines. These were merged into First Financial Savings Bank. Then Stanbrough bought several local insurance agencies and combined them into another subsidiary, First Insurance. The firm also included a property management unit and a construction firm, but the key asset was Stanbrough's real estate company. Rebranded as First Realty/Better Homes and Gardens, he expanded it by purchasing some smaller area competitors, most notably Ken Grandquist and Associates and James Conlin's real estate companies.[21]

By the time Stanbrough's first acquisition became public, Bill had already identified a potential partner. Sometime in mid-1983, he raised the subject at a lunch with Roger Brooks, the forty-seven-year-old CEO of Des Moines-based Central Life Assurance. The two had been acquainted since the early 1970s but became better friends several years later when Brooks joined the Breakfast Club and they began playing tennis. In fact, it was on the tennis court at Bill's Timberline property that the two discussed the idea in more detail.[22]

Bill caught Brooks at a good time. Ever since he returned from an executive seminar at Stanford University in 1978, he was convinced diversifying Central Life was critical for the long-term health of the company. To avoid remaining a "Johnny one-note company," Brooks went on a buying spree. He took his first important step in 1982, merging with Wisconsin Life Insurance, which added group insurance to the life insurer. Meanwhile, as a hedge against inflation, the company also went into real estate, and by the mid-1980s, it owned several hotels and was involved in development projects in Jacksonville, Florida, Austin and Dallas, Texas, Phoenix and Tempe, Arizona, Oklahoma City, Oklahoma, and Omaha, Nebraska. Up to that point, Central Life's real estate ventures had focused on the Sun Belt, and Brooks saw Bill's offer of Iowa Realty as an opportunity to buy expertise and experience in Central Life's home market. Bill saw Central Life's deep pockets as a way protect Iowa Realty and rapidly expand the number and size of its developments.[23]

Once the two concurred that combining was a good idea, Brooks bowed out of the talks to avoid any conflict of interest. Even as negotiations moved forward, Bill continued with other deals, one of which was finding a much needed larger corporate home. He initially looked downtown but eventually ruled that out because of limited parking. Instead he considered the western suburbs and in March 1984, he paid $2.5 million for the Eddie Webster's Motor Inn and Restaurant property across the street from Valley West Mall in West Des Moines. The restaurant was gutted and redesigned as Iowa Realty's new headquarters, nearly doubling the size of its former facility on Beaver Avenue, which became another sales office. Also updated and remodeled was the 141-room motel, reopened as the Iowa Realty–owned Valley West Inn.[24]

Just two weeks after the new headquarters opened, Bill Knapp and Roger Brooks announced a deal at a news conference arranged by the Greater Des Moines Chamber of Commerce, held at Bill's Hotel Savery. Central Life purchased 80 percent of Iowa Realty Co., Inc. for $6.8 million. The sale included the residential and commercial brokerage business, the property management division, Iowa Mortgage Corporation, and a recently established Iowa Realty Securities Company. No real estate was involved.[25]

Many were surprised that the independent Iowa Realty owner would sell and work for someone else; but Bill's childhood memories of financial insecurity on the farm coupled with the deep recession of the late 1970s through the early 1980s convinced him to consider a new path. Plus, Iowa Realty's continued dominance as the state's largest real estate company in terms of volume suggested the timing was right. Bill explained, "When you're up and going great is the time to sell. The time has come to be part of a strong financial organization like Central Life. It will enable us to become more aggressive and competitive." While Bill would actually work for Central Life, Brooks noted that he would have "free rein to do as he wishes," and Bill, Paul, and other key managers at Iowa Realty were given employment contracts. With access to Central Life's capital, Bill believed he could make more money owning 20 percent of the company than he had when he controlled all of it. Brooks suggested as much when he told the crowd, "Making Bill Knapp an employee is a little like hitching a race horse up to a plow."[26]

Brooks could not have been more right. The sale marked a turning point for Bill; it was as if he were unleashed. With internal financing provided by Central Life at below market rates, he initiated numerous projects, taking Iowa Realty to new heights. Developments sprung up all over the city, and the brokerage and mortgage business boomed.

In the midst of discussions with Central Life, Bill became a leading proponent of plans to revitalize the area around Drake University. The local business district—situated along Twenty-fourth and Twenty-fifth streets between Carpenter Avenue to the north and Drake Park Avenue to the south—had been deteriorating for years. The first moves to halt the decline were made in 1982, when J. Michael Earley became the president of Hawkeye Bank and Trust, which was headquartered in the heart of the flagging neighborhood at Twenty-fourth Street and University Avenue. He initially considered fleeing the area and relocating the bank's main office in West Des Moines but ultimately chose to stay put and work to rebuild the neighborhood. Since moving to Des Moines the previous year, Earley had been learning the lay of the land and making connections throughout the city. One of the most important was Monroe Colston, an executive with the Greater Des Moines Chamber, who introduced him to key business leaders. Another one was Bill Knapp, who was also a trustee of Drake University.[27]

159

Earley began by discussing restoration of the area with Drake University trustees and followed up the meeting by organizing a bus tour of the neighborhood for them. Although the Des Moines *Business Record* called the excursion "eye opening," two leading board members, chairman Ed Glazer of Central Management Corporation and Martin Bucksbaum of General Growth Properties, suggested separating the school from the spreading blight by "building a moat around the campus." Bill entered the discussion at this point. Although he had been on the Drake board since 1976, he had not been very active, but the comment angered him. At the time, his son Roger was attending USC, located in a poverty-stricken section of Los Angeles. In the 1960s and 1970s, the school and the city had worked together buying or condemning many old, decrepit structures adjacent to the campus and building outward as if to create a buffer zone between the university and local residents. Such action only created animosity and suspicion among those in the surrounding community, and it took years to rebuild relations with people in the neighborhood. Bill saw his fellow trustees' comment in this vein, and he did not want to see Drake make the same mistake. He went after Glazer and Bucksbaum, arguing that walling off Drake would only lead to alienation. Instead, Bill lectured, Drake needed to embrace the neighborhood and be part of its revitalization before it was too late.[28]

The decay in the university neighborhood struck a chord with him. It was bad for the school and, more broadly, bad for the city. Bill's argument before the board won the day, and by the fall of 1984, he and Earley along with Drake trustees Glazer, Bucksbaum, Ken Austin, chairman of the Equitable of Iowa, Jack Pester of Pester Corporation, and Bob Houser of Des Moines Development Corporation formed the Drake–Des Moines Development Corporation to oversee the neighborhood's rehabilitation. A Chicago consultant was hired and suggested a gradual redevelopment spanning several years, which would include renovating area homes, a new apartment complex, and providing a common façade for existing business buildings. Drake was a key player, but with its president Wilbur Miller retiring in 1985, the school was in a holding pattern; no one would commit to the project. From Bill's perspective, the proposal was not going forward anyway because plans were developed for land that had not yet been acquired. By the following summer, however, things changed. Michael Ferrari, Drake's new president, strongly believed the university should be partnered with the community and agreed with Bill on the urgency of rejuvenating the local neighborhood. He threw the university's full support behind the effort.[29]

That was all Bill needed. With characteristic impatience, he took action, prodding the Drake–Des Moines Development Corporation to move forward. He sent Pat Greene, a leading Iowa Realty commercial agent, to obtain the necessary pieces of property for redevelopment. Bill recalled that Greene was masterful, purchasing the land from "35 to 40 different landowners, an almost impossible job." As the real estate was being assembled, Bill called for expanding the project, which soon included a motel, more apartments, and a restaurant. The university stepped up as well with plans for building a legal clinic in the neighborhood.[30]

Besides being the front man and public face of the renewal, Bill worked behind the scenes putting together investors to finance the rebuilding. First to go up in 1986 was the Old Main Apartments, a four-building, 108-unit complex erected on the block bounded by Twenty-third and Twenty-fourth streets and University and Carpenter avenues. It was developed by Civic Center Court, Inc., the group Bill had established to erect Civic Center Court Apartments downtown. At about the same time, Bill led another limited partnership, erecting the fifty-two-unit Drake University Inn between Twenty-fourth and Twenty-fifth streets south of University Avenue. Meanwhile, Drake went ahead with its law clinic, located in the energized neighborhood just north of the motel. Then because the Old Main Apartments had been fully leased within several months, Bill and the Civic Center Court consortium built Drake Court and Drake Pointe, two additional twenty-four-unit apartment complexes in the neighborhood.[31]

Bill's piece de resistance was the restaurant. All agreed that an eatery was needed, but it was Bill who came up with concept of the Drake Diner. He had recently enjoyed the Fog City Diner in San Francisco, a nostalgic, bright reinterpretation of a 1950s diner. He was certain the concept would work in the Drake neighborhood. In the fall 1986, he gathered thirty-seven investors into the Drake Area Restaurant Corporation to build and then operate the $1.1 million Drake Diner, immediately west of the Drake University Inn on Twenty-fifth Street. With its art deco design, black and white tile, chrome, and lots of blue, pink, and white neon lighting, the eye-popping diner opened in the fall 1987 and was an immediate success.[32]

Drake University was clearly a major beneficiary of the revitalization. Ferrari noted that the renewal helped with recruitment. "Prospective students and their parents are impressed when they see this level of commitment to the area," he explained. Numbers verified his feelings: the entering freshman class in 1987 exceeded the number of new students enrolled the previous fall by 11 percent. Maybe even more important for Drake, however, were the bonds that Ferrari and other board members were forging with Bill; these would lead to his growing support and large financial gifts in the following decade. City officials also praised the effort. Gary Lozano, the assistant city planning director, called the revitalization "very successful" in bringing people back to the area and expanding the tax base. But as was typical, even as his guidance of the renewal was "breathing life back into the Drake neighborhood," Bill had moved on to other projects.[33]

These activities took him to the western suburbs as Bill stayed ahead of the movement of people and businesses heading in that direction. First was a 364-acre luxury residential development in Booneville, eighteen miles west of downtown Des Moines. Located on a ridge overlooking the Raccoon River Valley, the parcel was named Woodhill and rezoned for residential use in the 1970s. Owner Crawford Hubbell had put in some streets and added water lines, but the development came to a halt when he went bankrupt in the mid-1980s. Bill bought the land for $300,000 in 1986, and while considering a new moniker for the development, jokingly nicknamed it Boot Hill. Several weeks later, it was renamed Napa Valley. Bill's son-in-law Mark Haviland and nephew Mike Knapp came up with the idea while having dinner at Guido's. As Haviland remembered, after the waiter recommended a Napa Valley chardonnay, "a light went on for both Mike and me." The name Napa Valley proved perfect; it invoked the idea of rich rolling hills, expansive vistas, and elegance, and it was a tongue-in-cheek play on the Knapp name.[34]

Bill and his team revamped plans for the wooded acreage to include 155 large lots, ranging in size from one to four acres. An old farmhouse near the development's entrance was refurbished for use by residents, and other amenities including a swimming pool, two large ponds, tennis courts, a driving range and putting green, and picnic facilities were added to the common area. In a nod to the wine theme, a vineyard was planted on the grounds, while Napa Valley's streets were given such names as Bordeaux Circle, Chardonnay Point, Champagne Road, and Vintage Trail. Bill held several private showings and wine tastings at Napa Valley in the fall 1987 and then opened the development to the general public. Because of its distance from Des Moines and the development's large, expensive lots, Bill expected to sell only twelve lots per year, but by early 1990, nearly fifty lots had been sold and sixteen homes were built or under construction.[35]

Most buyers were movers and shakers from Des Moines and included trucking magnate John Ruan, who owned the 1,200-acre Jonbar Ranch immediately west of the development; David Kruidenier, former publisher of the Des Moines Register and Tribune Company; Drake's Michael Ferrari; Dave Miller, the president of West Bank; and Ed and Bonnie Campbell. But the most interesting new resident to Napa Valley might have been Kenny Grandquist. For years, he and Bill had been the closest of friends, but since Grandquist left Iowa Realty and started a rival company in 1977, the two had been at odds. The bitterness ran deep, but Bill finally reached out to Grandquist in the mid-1980s, and they gradually became friendly again. By 1989, their reconciliation looked complete when they returned to their old ways, becoming next door neighbors for the third time. Grandquist initially built a splendid 5,000-square-foot residence in Napa Valley, and although Bill spent most of his time at his Plaza penthouse downtown, he erected a virtually identical home next door to his old friend.[36]

Sale of lots in Napa Valley slowed after the initial couple of years, but then picked up again, especially after residential developments in West Des Moines began pushing toward Booneville in the early to mid-1990s. In both this project and the Drake neighborhood, Bill had invested his own money, not Iowa Realty's; and, although the company was involved and benefited from marketing, selling, and mortgage lending in the case of Napa Valley and property management in the case of the Drake apartments and motel, these were *his* ventures. Still, most of his undertakings from 1985 through 1989 involved Iowa Realty, where he used the financing assured through his deal with Central Life to buy and develop property. The readily available funds allowed him to expand his development efforts and led to Iowa Realty opening numerous subdivisions over the period, including Parkview on the south side of Des Moines; Ashworth Hills, Meadow Point, and Meadow Rue in West Des Moines; Meredith

Park in Urbandale; and Streamwood and Prairie Point in Polk City, twenty miles north and west of Des Moines.[37]

Though important, these housing developments were dwarfed by Bill's two biggest Iowa Realty projects of the decade, both of which proved hugely successful. Certain that population and businesses would continue trending in a westerly direction, Bill began looking at land along the western edge of Polk County and into Dallas County in the early 1980s. It was here he bought 570 acres of farmland straddling the two counties in 1987 for $2.77 million. Four hundred acres of this land was situated between University Avenue to the south, Hickman Road to the north, Northwest 128th Street to the east, and northwest 142nd Street to the west. The remaining 170-acre tract sat south of University Avenue.[38]

As the acquisition was being negotiated, the city of Clive—a narrow strip of a suburb with only 7,000 people sandwiched between the larger suburbs of Urbandale to the north and West Des Moines to the south—had run out of development ground and was moving forward with plans to annex 1,200 acres of unincorporated land from Interstate 35-80 west to the Polk County/Dallas County line. The move would increase Clive's size by 40 percent, encourage developers with the promise of extending municipal services, and included the 400-acre parcel Bill was in the process of buying. In November 1986, Clive residents overwhelming approved the annexation, shortly before Iowa Realty completed the purchase of the land.[39]

The following spring, Iowa Realty announced its plans for the land. The firm envisioned a $100 million development of 359 posh homes, 328 elegant townhomes, and an office park around a forty-five-acre lake that would be built from a Walnut Creek tributary. Named "Country Club" because it was located just north of the Des Moines Golf and Country Club, the community began generating a lot of interest while it was still on the drawing board. Other developers, for example, jumped at land in the area once they heard of Bill's purchase and plans. Their thinking was simple: if Bill thought it a good investment, it was wise to follow. Most notably, Marvin Pomerantz's Mid-America Group, a real estate and development company, bought 150 acres adjacent to Country Club on its northeastern boundary in 1988. Here Mid-America would build The Woodlands, an upscale subdivision of large, densely wooded lots. But more important for Iowa Realty, the announcement of Country Club received a warm reception from the public. By February 1988, the company had a waiting list of people who wanted to buy the development's lakeside lots. This was months before construction of the lake even began. Mark Haviland, then president of Iowa Realty property management division, noted the excitement surrounding Country Club: "Without any doubt, there has been more interest in this than any project we've had. We've had calls from the public, from our brokers, builders, just an incredible amount of interest. People say, 'When can we buy a lot where there's a lake?'"[40]

In addition to the lake, the community promised winding, tree-lined streets, a greenbelt with trails and bike paths, and large lots. While Iowa Realty would not construct the homes, it established restrictive building covenants—including minimum square footage and a wood shake shingle roof requirement—to maintain the development's exclusivity. And to emphasize the neighborhood's upscale nature, Country Club's southern entrance would feature an impressive brick colonnade and wrought iron fencing accented by a three-level, lighted fountain. In July 1988, Iowa Realty opened its first Country Club plat, putting seventy lots on the market. They sold out in a week. Kelly Bryant, Iowa Realty's marketing director, said it was "like an Oklahoma land-rush around here," while general manager Mike Knapp was caught off guard: "I was really surprised by how fast they went. We thought it would take a year to sell them." The average lot sold for $51,000 and the company expected the homes built in the area to range in cost from $150,000 to $500,000.[41]

The remaining twenty lots not offered for sale were held in reserve as part of the company's bid for the following year's Home Show Expo, the Home Builders Association of Greater Des Moines's annual fundraiser, which had been held since 1976. Designed to highlight the finest area builders and the latest trends in the industry, the Expo was essentially a week-long open house, allowing attendees to tour newly constructed, fully decorated and furnished model homes. Developers competed strenuously for the event because it drew a lot of public attention to the hosting subdivision. Iowa Realty's Country Club won the 1989 show, and sixteen builders erected custom-built homes valued at over $10 million for the June event. Nearly 30,000 people attended the Expo, and Mike Knapp believed the interest it generated put the development six months ahead of schedule. The Home Builders Association was pleased too and decided to hold the Expo at Country Club again the following year. It was the first time in more than a decade that consecutive home shows were hosted by the same development.[42]

Country Club went on to be Iowa Realty's largest and most successful residential community. By the mid-1990s, hundreds of upscale homes and townhomes dotted the development's nearly 1,000 acres in the original Country Club, Country Club Woods, and Country Club West. It also included office space, a bank, and the West End Diner, a replica of the successful Drake Diner. With nearly 3,000 residents, Country Club was larger than at least 800 towns in the state.[43]

While planning for Country Club continued, Bill was also working on developing the 170-acre Iowa Realty tract just to the south and east for commercial use. Originally called Westgate and then Country Club Business Park, the land sat between Sixtieth Street on the east, University Avenue on the north, Interstate 80 to the south, and extended about one mile west into unincorporated land in Dallas County. As a precursor to development, Bill and Bill II pushed to have the City of West Des Moines annex the land, which took place in 1988. It was zoned for office buildings, extending the city's existing 556-acre office park corridor by 30 percent. [44]

In the meantime, he sought tenants for the business park, and as was frequently the case, his relationships played an important role here. The first firm Bill won over was Iowa Methodist Medical Center. His long-standing connection with the nonprofit dated back to the late 1960s when he signed a contract with the hospital to take rooms in Iowa Realty's Inntowner apartment and motel complex. In June 1988, Iowa Methodist bought twenty acres in the business park and then bought an additional forty acres the following year. Here it would erect a number of buildings beginning with Lakeview Medical Park in 1991. Then one of Bill's oldest corporate partners, Hy-Vee, bought land in the development as well, acquiring twenty-one acres for a reported $1.6 million in December 1988. With two major firms committed to the park, Iowa Realty began preparing it for building, burying utilities and grading the land.[45]

Before any buildings went up, Bill partnered with Farm Bureau Life Insurance Company, Country Club Business Park's neighbor to the east, which also owned more than 100 acres of land abutting the Iowa Realty development. Under the arrangement, the two combined their land, which totaled 320 acres, and named the venture West Lakes Business Park. According to the *Des Moines Register*, the jointly owned West Des

Moines commercial development was "five times larger than any other of the suburb's office parks." For Bill, the benefits of the deal were similar to his arrangement with Central Life. "If we do more joint ventures," he noted, "we can do more projects." Farm Bureau, meanwhile, was new to the real estate business and was happy to tap into Iowa Realty's expertise.[46]

Once together, Iowa Realty/Farm Bureau vigorously pushed the development forward. In the spring of 1990, Bill announced plans for the first structure in West Lakes: a speculative $11 million office facility built by the Iowa Realty/Farm Bureau partnership. The crescent-shaped glass and brick structure would include 120,000 square feet of office space and feature a rotunda with a sixty-five-foot skylit dome. A year later, Bill landed another major tenant for the commercial park when Kirke-Van Orsdel, Inc. announced it was leaving Capital Square downtown and developing a $20 million office building in West Lakes. Then in September 1991, Bill added to the office park, buying the LakePoint development from a joint venture of Hubbell Realty and Allied Group, Inc. The ninety-five acres extended the West Lakes Business Park west to Seventy-fourth Street.[47]

He paid $4 million for the land—then the market price—but that was not the most interesting detail about the acquisition. Bill had owned the ground years earlier and was buying it back. He originally purchased the land in two transactions in 1970 and 1973, paying $1,475 per acre or a total of $140,125. Then in 1979, he transferred it (valued at $607,500, or roughly $6,400 per acre) to Kenny Grandquist as part of the settlement with his former partner. This did not fit his usual pattern of buying low and selling high. Instead, Bill explained with a laugh, "I bought it low, sold it low edge, and bought it back high." But when asked about regretting the move, he was definitive: "No. I never look back. I never second guess a decision I've made. If I'd kept the land then, I wouldn't have been able to buy other things." The answer was revealing and reflected his realty; Bill was pragmatic and lived in and for the moment. Once a deal was concluded, good, bad, or indifferent, he moved on to others and did not dwell on what was done. In this case, the land had quadrupled in value during the time he held it, and it looked like he had made a handsome profit. No one, not even Bill, could have imagined how the property's value would soar over the next dozen years.[48]

If he had guessed wrong on LakePoint, he did not make such mistakes very often. In fact, after he sold the 80 percent stake in Iowa Realty in 1984, his aggressive development of Country Club, West Lakes, and numerous smaller subdivisions pushed the company to new heights. At the time, Iowa Realty had 346 agents and a 38 percent share of the Des Moines real estate market, while leading competitor Stanbrough's First Realty had 339 agents in the metro area and roughly 32 percent market share. From that point on, the fortunes of the two moved in opposite directions.[49]

The many subdivisions Bill was opening for Iowa Realty gave it an edge over its competitors, which had done little in the way of land development. Paul Knapp explained, "Being a developer allows us to provide inventory for our agents." With this ever increasing stock of new homes to sell, Iowa Realty added to its sales force. By the end of 1987, the company had 400 agents, and a year later nearly 500. More agents meant more sales. In 1985, company sales volume stood at $169 million, up more than 10 percent from the previous year, but then it soared, rising to $250 million in 1986 and $341 million in 1988.[50]

First Realty, meanwhile, stagnated. It began losing market share, although a forceful 1987 advertising campaign argued otherwise. Based on responses to a survey sent to Polk County home buyers, company billboards featured a pie-chart claiming that First Realty had 40 percent of the local market and was the "First Choice" of area buyers. Iowa Realty's share, which First maintained was 42 percent, was lumped together with all other local real estate firms. Iowa Realty responded with ads of its own, showing its market share at 53 percent, while putting First Realty's at 29 percent. Real estate expert Jay Hytone offered an explanation for the discrepancy. At the time, about 30 percent of Polk County homes sold were listed by one company and sold by another, and market share statistics varied depending on whether or not the listing and selling firms both took credit for the sale. Iowa Realty statistics were based on sales reports from the multiple listing service (MLS) and relied solely on sales volume. For a while, each threatened to sue the other, but the issue gradually faded away when Stanbrough's firm dropped the campaign in early 1988. Later that year, its parent company found itself in serious trouble, and Gene Stanbrough conceded that his real estate operation had been losing market share since 1985. Iowa Realty's numbers on market share had been correct.[51]

Actually, Stanbrough's First Financial Group, the holding company he established in 1983, had faced major difficulties from the outset. Stanbrough had underestimated the financial woes of the two troubled savings and loans he bought and merged into First Financial Savings Bank. The situation was so grave, the *Des Moines Register* later reported, that when he acquired them, Stanbrough "should have asked for at least $30 million in assistance from the Federal Savings and Loan Insurance Corporation." Instead, he received only $3.4 million. Not surprisingly, the depth of the problem distracted him from focusing on First Realty. At the same time, negative publicity about the savings and loan discouraged people from listing property with the firm. Taken together, these factors hurt First Realty's sales and market share. Meanwhile, try as he might, Stanbrough could not save his thrift. A proposed merger never occurred, and federal regulators prohibited the capital infusion he had arranged from Principal Financial Group. In December 1988, First Financial was declared insolvent and sold by federal regulators to Metropolitan Financial Corporation. Its real estate arm, Edina Realty of Minneapolis, took over First Realty/Better Homes and Gardens.[52]

Then Stanbrough surprised the local real estate community. Instead of doing what most expected, either staying with First Realty or trying to buy it back from the new owners, he started a new local real estate brokerage. He had been contacted by Pomerantz of Mid-America, and the two partnered to create Stanbrough and Associates, Realtors. Bill did not think the new alliance could make much of an impact. Paul Knapp agreed. With Iowa Realty's 54 percent of the market and First Realty's 25 percent, he thought Stanbrough would have a "tough sell" getting the large sales force he needed to mount a serious challenge.[53]

Just months after Stanbrough's two bombshells, Bill announced his own; he and minority shareholders were selling their stake in Iowa Realty. Roger Brooks had initiated negotiations in late 1988. He was preparing to take Central Life public, but before doing so, he needed to buy the subsidiary's outstanding 20 percent. Discussions soon bogged down over the valuation of the remaining Iowa Realty stock. The original purchase agreement set Iowa Realty's goodwill, or the firm's intangible assets, at ten times its earnings. The same calculation was to be used if or when Central Life exercised its option to purchase the outstanding shares or minority shareholders used their option to sell the remaining 20 percent to Central Life after January 1990. When Brooks opened talks about buying the rest of Iowa Realty, the key question was how to value the company, especially because of its earnings after it became part of the Central Life family in 1984. This made the value of the outstanding Iowa Realty stock worth much more than anyone had expected.[54]

Talks came to a head in the spring of 1989 in what Bill Knapp II described as "a knock-down, drag-out" Saturday morning meeting at Iowa Realty's West Des Moines headquarters. Sitting around the conference room table for the minority shareholders were Bill, his brother Paul, nephews Bill Knapp II and Mike Knapp, Daryl Neumann, and the McGladrey accountant, Jack Wahlig. Central Life was represented by Brooks, D.T. Doan, executive vice president, Keith Gunzenhauser, senior vice president of finance, and James Smallenberger, corporate counsel. The meeting was contentious from the start. Although both parties eventually agreed to estimates of the company's future earnings potential, they could not agree on its present value. Bill and Iowa Realty managers maintained that the formula used to value goodwill set forth in the 1984 document was clear. Brooks and his team balked, explaining that this was not the intent of the language. They also argued that the real estate firm had only grown because of its use of Central Life's financing. At loggerheads, the two sides took a break. An hour later, they rejoined the discussion without Bill, who had not yet returned.[55]

On his way back to the meeting, Bill stopped by Tim Meline's office, where he picked up a rubber chicken, a prop the company trainer sometimes employed in his courses. So armed, he marched into the conference room grasping the chicken by the neck, and without saying a word, shook it at Brooks and the others from Central Life. The stunt provided some much needed comic relief, but Bill's message was clear: We have you by the neck on how the firm should be valued. A short time later, Brooks assented to Iowa Realty's position and asked Bill to meet him at his office downtown that afternoon, where the two hammered out the broad outlines of the deal. Central Life purchased the outstanding 20 percent of Iowa Realty for $7.99 million or $1.2 million more than it had paid for 80 percent of the company. With an agreement on the details, the sale price was met through a combination of immediate cash payments, compensation packages—Bill and the rest of Iowa Realty's top managers signed contracts to stay in place for the next few years—and high-interest debentures notes.[56]

Bill's flurry of activity from 1985 to 1988 had paid off handsomely, and the sale of his remaining interest in Iowa Realty capped a long period of success. Thirteen years earlier in 1976, he had been identified by the *Des Moines Register*'s "The Powers That Be" poll as the fifteenth most powerful figure in the city, certainly an up-and-comer to watch. Since that time, Bill became much more prominent in and around Des Moines. He was a major figure in the city's continuing downtown renaissance, led the charge to restore the Drake neighborhood, and remained a leading influence in the Iowa Democratic Party. All the while, he shaped and extended the metro area with residential developments here and commercial developments there, as he oversaw the expansion of Iowa Realty. Several months after he sold the last shares of the company, the *Des Moines Register* published its second "The Powers That Be" poll in January 1990. This time, Bill landed on top; he was now regarded as the city's foremost business and community figure. Although he said he was embarrassed by the designation and believed such lists only alienated people, he must have smiled for a moment. It had been a long journey for the poor farm boy from Allerton, but it was clear the sixty-three-year-old had no intention of slowing down. He enjoyed doing deals; that was what kept him going. "What else would I do?" Bill responded, when asked about retirement. "Walk the beaches and play tennis all day?"[57]

Chapter Nine

Act Two

Like other self-made business figures, Bill was proud of his accomplishments and spent lavishly on items that announced his success. He wore finely tailored suits and owned homes in fashionable areas such as Palm Springs, California; Naples, Florida; Chicago, Illinois; and Aspen, Colorado. When in Des Moines, he was often seen holding court at his elegant Hotel Savery, and he drove about town in one of his attention-getting automobiles. By the early 1980s, these included a high-end Mercedes Benz, a DMC-12—the gull-winged, stainless steel sports car built by John DeLorean—a Corvette, and a two-toned burgundy and black limousine. Sometimes, his showy display seemed insensitive and bordered on bad taste. Bill had been a longtime patron of the Door of Faith Mission, a downtown charitable organization that provided free food and housing to the homeless. He wanted to interest others in supporting it as well. He asked David Kruidenier, a good friend and former publisher and chief executive officer (CEO) of the Des Moines Register and Tribune Company (R&T), and his wife Elizabeth (Liz) to join him at the Mission for lunch. They agreed. Bill picked them up in his limousine and headed toward the ramshackle center. Kruidenier was mortified and told Bill, "Don't pull up in front of the door, for heaven's sake."

But Bill did and thought nothing of this over-the-top display of wealth amid the impoverished.[1]

Bill enjoyed the finer things money could buy, but his interests beyond work were narrow. He had no desire to follow successful peers who transitioned from working to the more leisurely pursuits of the wealthy, such as collecting art and books or frequent and extravagant travel. Some did try to broaden Bill's horizons by encouraging him to cultivate an interest in the arts, but they held no appeal for him. He traveled to Europe several times but found touring the historic sites, castles, cathedrals, and museums tedious. He also began vacationing more often in Florida but when there, Bill spent a lot of time on the telephone talking with his managers or working on deals. He even opened and briefly maintained a real estate operation in Naples, Florida, to "stay involved while I was away from home." Clearly, Bill needed to be in the middle of the action, and he was happiest when engaged in a transaction.[2]

He remained a man in motion, looking at properties, meeting with people, inspecting buildings, negotiating deals, or talking incessantly on the telephone. Cecilia (Cee) Gentry, Bill's longtime administrative assistant, noted that he did not really require an office; all he needed was a telephone. "It was his lifeline; he kept abreast of things on the phone" she recalled. He was one of the first in Des Moines to get a mobile phone. "It was a big clunky brick of a thing," Gentry remembered, "and he would always answer it, whether he was at home, on the tennis court, or in his car."[3] Bill especially liked the efficiency of the telephone. "It was quick, and it was easy. I could find out information, get a donation, or close of deal all in a matter of minutes. Then I could hang up, dial another number, and talk to someone else."[4]

For all his success, though, Bill felt something was missing and during these years, he considered trying something else or doing something new. He never found a new career, but he did become increasingly involved in philanthropic endeavors. These activities and new relationships, as well as some important changes in existing ones, including his breakup with Connie and his later marriage to Susan Terry, set him on a new course. All the while he remained engaged in the real estate business, but eventually, more and more of his time was devoted to Knapp Properties, a new company he created in 1992.

Generally sanguine, Bill had turned more melancholy by the late 1970s and early 1980s. The terrible economy certainly took its toll, but journalist and friend Walt Shotwell believed it was more complicated. Shotwell remembered Bill as unhappy with himself. "He talked of feeling empty, dissatisfied, [and] uneasy. He seemed very sad and couldn't understand why." Bill was still married at the time, and part of the dissatisfaction was tied to his ongoing affair and the strain it put on his relationship with Ginny and Roger, but it went deeper. Kruidenier speculated that Bill concentrated too much on real estate and needed to develop other interests. There was surely some truth to this as well; Bill was known for his single-minded devotion to the land business. "He lives and breathes real estate," Bill Knapp II once explained. Bill was certainly aware of this fixation and could eventually laugh about it. When recovering from knee surgery in 2004, he later joked with Michael Gartner, currently the majority owner of the Iowa Cubs, "I was so sick, I wasn't even thinking about real estate."[5]

Bill thought maybe a second career was in order and might lift him out of his funk. He talked frequently about taking up another vocation, and Connie Wimer remembered him becoming frustrated when he could not find it. About the same time, however, Bill gradually became more engaged with local nonprofits, and these activities substituted for the second career not found. Gartner thought this step was natural: "He was already successful, had plenty of money, and had proven himself to the community. Or maybe he was confronting his own mortality, but whatever it was, he began focusing on giving back." He had given to charitable causes throughout his career, but his interest in donating money and participating in fundraising efforts intensified in the early 1980s and gave him increasing satisfaction.[6]

Not surprisingly, this involvement coincided with his commitment to revitalizing downtown Des Moines. It began when Bill inserted himself into the debate about where to locate the new state historical building. The Iowa museum had outgrown its turn-of-the-century facility just north of the Iowa State Capitol, and discussions about a new building began in the late 1970s. Governor Robert Ray supported plans to locate a new museum in the Japanese Gardens immediately south of the Statehouse. He was opposed by Bill and most Des Moines business leaders, who wanted the structure on the business block west of the Capitol between Grand Avenue to the north, Locust Street to the south, Pennsylvania Avenue to the east, and East Sixth Street to the west. Bill believed this latter location was better because it was more accessible from the downtown core and nearby parking was available. He also thought putting the museum there "would spark redevelopment" in this eastern section of downtown. The standoff ended in the spring of 1983 when Bill, along with insurance executive Gary Kirke and Marvin Selden, a former state comptroller, worked behind the scenes to convince the new Governor Terry Branstad that the business block site was preferable. The Capitol Planning Commission and the legislature soon agreed, and plans moved forward for a new historical building west of the Statehouse.[7]

The new facility would cost just over $25 million. The state had received a $5 million gift from the estate of businessman and road builder Glenn Herrick, which was set aside for the building, and the 1983 legislature funded Branstad's $10 million request for the project. This left $10.4 million to come from private donors. It was here that Bill played a leading role on the committee established to raise funds from the business community. Over the next few months, he spent hours on the phone, soliciting donations by describing benefits the new museum would bring, explaining that he "had skin in the game," and then asking his friends or colleagues to give as well. The technique was most often successful, and Bill would use it many times over in future fundraising campaigns. In this case, Bill and the committee met their goal of raising $3 million by December 1983, and as a result, the City of Des Moines pledged $1 million toward the building fund.[8]

Groundbreaking for the structure took place the following winter. The stunning building of light and dark pink granite opened with great fanfare in December 1987. Bill was glad the museum was finally completed, but he had already moved on to other downtown charitable projects. Most noteworthy of the period was his whirlwind effort to save the Tiny Tots Childcare Center.

Tiny Tots, a nonprofit daycare center, was founded in 1967 by a determined woman named Evelyn Davis. It provided quality childcare to low-income families who could not otherwise afford it. The center had no significant budget, and from the beginning, Davis struggled to keep its doors open. As of 1976, the center was located in the former Washington Irving Junior High School building, which the Des Moines school district rented to Davis for $1 per year. Still, the center was almost always behind on its bills, and by summer 1984, it owed $80,000 in Social Security payments and $130,000 to the Iowa Power and Light Company (now MidAmerican Energy). The utility firm had carried the debt for years but now threatened to shut off Tiny Tots' electricity and natural gas. Meanwhile a Des Moines-based seed company, Pioneer Hi-Bred International, was no longer willing to act as the center's only major supporter. Charles Johnson, the firm's vice president for finance and treasurer, was certain Tiny Tots would close without significant cash contributions. That was when Lu Jean Cole, Pioneer's director for community investment, took action; she believed Bill might be interested in helping, and so she arranged for Davis and Bill to meet at his Hotel Savery. The visit went well. Bill knew of the Tiny Tots founder and thought her work important for downtown. He was immediately impressed with Davis and jumped at the opportunity to help the center.[9]

One September morning shortly after meeting Davis, Bill called Gartner, then the president of the Des Moines Register and Tribune Company, and said simply that he was getting in his car and would soon be on his way to pick him up. He then explained that the two of them were going out to raise $250,000 to save Tiny Tots. And they did. Bill put in $15,000, he got Gartner and the R&T to kick in $20,000, and then he and Gartner asked community business leaders for the rest of the funding. By the end of the day, they had pledges for $206,000. Monroe Colston of the Greater Des Moines Chamber of Commerce was amazed: "You and Mike should be titled 'Mega Men' for raising over $200,000 in one day. That was incredible." Three weeks later, they had exceeded their goal. With the money in hand, Bill, Gartner, and other business leaders in the group who supported the effort—including Orville Crowley of Ringland-Johnson-Crowley, Charles Johnson, and Colston—arranged a program for the center to pay down its delinquent bills. The group also negotiated a new, more energy efficient space for the center in Mercy Hospital's old Bishop Drumm's facility near Fourteenth and Clark streets in Des Moines. It moved to the new location in November, once some renovations were completed. Bill remained a key supporter of Tiny Tots, and in December 1986, Davis wrote him a heartfelt note: "I can never thank you enough for being my friend. I don't know how or why you do all you do for us and others, but I am more than glad the Lord sent you my way."[10]

A growing number of people would have agreed with Davis, especially as Bill's largesse and fundraising activity increased over the next decade. This would include those in his hometown as well. A couple of years before Bill's fundraising feat for Tiny Tots, he was in Allerton at a reception following his father's funeral. While there, he gazed at three ramshackle buildings that stood vacant along Central Avenue, the town's main street. "A good part of my life was spent in and around those buildings," he remembered. "You kind of hate to see them sitting there as eyesores...A lot of times, nobody can come up with the money needed just to clear them out of the way."[11]

After thinking about it and talking with his brother and sisters, Bill took action. He quietly bought the three buildings and then had them demolished. The rubble was cleared away and the ground prepared for sod. Bill then donated the land to the town for a mini-park, which he hoped would be named in honor of his parents. Allerton officials were happy to do so, and donations poured in to outfit the park with a gazebo, a water fountain, a children's play area, and a 50 × 17 foot mural on a blank brick wall of a building adjacent to the park, which depicted the history of the community. In September 1985, Bill was given the key to the city during Allerton's dedication ceremony for the Bill and Anna Knapp Park. In his brief comments, he told the crowd, "I have never forgotten the people in this town and never will."[12]

Nor did Bill forget where he came from. Memories of hard times growing up on the Depression-era Allerton farm remained with him and gave him empathy for the less fortunate. His close association with Harold Hughes, former governor and then senator, had expanded this compassion. It was not at all surprising that his early impulses were to assist organizations such as Tiny Tots or the Door of Faith Mission that helped those in need. This instinct soon coalesced with the notion of giving as a social obligation, which was reinforced through his growing friendship with David Kruidenier.

Kruidenier was yet another prominent person that Bill met through Bill and Connie Wimer. The two did not become immediate friends though, largely because Kruidenier was the publisher of the Register and Tribune (R&T) and assiduously avoided any close associations with businessmen that could be construed as a conflict of interest. In fact, friendship between the two appeared implausible. Kruidenier was a member of the old money Cowles family, which had owned the *Des Moines Register* since 1903 and later acquired the *Minneapolis Star and Tribune*. Educated at the exclusive eastern institutions Phillips Exeter Academy and Yale, Kruidenier then earned a master's degree in business administration at Harvard. He started his career at the family's Minneapolis newspapers before returning to Des Moines in 1952, when he began moving up the ranks at the R&T. Kruidenier was sophisticated and well traveled, but he was shy in social settings and could be abrupt and aloof. He appeared to be everything Bill was not. Yet, once the R&T was purchased by Gannett in 1985, Kruidenier felt free to associate with whomever he pleased, and over the last half of the 1980s, he and Bill developed an unlikely close bond.[13]

Despite their vastly different backgrounds, Bill and Kruidenier shared a number of traits. Both were smart and cared deeply for Des Moines. They soon discovered they enjoyed needling each other, and even shared a July 18th birthday, although Kruidenier was five years older. Kruidenier's wife Liz found the relationship interesting. "For Bill," she thought, "David represented approval of the establishment, and he was someone Bill could go to for advice. David was drawn to Bill's quick mind and his unpolished outrageousness." Over the years the two had butted heads over some downtown projects. In the late 1970s, for example, Kruidenier was a key sponsor of the Civic Center, which Bill initially opposed, and while Bill backed John Ruan's Marriott Hotel plan, Kruidenier did not. However, these disagreements were in the past by the late 1980s, when the two found they enjoyed each other's company. Soon they were traveling together. In 1990, for example, Bill and Connie went to Egypt with the Kruideniers for a Nile River cruise. Later, in the mid-1990s, Bill and Kruidenier were both in France during their shared birthday and decided to have a party in a chateau. They held joint parties from then on. One year they celebrated their birthdays with a trip to London. But especially noteworthy was the huge bash their families threw for them for Bill's seventy-fifth and Kruidenier's eightieth birthday in July 2001. The event was held at Bill's River House, just west of the Napa Valley development. There Bill, Kruidenier and roughly 300 guests ate barbeque and enjoyed listening to country music legend Willie Nelson.[14]

The two business leaders talked frequently, most often about the Des Moines community and philanthropic opportunities. As a member of the Cowles family, Kruidenier had been imbued with a variant of noblesse oblige, the notion that the wealthy had a responsibility to give back to the community. They discussed this idea of social obligation as well, but even if they had not, Bill was impressed with the Cowles's long tradition of supporting many of the city's nonprofits. It was during this growing friendship with Kruidenier that he began speaking of giving back to the community as a social duty.[15]

Bill said that giving back financially made him feel good and Connie Wimer noted, "The more he gave, the happier he became." Earlier in the decade, Bill had formalized the way he and his company made contributions. In 1983, he established the Iowa Realty Foundation, and from then on the firm became a more consistent donor to local causes. Annual recipients of the company's generosity included United Way of Central Iowa, Living History Farms, the Civic Center of Des Moines, the local chapter of Planned Parenthood, and Drake University. Two years later in 1985, Bill created the William C. Knapp Charitable Foundation through which to make his personal contributions.[16]

Most of Bill's assistance for the rest of the decade went to organizations that served the less fortunate. This was the case when he lent a hand to downtown Des Moines's Bethel Mission, which provided shelter for indigent men, hot meals, and a drug and alcohol rehabilitation program. Bethel Mission had been looking to move out of its dilapidated building on Sixth Avenue south of School Street for several years, and in 1986 its board decided that $650,000 needed to be raised for a new facility. Mission director Ralph Huff asked Jerry Schmalenberger, pastor of St. John's Lutheran Church, to head the fundraising campaign, and Bill; Fred Hubbell, chairman of Younkers Department Stores; Charles Edwards, publisher of the *Des Moines Register*; and Sam Kalinov, chairman of American Mutual Life Insurance were asked to raise $450,000 or two-thirds of the campaign's goal from the downtown business community. Bill contributed $25,000 of his own money (the largest private gift to the campaign) and led the successful fundraising effort. But finding a location proved difficult as some did not want the homeless shelter in their neighborhoods. Eventually, Bill stepped in and helped the mission find a new site—where it remains today, 1310 Sixth Avenue—and raised additional funds needed for the new building, which opened in March of 1988.[17]

Predictably, as Bill's philanthropic efforts became well known in the nonprofit community, he received an increasing number of requests for assistance. Later that year, Margaret Toomey, the director of the Homes of Oakridge, a low-income housing project in downtown Des Moines, called on Bill about building a much needed community center. There she planned a childcare facility, a library, an art and ceramics area, and a multipurpose room for adult education and vocational training. She had come to know Bill earlier in the decade, when the Homes of Oakridge, which frequently struggled financially, found itself strapped for cash. Her board of directors suggested Toomey seek help from Bill. She went to his Iowa Realty office, visited with him a few minutes, and then left the room, Cee Gentry remembered, "visibly shaken and pale." Gentry ran to assist her, getting her a chair and some water. "Are you okay?" a concerned Gentry asked. "Oh, yes," Toomey replied, "I'm just overwhelmed by Bill's generosity." After telling him of her money woes, he gave her $25,000.[18]

But on the issue of the community center, Bill hesitated. He regarded Toomey and the Homes of Oakridge in much the same way he saw Davis and Tiny Tots. Both women were good, strong-willed leaders, and both headed organizations that provided invaluable services for the city's poor. He liked Toomey and thought the project worthwhile, but he had just finished raising money for the Bethel Mission and did not think he could "go back to the well" so soon. Bill sent Toomey to see Fred Weitz, the CEO of the Weitz Corporation, but he turned her down as well. Each, however, had agreed to another visit with Toomey at the Homes of Oakridge.[19]

Toomey and the two businessmen met in one of the three tiny efficiency apartments she had converted into a makeshift community center for 800 residents of the Homes of Oakridge. That cinched it. The need was obvious, and Bill decided he had to help. As Toomey recalled, his response was instantaneous: "You build the building," Bill told Weitz, "and I'll raise the money." Just like that, the project was launched. Bill initiated a $1.5 million drive by contributing $50,000, Iowa Realty added another $10,000, and US West Communications (now Century Link) donated the land immediately to the east of the complex. Soon Bill had another $150,000 from the Variety Club of Iowa. Then he sold his friends and contacts in the business community on the urgent need for the center. In just two weeks, he reached the fundraising goal, which included commitments from over sixty individuals and companies.[20]

The groundbreaking ceremony took place in June 1989, and the facility opened the following year. At Bill's suggestion, it was named the

Variety Center, in honor of the Variety Club of Iowa's large donation. He correctly believed so naming the building would help ensure the club's continued financial support of the center. The completion of the facility thrilled Toomey, who had dreamt about such a building for ten years. Shortly after Bill decided to lead the fundraising drive, Des Moines City Councilwoman Connie Cook thanked him and summed up his significance: "Once again, you have agreed to take on a project that others backed away from. You are a real deal!" She added, "Margaret Toomey and others of us know what a good man you are—and what compassion you have for poor people."[21]

This empathy led to his continued support of charitable organizations downtown. He remained an important financial backer of the Homes of Oakridge and a major supporter of what he called "safe, quality child care" for the inner city. By the mid-1990s, Bill saved two nonprofit child-care centers slated to close with a $100,000 gift and then led a fundraising effort for the Affordable Child Care Coalition, a group headed by former Iowa Governor Robert Ray. In 1994, he also accepted a request to chair the fund drive for a homeless shelter project sponsored by Churches United—a coalition of Des Moines churches created in 1991 to provide housing and meals for the indigent. The *Des Moines Register* commended Bill's "decisive, problem-solving action that social issues crave but rarely receive."[22]

In what was his modus operandi, Bill gave to the cause, in this case it was $25,000, and then canvassed the business community for the rest of the needed funds—$510,000; he reached the goal a few weeks later. In explaining why he helped, he said: "I've been in the real estate business for forty years, finding homes for people who have money and can afford to buy a home. There comes a time to help people who can't afford a home. I have a real interest and obligation to do something about the homeless."[23]

As one might expect, Bill's contributions were based on the confidence and respect he had for the people who sought funding and his interest in particular causes. These factors pushed him to expand his giving in the early 1990s, when he made the first of two large gifts to Drake University. His relationship with the school and its leadership had been growing since the mid-1980s, when Bill spearheaded the remarkable turnaround of the increasingly blighted Drake neighborhood. This effort drew him closer to Drake's president, Michael Ferrari, who further cemented Bill's relationship with the school by hiring Roger Knapp as the men's tennis coach in 1989. Bill was delighted to have his son back in town, and after Roger and his wife Amy had two children in quick succession—Sable Noel in August 1989 and Montana Michelle in July 1991—it looked like they were settling into the Des Moines community.[24]

Meanwhile, Drake launched a $115 million fundraising drive in October 1989 and named Des Moines civic leader Maddie Levitt the campaign's chairperson. Levitt was one of the city's leading philanthropists and fundraisers, and Ferrari remembered that she and Bill "hit it off immediately." Forty million dollars of the campaign was earmarked for an extensive campus building program, including plans for a new $12 million sports and convention complex. Besides housing a 7,000-seat arena for basketball and other athletic events, the facility was also to include six courts for basketball and volleyball, four racquetball courts, six tennis courts, a fitness center, and a jogging track. Given Bill's personal commitment to fitness, his ties to the Drake tennis team, and his enthusiasm for the project, he was recruited to co-chair the fundraising effort for the complex in October 1990. The two other co-chairs were his good friends David Miller, president of West Des Moines Bank, and Jim Cownie, former president of Heritage Communications, Inc.[25]

As always, Bill was intent on closing the deal quickly, and he along with Miller and Cownie went to work immediately. In just two months, they had pledges for $6.7 million toward the center. Then in January 1991, Bill added his own $3 million contribution. His gift brought the fundraising total to nearly 80 percent of the estimated cost of the building, the amount the board of governors had required before construction could begin. Bill explained the reasons for his extraordinary gift: "It was not hard for me to decide to make this kind of contribution. I'm not a Drake alum, but I know how important Drake University is to the city and state. This building is going to be good for the economic development of Des Moines, and it's going to be a major step to the continued revitalization of the Drake area." While a *Des Moines Register* editorial commended Bill for his generous gift, Eliot Nusbaum, the paper's society columnist, jokingly reminded readers that Bill's son was Drake's tennis coach, and the complex was to include six tennis courts.[26]

Nusbaum's comment was telling. Several months after the announcement, Drake's plans changed. Instead of including the tennis courts in the arena building, a separate $1.2 million tennis facility was envisioned. Bill immediately donated an additional $100,000 to the new complex, which would have six indoor and six outdoor tennis courts. When it was completed in October 1992, Bill addressed the crowd at opening ceremony, saying, "I like this tennis facility, I like the Drake tennis program, and I really like the Drake tennis coach!"[27]

The sports complex was soon completed as well. But the arena's formal dedication scheduled for November 30 was postponed when a shooting rocked the neighborhood. The preceding evening, Cara McGrane and Tim Burnett, two managers at the Drake Diner, were shot and killed during a robbery at the restaurant. The suspect, seventeen-year-old Joseph White, Jr., fled with roughly $500. Although he was soon apprehended, the bloody incident shook Bill and the entire neighborhood. He and Ferrari, along with other Drake officials and community members, worried that the violence would stymie the neighborhood's recovery. Fortunately, students and area residents were emboldened, and they continued patronizing the diner and other businesses around the college campus.[28]

Part of the neighborhood's healing necessitated a return to normalcy, including moving forward with the dedication ceremony of the new sports arena, which was rescheduled for January 29, 1993. For months there had been rumors that the center would be named after Bill. Many believed this was something he sought, but it was really the idea of Drake president Michael Ferrari, who wanted to recognize the businessman for his major gift and fundraising effort on behalf of the complex. Actually, Ferrari noted that it required "considerable effort to convince Bill that the 'The Knapp Center' [designation] was appropriate and desirable for our university and the community." After several long conversations, Bill finally consented to his name being placed on the building. At the dedication ceremony, Bill joked that he had agreed to the facility bearing his name only after threats that the arena might be called "the Dog Pound" or "the Dog House" after the school's mascot, the Bulldog.[29]

Bill's involvement with Drake continued growing over the decade, despite the fact that Roger soon left the university. Since taking over as head coach in 1989, Roger had "transformed a downtrodden Drake's men's tennis program into Missouri Valley champions the last two seasons," wrote the *Des Moines Register* in 1993. But in December of that year, the thirty-four-year-old resigned, explaining that he wanted "to spend more time with his family and pursue other interests," and the following spring, he and his family moved to Sarasota, Florida. Bill had discussed the move with Roger, and although he hated to see his son leave, he understood and told the *Register,* "People have to do what they want to do in life. Roger has been in tennis all his life. I think he's ready to move on to different things. He's done a good job at Drake....He's accomplished some big goals." But then, much to the relief of everyone at the university, Bill emphasized that his son's leaving did not alter his relationship with the school: "It was interesting to me when Roger was there, but that doesn't diminish my commitment to Drake now." This became clear in 1998, when Bill, Maddie Levitt, and David and Liz Kruidenier, as a couple, each gave $5 million to a new Drake fundraising campaign.[30]

Of course, most of Bill's time was taken up with the real estate business from his base of operations at Iowa Realty's corporate headquarters in West Des Moines. But some important changes were taking place at the company. Nephews Mike Knapp and his brother Bill Knapp II continued moving up in management. They were clearly the heirs apparent. In 1991, Mike was named senior vice president of the brokerage business, while Bill II became the senior vice president of operations, overseeing the finance, property management, and development business. The following year there was a corporate reorganization and more promotions. First, Mike was advanced to the presidency of Iowa Realty, which spun off its commercial property management and development businesses into a new firm called Central Properties. Bill II was to head that company. Paul and Bill, meanwhile, signed new five-year contracts to stay with the firm as Paul was advanced to vice chairman of both Iowa Realty and Central Properties and Bill remained chairman.[31]

A bigger change was the creation of Knapp Properties, a new venture wholly owned by Bill to oversee his personally owned properties, which to that point had been managed by Iowa Realty. The move was, in the words of Bill II "a friendly separation" from the parent company, Central Life. At the time, Central Life was pursuing a public offering of stock, and management believed it necessary to separate Bill's personal interests from those of the soon-to-be publicly held firm. Bill served as Knapp Properties' chairman, and Bill II was vice chairman. Others moved from Iowa Realty to Knapp Properties as well, included Bill's son-in-law Mark Haviland, who was named president, and Daryl Neumann, who became secretary/treasurer. Knapp Properties' office was established downtown in

The Plaza condominium building; two years later, it moved into its own building on Westown Parkway in West Des Moines.[32]

Regardless of these changes, Bill continued working on deals and overseeing the companies with a level of intensity that his secretary Cee Gentry believed was unequaled. She had never seen anyone so single-minded or singularly focused. Bill knew he could be obsessive and impatient: "I have a personality that is probably type-A—if there's something I need to do I feel pressure to get it done quickly. I always want everything done very fast, even if it doesn't need to be that way. So I feel pressure all the time. When a project has been picked, I can't relax. I've got to move on it, move smart, and get it done." Clearly, this determination had pushed him to success, but it also caused some hiccups. Despite a rigorous exercise routine, Bill began experiencing shortness of breath and then some chest pains in the spring of 1991. A checkup revealed a 90 percent blockage of his right coronary artery, which was successfully treated with an angioplasty. Although the incident gave him pause, Bill had no further heart problems.[33]

Bill's intensity also impacted his business relationships, which had always been paramount to him especially when people broke his trust. He hired people and made deals with those he judged reliable and responsible. Over the years, this led to a reliance on family members in top positions at Iowa Realty. First and foremost there was Paul, then brother-in-law Clair Niday, and later, nephews Mike and Bill II. Of course, Bill employed and dealt with many others beyond family, but when someone broke his trust, Bill often exploded and rarely worked with that person again. This was the case with longtime hotel manager Gene Moore. Moore had been hired in 1979 to manage the Savery as well as the other hotels Bill owned. Moore's job soon entailed much more; in reality, he was almost a fulltime assistant to Bill. He sometimes chauffeured Bill or his friends in the limousine, accompanied Bill on business trips, and was a frequent tennis partner for his boss. Moore came to see Bill as a friend; Bill saw Moore as a friend as well, but business came first. By the end of the 1980s, Moore was increasingly discontent, believing too much was expected of him. Bill, meanwhile, thought Moore was losing interest in the job and should be replaced.[34]

In January 1991, Bill suggested that the soon-to-be sixty-five-year-old Moore retire in favor of a younger manager. Moore went back and forth on the idea but decided against it. Several months later, there were rumors circulating that Carole Baumgarten, who had served as a Drake women's basketball coach, head of downtown's YWCA, and then manager of Prairie Meadows Race Track, would soon run the hotels. Bill eventually told Moore the rumors were true, and he dismissed Moore because of his age. Soon, Bill learned he had violated the age discrimination laws, and in January 1992, Moore sued him for wrongful termination. Initially, Bill was angry with himself: "I fouled up," he said. "I was just plain ignorant." But he became enraged when he discovered Moore had worn a wire and tape-recorded the conversation when Bill fired him.[35]

The situation grew worse when an anonymous typewritten letter arrived at Iowa Realty threatening the lives of Bill, Bill II, and Baumgarten. Security was hired for the Iowa Realty's corporate office, Baumgarten wore a bullet-proof vest, and the police were called. Several misshaped characters in the letter proved that it had come from the typewriter in Moore's office. While Bill believed he and Moore could have gotten over the lawsuit—settled out of court in March 1993 for $200,000— he could not abide Moore's secret taping or the menacing note. "I was done with him at the point," Bill remembered. The two never spoke again.[36]

Then there was the situation with Mark Haviland, who in late 1992 left Bill's daughter for another woman. He resigned from Knapp Properties, divorced Ginny, and moved to Arizona. Ginny was devastated, and although Bill had behaved similarly years earlier, he now saw the situation from the perspective of a father. He was livid. A little over a year later, Haviland and Ginny reconciled and even remarried in the summer of 1994. Ultimately, Bill accepted the repentant son-in-law back into the family. He eventually reestablished a close relationship with him, but Bill would not bring him back into the company. To fill the vacated position, Bill wanted a person he knew and trusted. He initially considered Baumgarten, his new hotel manager, but in the end he followed Bill II's advice and asked attorney Gerry Neugent to take over the day-to-day leadership of Knapp Properties. A law school classmate of Bill II's, Neugent had specialized in real estate law and had done a large portion of Iowa Realty's legal work since the late 1970s while with the Wimer and then Belin firms. Neugent accepted the offer, becoming Knapp Properties' president and chief operating officer in September 1993. This would prove to be one of Bill's most significant hires.[37]

With Neugent filling out a team of real estate veterans that already included Bill II and Daryl Neumann, Bill began moving Knapp Properties from managing his holdings into land development. This shift took place amidst many changes at Iowa Realty. In late 1993, the company started growing through acquisition, doubling its presence in Cedar Rapids by purchasing the Byers & Happel real estate agency. Iowa Realty continued this strategy the following year, buying Carol Jones Realtors, the largest real estate company in Springfield, Missouri. Later in 1994, parent company Central Life merged with American Mutual Life Insurance Company and was soon rebranded AmerUs. In August 1995, Iowa Realty continued its expansion, this time by acquiring longtime rival First Realty/Better Homes and Gardens (the company originally founded by Stanbrough in 1960) from Hubbell Realty. All together, Iowa Realty/First Realty controlled over 70 percent of the Des Moines realty market. That December, Bill stepped down as chairman of Iowa Realty, becoming chairman emeritus, and Paul moved into the chairmanship. Two years later in 1997, Paul retired, and Mike Knapp, who was already company president and CEO, was named chairman as well. Through all of these changes, Bill's ties with Iowa Realty slowly loosened until, as chairman emeritus, he announced that Knapp Properties would be his main focus. To that end, he bought Iowa Realty/AmerUs Properties' (the new name of Central Properties) share of the West Lakes development in 1997. From that point on, Knapp Properties and FBL Financial Group—the holding company of Farm Bureau Life Insurance, which had been Iowa Realty's partner in the commercial park—would expand and develop the property.[38]

In addition to buying half interest in the West Lakes development, Bill bought Iowa Realty's stake in two commercial parks on the city's south side near the Des Moines airport. In these, too, Knapp Properties was partnered with FBL Financial. Other purchases included more than 300 acres in Grimes and the Metro East Business Park in Pleasant Hill. By 1999, Bill had developed or was developing thirty-one commercial and residential projects and had another 3,000 acres ready to develop. He had also developed thirty commercial buildings, twenty-seven apartment complexes, and completed seven condominium conversions. All the while, he still owned three hotels and a handful of restaurants in town. However, this asset mix was undergoing change.[39]

By the mid-1990s, Bill had begun estate planning, and as he and Bill II reviewed his portfolio, they decided Knapp Properties was involved in too many different areas. To streamline it, they would shed what Bill II termed "cash register businesses"—hotels, restaurants, and apartments— to focus on land acquisition and development. The shift also aligned the company with activities Bill enjoyed: negotiating deals, buying land, and envisioning the future use of virgin ground. Although he was certain it was the right move at the right time, unloading one property was particularly difficult for Bill. "Selling the Hotel Savery," he recalled, "was one of the hardest things I ever did. I loved the place; I loved the business; and I loved all the people." Mike Knapp remembered, "He usually made decisions quickly, effortlessly, but with the Savery, it was different. He really struggled with that." By April 1996, though, it was clear Bill was going through with the sale. Shaner Hotels of Pennsylvania wanted the Savery, and the following month, Bill sold the venerable, old hotel for $7,450,000. Six years later with the sale of the Valley West Inn and the West End Diner in West Des Moines, Bill was completely out of such businesses.[40]

There was one more major move on the business front. It was set in motion in the fall of 1997, when Roger Brooks decided AmerUs should focus on its core life insurance business and put Iowa Realty up for sale. In the midst of this process, Bill stepped down as the company's chairman emeritus, completely severing his personal relationship with the business he had founded in 1952. Five companies expressed interest in the real estate firm. Brooks ultimately sold it, along with a majority stake in Edina Realty, which AmerUs had acquired in 1996, to the only Iowa-based suitor, MidAmerican Energy Holdings, headquartered in Des Moines. The sale price, estimated between $75 and $100 million, was announced in April 1998. Brooks and Bill were happy with the deal: Brooks because he had sold the company at a healthy profit, and Bill because the buyer was a local company interested in helping Iowa Realty grow. "Growth is what it's all about," he said. Bill was also pleased that the company's current management, headed by Mike Knapp, would stay in place.[41]

Important changes were also taking place in Bill's personal life. By the early 1990s, his love affair with Connie Wimer was winding down. Problems began when it became apparent that the two were at very different points in their lives. Bill was hugely successful and widely recognized as one of the most prominent and influential businessmen in the area. He remained interested in work and enjoyed it, but he talked about slowing down and his schedule was increasingly flexible. Connie, on the other hand, was climbing in the business community and fully devoted to her companies. She was still president of Iowa Title, an abstracting firm, although she had sold it to Central Life shortly after Bill sold his stake in Iowa Realty to the same company. More importantly, she was focused on expanding her publishing enterprise, which at the time included the *Business Record* and *Cityview*. Bill recalled that these issues spilled over into their relationship, and he noted, "We began growing apart." Connie's recollection was similar: "I was working all the time and becoming more independent, while Bill was looking to relax a little." These differences led to an increasing number of disagreements, which in earlier years might have faded away but now escalated into full-blown arguments. The relationship became increasingly strained until it finally ended in 1992.[42]

Late that year, Bill began seeing forty-one-year-old businesswoman Susan Terry. Des Moines clothier Bill Reichardt had introduced them in 1988. Each was in a relationship at the time, and the meeting did not lead to anything until 1992, when they began dating.[43]

For Susan, the blossoming relationship represented good fortune, something that had been lacking in her life. Born in Des Moines, Susan and her family moved around the city and suburbs before finally settling in West Des Moines. After graduating from Valley High School in 1970, Susan married boyfriend Larry Carley and took some classes at Des Moines Area Community College's Boone campus, before deciding to work full time. She held several jobs before divorcing Carley in 1974 and taking a secretarial position at her brother-in-law's Rhiner Plumbing Company in West Des Moines. There she met and married plumber Wendell Terry the following year. But Susan had greater ambitions. After dealing with building contractors at the plumbing firm, she began thinking about building homes herself. She read up on the business, built a "speculative" home, and in 1977 established SKT Construction. Susan and her husband left Rhiner to build homes and later commercial properties. Five years later, tragedy struck. Terry was killed in a construction accident, leaving Susan with two daughters, three-year-old Sara and newborn Anna.[44]

She pressed on, running her company and raising her daughters alone until 1984, when Susan married accountant Norton Gegner. Her life seemed back on track; SKT netted $1 million in sales in 1987, and

Susan was recognized as an "up and comer" by the *Des Moines Register.* The following year, Susan was one of five recipients of the Women of Enterprise award given by the U.S. Small Business Administration and Avon Corporation. But then the bottom fell out in September 1989, when Susan was caught in the middle of a federal probe and indicted in a money-laundering scheme with business partners Dennis Harker, a Drug Enforcement Agency agent, and his wife Mary Ann Harker. The crux of the case against Susan focused on $85,000 the Harkers had not reported to the Internal Revenue Service (IRS) and sent to her to be used in several business partnerships the three shared. Susan deposited the money in her checking account gradually, always making deposits under $10,000. This was done, according to investigators to "circumvent currency laws requiring participants in cash transactions of $10,000 or more to file a currency transaction report [with the IRS], a practice known as 'structuring'." [45]

Susan's trial began in late January 1990. She pleaded innocent, arguing that she completely trusted Harker, who had been her late husband's best friend and a business partner of hers for years. She also explained that she saw nothing strange about the way she deposited the funds. A banker had advised her to make a number of smaller deposits rather than a few larger ones. Susan was acquitted of the charge of conspiracy to defraud the government but convicted on three technical felonies of evading bank reporting laws, which did not require proof of criminal intent. In March, she was sentenced to one-year probation and fined $20,000. Thrilled to avoid prison and separation from her children, Susan blamed herself for blindly trusting the Harkers and accepting bad advice but maintained that she had been unaware of the bank reporting requirement and had not intentionally broken the law. With the case behind her, Susan was ready to move forward, and by the end of 1992, it was clear she was on a new path. She and Gegner divorced, she left SKT Construction, and she and Bill began seeing each other. [46]

Bill was attracted to the tall, svelte businesswoman's savvy, her entrepreneurial spirit, her competitiveness, and, he remembered with a smile, "She was good looking and full of life." Of course, Susan could not avoid noticing Bill's wealth and power, but she was also drawn to his quick mind, raw intellect, and compassion, which she often described as "softness." After the two began seeing each other in the fall 1992, the relationship quickly moved from friendship to romance. Bill was pleased that Susan had a rapport with his adult children, Ginny and Roger, while her young daughters enjoyed Bill as well. This compatibility made the couple's 1995 decision to live together simpler, and as Susan remembered, "We were really surprised at how easy the transition to a blended family was once we moved in together." They initially lived at a home in Glen Oaks, an upscale, gated community in West Des Moines, before moving fifteen miles west to an acreage in Van Meter ten years later.[47]

After Bill started seeing Susan, he took up two new activities, which would remain very important to him. First was the Iowa State Fair, a regular event for Susan since childhood. She especially enjoyed the horse shows and had entered and won a number of baking and cooking contests over the years. Bill, on the other hand, had only attended sporadically. Susan first took him to the fair in 1994, and from then on, it became an annual trip for the couple. That year, during the last day of the fair, Bill and Susan were walking by the Swine Barn when John Putney, director of the Blue Ribbon Foundation, the Iowa State Fair's fundraising arm, saw them, introduced himself, and offered the couple a golf cart tour of the fairgrounds. This marked the beginning of a close friendship between Bill and Putney, which over time reinforced the real estate man's increasing interest in the fair. Three years later in the summer of 1997, Susan convinced Bill to camp at the fair for the duration of the eleven-day event.[48]

The couple stayed at the fair's campgrounds, along with roughly 15,000 others. But unlike many at the site, Bill and Susan resided in a luxurious, air-conditioned 500-square-foot trailer, which provided all the amenities of home; and, with several cell phones at his side, Bill could conduct business. The arrangement was perfect: Bill could enjoy the fair but also stay in touch with employees, colleagues, or partners; thus, the trailer served as both a home and office away from the home. Bill was growing fond of the fair; he especially liked "to go out real early, before folks get up and see the kids sleeping [in the barns] alongside their animals." In fact, several months earlier, he made his first of what would be several large contributions to the fair.[49]

Over the previous couple of years, he and Putney explored the fairgrounds together, and Bill noticed that many of the fair's major buildings were in disrepair. As the two became better friends, the foundation director told Bill about his long-range plans to refurbish many of the facilities. Late in the fall of 1996, Putney approached him for a significant donation. He asked Bill for $1 million dollars to go toward the renovation of the Varied Industries Building, which had been built in 1911 and was showing its age. Bill responded that he was thinking about giving a couple of hundred thousand, but Putney persisted. He knew a big gift from Bill Knapp would garner a lot of attention and attract other donations. It would also help convince the legislature of the private sector's interest in the fairgrounds, something lawmakers wanted to see before committing more public funds to the fair. Bill agreed, and in February 1997, he gave $1 million to the fair; the largest private donation to date. At the announcement, he explained: "When you're successful, you owe some of that back. I've been involved in a lot of things in the greater Des Moines area, but I've always wanted to do something for the state."[50]

Just as Putney expected, Bill's gift led to other contributions, and the $10 million renovated structure was renamed the William C. Knapp Varied Industries Building and dedicated in August 2001. Originally an open-air facility, the building had been enclosed, the floor was replaced, and much to the delight of fairgoers, the remodeled facility was now fully climate-controlled with air-conditioning and heating. Following that year's fair, an additional 16,000 square feet of space was added to the structure's south side, making it, according to Kathie Swift, the state fair marketing director, "the largest enclosed single-level exhibit facility in Iowa."[51]

Much more surprising than Bill's involvement with the fair was his new-found interest in golf. He had always detested the sport because it was slow and not much of a workout. Worse, it took hours to play, eating up time when he or others could be working and making money. It had especially bothered him when his real estate agents spent time on the golf course instead of selling homes. Former Iowa Realty agent Roger Cleven was particularly notorious for playing golf during business hours. One day in the late 1970s, Bill became so fed up with Cleven's golfing that he grabbed the agent's car keys from his office desk, marched out to the parking lot, and removed Cleven's golf clubs from the trunk. He then took the clubs and locked them in his car, telling Cleven he would get his clubs back when he started working. Bill's message to his agents was clear: Stay off the golf course and sell homes.[52]

Then while visiting his son Roger in Florida in 1996, Bill discovered he liked the game. An avid golfer, Roger took his seventy-year-old father out for several rounds that year. Bill loved his time on the course with his son, and the sport appealed to his competitiveness. He and Susan both took lessons, and he was hooked. Bill began playing religiously several times a week, depending on the weather. He loved the challenge of the game and the camaraderie on the course, which he soon realized was a perfect place for doing business and making deals. Over the years, he played regularly with a number of friends, but later in life his golfing partners usually included Jim Cownie, Mark Oman, retired senior executive vice president of Wells Fargo & Co., or John Mauro, a Polk County supervisor.[53]

Golf became even more important to him after he tore the rotator cuff in his right shoulder in the late 1990s. It required two surgeries to repair but left him unable to play tennis. After that, besides working out, which he still did several times a week, golf became his sport of choice. Sometimes, he went to extraordinary lengths for a round of golf. Once, he and Mauro had planned to play, but Bill could not get a tee time at Glen Oaks, his preferred club. When he called Mauro and explained the problem, his friend teased him: "What happened? A big shot like you couldn't get a tee time?" Ten minutes later, Bill called Mauro back and announced, "We're playing in an hour. I got a tee time at Des Moines Golf and Country Club." Mauro was dumbfounded, "But you don't belong to Des Moines Golf." "I do now," Bill responded, "I just joined!"[54]

Bill was content. He was enjoying new pastimes and life with Susan. By 1997, they began discussing marriage. When she had moved in with him, Susan told her daughters that she and Bill would probably marry if living together went well. It had, but Bill's memories of his bitter divorce kept him from marrying again. As if to confirm his concerns, his son Roger and his wife Amy were having marital problems and divorced in December 1997. But earlier that year, Bill's granddaughter Kendy Haviland married Tyler Granzow, and the couple had two children, son Cole born in 1997 and daughter Brooke the following fall. Bill and Irene became great-grandparents.[55]

Yet Bill remained uneasy about marriage. Susan raised the issue several times to no avail until she asked in frustration, "Who in the hell are you saving yourself for?" He laughed and said he "had no good answer" but could not marry again. Then Susan drew the line. She and Bill were vacationing in Venice, Italy, in the summer of 1998. While dining at the elegant Hotel Danieli's rooftop terrace overlooking the city's Grand Canal, Susan told Bill, "It's time we get married. Can you do this or not? If not, it's fine, but then I need to move on." Bill responded, "I just can't do it." The two finished their meal and started to leave when Bill went to the restroom. He returned and insisted that they go back to the table to have their photographs taken. Then he took Susan on a gondola ride. There Bill handed her a note that read, "Susan, will you be my wife?" She said he had to say the words. He did, and the couple eloped that fall. They had a small wedding ceremony at the picturesque Aspen Chapel in Colorado. It was the same place Roger Brooks and Sunnie Richer had wed in 1990, when Bill had been Brooks' best man. This time, Brooks and Richer stood up for Bill and Susan. They held a Des Moines reception for friends and family when they returned.[56]

The union raised some eyebrows; Susan was twenty-five years younger than Bill, and there were murmurs that she was a trophy wife who married for money and social position. But friends dismissed these ideas. It was clear the two cared deeply for each other and enjoyed spending time together, whether it was in Des Moines, their home in Florida, the condominium in Chicago, or later traveling in a mobile home to horse shows where Susan rode in quarter horse competitions. Bill's eyes sparkled whenever he spoke of Susan, and Susan doted on him, often checking on him by calling or dropping by the office. She even called him while he was on the golf course. Susan was also happy to take care of all the details in life that Bill detested: scheduling events, organizing parties, arranging trips. "Susan," John Putney observed, "takes very good care of Bill; she keeps him active and interested." Likewise, he explained, Bill "is very supportive" of Susan and made it possible for her "to live her dream of competing" with the best horses at national events. They were, friends agree, well suited for each other.[57]

Marriage to Susan was a high point for Bill, but the decade ended on a more somber note. In April 1999, Bill's longtime partner Kenny Grandquist had a stroke while watching the home opener of his Iowa Cubs baseball team at Sec Taylor Stadium (now Principal Park). He was rushed to Iowa Methodist Medical Center but never regained consciousness. Years earlier, he had played a key role helping Bill build Iowa Realty into the state's largest real estate company, and they had been the closest of friends until Grandquist quit the company and became a competitor. They eventually made amends, but their friendship was never quite the same. Still, Bill and Paul had just enjoyed lunch with Grandquist at the ballpark three days before he was stricken. Bill and Susan rushed to the hospital when they heard the news. They visited Grandquist and his wife Linda daily until the Iowa Cubs owner succumbed and died eight days later.[58]

Bill had recently lost two other people close to him. In the fall of 1994, his ninety-two-year-old mother Anna had a stroke and required around-the-clock care thereafter. She died of a heart ailment the following October. The next year, his good friend, Iowa Governor and U.S. Senator Harold Hughes, passed away. He grieved over both these deaths, but Grandquist's loss was different. This was his first very close associate to die, and Bill was stunned. Grandquist was a peer and had been essential to Bill's rise in the business. They had been like family. The loss forced Bill to consider his own mortality. He had already started thinking about his legacy, and curiously, Grandquist's death reinforced his future orientation. Bill had always lived for the next project and took to heart the old maxim, which he started to quote: "The only thing you take with you [when you're gone] is what you leave behind." If his time were limited, he needed to press forward; he needed to make things happen.[59]

Chapter Ten

Remaining Relevant

Suggestions of Bill Knapp's retirement had been around a long time. In 1983, he told the *Des Moines Register* he intended to spend much more time in Florida.[1] His sale of 80 percent of Iowa Realty the following year and the remaining shares in 1989 seemed to indicate he was moving away from business. A decade later, he stepped down as the chairperson of Knapp Properties in favor of his nephew, Bill Knapp II.

At the same time, he received a spate of business, civic, and philanthropic awards, usually reserved for the end of one's career. He was named Des Moines Citizen of the Year for Public Service in 1984 and was inducted into the Iowa Business Hall of Fame in 1991. Two years later, he received the Ernst and Young Entrepreneur of the Year Award, and in 1994, the Boy Scouts Mid-Iowa Council honored him with the Distinguished Iowa Citizen Award. More recognition followed, including the Outstanding Volunteer Fund Raiser Award from the Central Iowa Chapter of the National Society of Fund Raising Executives, and West Des Moines Citizen of the Year.[2]

Yet Bill did not retire. Although he halfheartedly tried a couple of times, he missed the excitement of putting together projects. "His idea of entertainment," Bill Knapp II once noted, "is to put a bunch of business people together and go to dinner and talk business issues." Bill remained engaged but did so on his own terms, settling into a daily schedule with most of his meetings in the morning. This kept his afternoons free for mixing business with other activities.[3]

When he owned the Hotel Savery, he frequently spent his afternoons there, where he worked out in the downstairs exercise room, enjoyed a massage or sauna, and then milled around with people in the hotel's lobby or bar. After he sold the Savery, he was often on a golf course in the afternoon. But whether at the hotel or playing golf, Bill still spent a lot of time on the telephone, checking in with his wide network of friends and colleagues. He was obsessed with staying connected. Even when he took up hunting late in life, he sometimes could be found up in a tree stand looking for deer and talking on the telephone. This preoccupation was part of Bill's very makeup, and these conversations were important, for they often provided him with the latest information from the local world of business and politics. Knowledge thus gained regularly led to fruitful deals.[4]

This schedule was only possible because Bill always had close colleagues to handle the day-to-day details of his operations. By the late 1990s, it was Bill Knapp II and Gerry Neugent who filled this role at Knapp Properties. He had complete confidence in both, and believed that without them, he would have had to retire. Bill II had long been Bill's trusted associate; competitor James Hubbell III of Hubbell Realty once explained, "For many years…he basically did a lot of Bill's [Knapp's] work. Bill would come up with the deal, and Bill II would wrap it up." Bill had equal faith in Neugent, and by 1999, he found himself in an ideal situation: "I've never been happier, and I've never been more confident with my business life and my personal life, and a lot has to do with these two fellows [Bill II and Neugent]." Then passionately, he added: "Development is exciting. Real estate is exciting.…It is different every day. I enjoy this company. This is not like Meredith [the publishing company]; at 65 and you're done. In owning this company, you have more of an opportunity to continue."[5]

And continue he did. Through his seventies and into his eighties, Bill remained a key individual in the Des Moines business circles, even though leadership had clearly been passed to a generation of men and women in their forties and fifties.[6] People looked to him when they wanted to get something done. He took on big projects, working with both aging peers and emerging business leaders. In the words of Fred Weitz, Bill was a "spark plug." When involved, Weitz once explained, Bill was the one who "kept everybody charged up" and moving forward to a successful conclusion.[7] His giving continued apace as well. Nothing seemed to slow him down until he was struck by a particularly painful loss.

His immersion in big civic undertakings persisted. First was the revitalization of Gray's Lake. Situated just southwest of downtown Des Moines, the lake was originally a small U-shaped pond on the Raccoon River. Decades of sand and gravel mining transformed it into a 100-acre lake. Once quarrying stopped, a private company leased the eastern half of the lake and operated Marine Beach; and in 1959, a Holiday Inn was built on the southwest corner of the lake. In 1970, a small city park and picnic area was established on the western shore. Sadly, the historic floods of 1993 destroyed the park and badly damaged the hotel, which stood vacant for several years. The lake area had become an eyesore, and a number of people began calling for its renewal.[8]

As city leaders drafted such plans, businessmen David Kruidenier and later John Grubb came forward with pledges to be used for the lake's rehabilitation. In 1998, Kruidenier and his wife offered the city $1.5 million to build a trail around the lake, and then Grubb promised $1 million toward the park's restoration. Bill saw great potential in the project and became involved as well. All three agreed that it should be a public park free of commercial development, but Bill saw a problem. The Weitz Company owned roughly one-third of the lake and another 30 acres of adjacent land.[9]

Ever the dealmaker, Bill sprang into action. He kept the project alive by raising money to purchase the Weitz-held property at Gray's Lake. He contributed $100,000, had Grubb put his $1 million donation toward the effort, and convinced Kruidenier to throw in $200,000 from his $1.5 million pledge for the trail. Other major donors from the private sector included Jim Cownie, the Meredith Corporation, Pioneer Hi-Bred, and Principal Financial Group. Polk County donated $500,000 to the effort. Meanwhile, Bill negotiated with Weitz executive Dick Oggero, eventually convincing him to take $2.2 million for the property, or $1 million less than its market value. The funds were then turned over to the city, with the provision that no commercial development would be part of the park. By March 1999, the city owned all of Gray's Lake.[10]

Cleanup and construction soon began, and in 2001, an enlarged gem of a park reopened. A new playground, picnic area, and public beach were added, and the two-mile Kruidenier Trail went around much of the lake. It was connected by a stunning, illuminated 1,400-foot pedestrian bridge. A decade later, the success of Gray's Lake Park was evident: it was attracting more than a million visitors a year and was named one of the ten great public spaces for 2011 by the American Planning Association.[11]

Bill was also involved in the creation of Choose Des Moines Communities, a new regional development group established in 1999 to attract new businesses to the area and develop and expand existing ones. He was then recruited to head its fundraising campaign. It was an easy sell; Bill did not believe there was a "fund drive or cause more important to the community [than Choose Des Moines Communities]." In just two years, Bill raised the five-year goal of $10 million, and by 2004, the Choose Des Moines recruitment program had enjoyed substantial success, bringing in forty-seven new businesses to greater Des Moines and helping ninety-two area companies expand. This activity generated $976 million in new investments by 2004.[12]

In addition to these and other civic endeavors, Bill continued making large charitable donations. Because he remained interested in doing "something that was good for all of Iowa," he focused more attention on the Iowa State Fair. He and Susan had become fixtures at the annual summer event, and in 2007, they served as marshals for the Iowa State Fair Parade. While they still camped at the fair, they had moved to a much more exclusive location. Beginning in August 1998, John Putney, head of the fair's fundraising Blue Ribbon Foundation, arranged a special campsite for the Knapps, situated just east of the of the fairground's Livestock Pavilion and kitty-corner from where Putney camped during the fair. Over the next few years, improvements to the campsite included a concrete slab, artificial turf, and potted plants. A party tent was installed adjacent to the space where Bill and Susan parked their upscale trailer and later their $1.2 million luxury motorhome for the fair's duration. Bill acknowledged his swank campsite, telling a *Des Moines Register* reporter, "It's pretty nice when your house goes with you." Several years later, other donors came forward with a million dollars or more for the fair, and they were accorded similar campsites just up the hill from Bill's location.[13]

The campsite proved a great investment for Putney, who realized that in terms of fundraising, "Bill Knapp's involvement was a turning point for us at the fair." Besides his initial $1 million donation, he made two more substantial gifts. In 2005, Bill gave $750,000 toward a new $1.3 million outdoor stage, which opened the following year as the Susan Knapp Amphitheater, and in 2006 he donated another $750,000 for a new $2 million facility, known as the Paul R. Knapp Animal Learning Center, devoted to educating children about animal husbandry.[14]

More importantly, Bill's close ties to the fair encouraged others to make sizable donations. Putney estimated that his involvement probably led to $30 million in appropriations and gifts to the fair. Sometimes, Bill even made the "ask" on behalf of the Blue Ribbon Foundation. During the 2008 fair, Putney, fair manager Gary Slater, and Bill took a golf cart to visit Jim and Patty Cownie, who were having a drink at the Bird's Nest, their son's concession stand on the fairgrounds. The three had been discussing going after a large gift from Cownie. Once sitting with Jim and Patty, Bill figured the time was right to solicit a big donation to the fair. He asked the Cownies for $750,000; they agreed and subsequently gave an additional $250,000 to the cause. The fair's Cultural Center building would be named in their honor.[15]

Many additional central Iowa organizations benefitted from Bill's largesse as well. His biggest donation of the period was $2 million to Des Moines's Blank Park Zoo, but he gave major gifts to others as well, including his alma mater, the AIB College of Business, the YMCA of Greater Des Moines, the city's Principal River Walk—a 1.2 mile trail on both sides of the Des Moines River, including pedestrian bridges, public art, landscaped public spaces, and a skating plaza—a boxing club on the city's east side, and local chapters of Planned Parenthood and United Way.[16]

At mid-decade, Bill made another large donation, and like his gifts to the fair, this also had statewide implications. Iowa was one of only thirteen states lacking a state veterans cemetery, and its only national veterans cemetery in the eastern Iowa city of Keokuk was nearing capacity. The United States Department of Veterans Affairs had identified the need in 2001, when a study found that over 280,000 veterans lived in Iowa, with roughly 92,000 residing within seventy-five miles of Des Moines. By 2004, the Iowa Department of Veteran Affairs (IDVA) began a fundraising campaign for the cemetery. A federal grant would cover the cost of its standard cemetery buildings but not the land or any design upgrades.[17]

Bill was interested. Although he was not one to look back, the sixtieth anniversary of the World War II Battle of Okinawa in 2005 brought back memories of his wartime service, especially his days as a landing craft pilot during the attack. That year, he read a *Des Moines Register* story about the campaign to build the cemetery and called Patrick Palmersheim, the director of the IDVA. He invited Palmersheim to visit him on some land he owned about ten miles west of Des Moines just off Interstate Highway 80 near the Van Meter interchange. Palmersheim found the acreage on the hill beautiful but said that the state could not afford it. Bill quickly responded, "I'm not talking about selling. I'm talking about donating."[18]

Bill's gift, which was appraised at just shy of $1.1 million, got even better. In typical fashion, he leveraged it for a bigger gift. He began talking to Ron Kenyon, a friend who had a successful construction company, telling him of the cemetery plans and his gift. Kenyon owned an adjoining piece of land that would be needed to access Bill's donated ground. He asked Kenyon about giving 20 or so acres for the cemetery. Kenyon refused but decided to grant access. Bill persisted, though, continuing to talk with Kenyon until he finally agreed to donate the land. By February 2006, the deal was complete; Kenyon's 24 acres combined with Bill's 76 acres gave the cemetery 100 acres of land overlooking the rolling Iowa countryside. The groundbreaking ceremony took place that November, and the cemetery was dedicated in July 2008.[19]

Of course, Bill also continued making money in some highly profitable deals. The transactions generally involved his proven formula of buying and holding property until finding the right buyer, and all received wide coverage in the *Des Moines Register*. A year after the highly successful 1999 U.S. Senior Open Tournament at Des Moines Golf and Country Club, Minneapolis-based Enebak Construction and its subsidiary, Traditions Golf, came to talk with Bill and Knapp Properties about building an Arnold Palmer–designed golf course and residential community in the Des Moines area. They formed a partnership and decided to build such a project on 1,000 acres of Knapp-owned land on the bluffs south of the Raccoon River in an unincorporated area of eastern Dallas County. Plans went ahead until Dallas County supervisors allowed Hallett Materials to operate a sand and gravel pit across the river from the planned development site. Bill was disappointed. He always thought that land "would be perfect for a golf course and upscale development," but ultimately nixed the location because the heavy truck traffic, dust, and noise associated with the mining operation were not conducive to the atmosphere the partners desired.[20]

Instead, the group chose to build on 570 wooded acres Bill had acquired during the 1980s just north of Des Moines in Polk City. Plans called for a residential golf community featuring an eighteen-hole course and 600 single-family homes and townhomes near the Big Creek Reservoir. As construction began, dozens of people signed a waiting list to purchase home lots in the community, and Arnold Palmer visited the course while under development. He was pleased: "I think this is going to be something very spectacular for Iowa." The course opened the summer of 2003 and was soon recognized by *Golf Digest* as one of the best new courses in America and one of the best courses in Iowa. Lot sales to individuals and developers were brisk until the market downturn in 2007. They recovered several years later, and by 2012, the original subdivisions were sold out.[21]

At about the same time, Bill negotiated his most profitable deals ever. Years earlier in 1987, he had purchased the 375-acre Staples farm in what was then an unincorporated eastern portion of Dallas County. He paid $1,100 per acre and held the land. Development pushed westward over the next decade, but area land prices jumped in 2002 when General Growth Properties bought 216 acres at $81,000 per acre for the 1.2 million-square-foot Jordan Creek Town Center mall, located just north of the Staples farm. Meanwhile, Wells Fargo Home Mortgage, headquartered in West Des Moines, was looking to expand. Although it had strong ties to Iowa, Wells Fargo considered locating the new facility in another state—Arizona, Illinois, South Carolina, and Texas were also possibilities. Bill happened to be a next door neighbor to Mark Oman, the head of Wells Fargo's home lending and consumer finance operations, which oversaw the home mortgage division; and whenever the subject came up, he strongly encouraged Oman to build the new complex in Iowa.[22]

His friendship with the Wells Fargo executive did not hurt, but Oman was not involved in the details of where the new complex would be located. By August 2003, it appeared that Iowa, with its generous incentive package of state and local monies ultimately totaling over $54 million, had edged out the other states in the competition. Several months earlier,

Wells Fargo had retained Doug Siedenburg (who had formerly worked for Iowa Realty Commercial) of the Siedenburg Group to locate suitable land in the greater Des Moines area. Siedenburg contemplated sites in the suburbs of Ankeny and Urbandale, as well as downtown and in West Des Moines. Bill lobbied Siedenburg and Wells Fargo hard. At one point he offered them 100 acres of the Staples farm at no cost, but he wanted to keep the frontage land for commercial development. He reasoned that the gift would pay off by handsomely increasing the value of his commercial land that would front the banking complex. Siedenburg responded, "A bold move; I expected nothing less." But Wells Fargo wanted the frontage land and did not bite.[23]

Negotiations continued with Bill eventually selling Wells Fargo 136 acres of the Staples farm for $121,000 per acre in 2004. As the Wells Fargo deal neared completion, Knapp Properties joined with Ron Daniels' Buyers Realty group in a the development consortium and sold the partnership 73 acres of the remaining Staples farmland at $300,000 per acre. Together, they built the Galleria shopping area, soon anchored by a Wal-Mart Supercenter, TJ Maxx, OfficeMax, Trader Joe's, and Pier 1 Imports. While Bill was renowned for his foresight and vision when buying land, these two deals were extraordinary. Bill Knapp II explained simply, "We've had some great luck."[24]

In the midst of these successes, Bill was also involved in what became his most controversial set of transactions, leading to stories that challenged his integrity. In 1999, he partnered with commercial real estate developer Denny Elwell and bought 84 acres of land (paying just over $15,000 per acre) in Ankeny from the bankrupt Ankeny-Des Moines Aviation Exposition. The nonprofit group had held an annual air show, which featured radio-controlled model airplanes reenacting historic battles and actual aircraft doing precision flying stunts. In early 2004, Bill and Elwell sold seven acres of the land for $130,000 per acre to the Iowa Department of Transportation (DOT) for a new driver's license station. Questions arose when the *Des Moines Register* ran several stories about the deals after the announcement of plans for the new DOT license station.[25]

The investigative series suggested that the initial land sale in 1999 was an insider deal because Paul Knapp was the president of the Aviation Expo, and Bill had access to information about the land sale that others did not. Jeff Segin of Knapp Properties was retained to market the land,

and he also acted on behalf of the purchasers, Bill and Elwell. Further-more, the sale was never publicly announced and the land was never ap-praised, raising questions of whether or not fair market value was paid for the land. It also noted that Knapp Properties president Gerry Neugent served as the expo's attorney as well.[26]

These connections raised red flags for *Register* reporters Bert Dalm-er and Tim Higgins, who also questioned the nature of the relationship between Mark Wandro, the assistant engineer of Polk County and later head of Iowa's DOT, and Bill and Elwell. Wandro had been involved in planning a new Interstate Highway 35 interchange to be built near the Aviation Expo land (which would drastically increase its accessibility and value) shortly before Bill and Elwell purchased it. As head of the DOT, he had rejected all fifteen proposals submitted for the new license station and later purchased the seven acres at the Ankeny I-35 interchange for the facility from Bill and Elwell.[27]

Bill was angered by the articles. He felt they unjustly attacked him and wrote a guest editorial defending his and his company's actions. He even offered to release the DOT from the deal. Meanwhile, the Iowa at-torney general, Tom Miller, launched an investigation into the terms of the initial sale between the Aviation Expo and Bill and Elwell. The state auditor, David Vaudt, promised to monitor the situation and "see whether further issues should be examined."[28]

In April 2006, the attorney general concluded his investigation, find-ing that no state laws had been violated. Based on a twenty-nine-page opinion by an independent appraiser, Miller explained, "Regardless of the relationships between the buyer and the expo, the buyer did not receive a discount," and paid close to fair market price for the land. He did note, however, that the expo had not used best practices that would have dictat-ed obtaining an independent appraisal of the land and advertising the sale publicly. But it was not quite over. Vaudt followed up with his own inves-tigation. It took more than a year, but by August 2007, he also found that no legal or ethical violations occurred in the transfer of land between the Aviation Expo and Bill and Elwell. *Des Moines Register* business writers Lynn Hicks and Dave Elbert concluded, "The auditor's finding is likely to carry more weight because Vaudt is a Republican, while the attorney general is a Democrat. Knapp over the years had been a significant con-tributor to Democratic causes and candidates."[29]

He had been stung by the allegations and although pleased by the vindication, Bill thought it merited more ink than the four short paragraphs the *Register* devoted to it. Still, in typical fashion, he had moved on to other projects until a tragic death stopped him in his tracks. As Bill grew older, longtime friends passed away with greater regularity. Businessman, lawyer, and Democratic supporter Joe Rosenfield died in 2000, childcare activist Evelyn Davis in 2001, clothier Bill Reichart in 2004, and former *Register* publisher and philanthropist David Kruidenier died in 2006. He mourned their losses, but these deaths only reinforced his natural inclination to keep moving forward. This came to a halt in 2008.[30]

In March of 2007, Bill's son Roger had just finished a round of golf at the Tournament Players Club (TPC) Prestancia in his gated community in Sarasota, Florida. He and the rest of the foursome were returning to the clubhouse in a golf cart when Roger slumped over in pain. He was rushed to the hospital where he underwent open-heart surgery for an aortic aneurysm. Doctors gave him a 20 percent change to live, but Roger survived the six-hour operation, only to battle complications and an infection that kept him hospitalized for weeks. Amazingly, however, he was back on the golf course by the end of the summer.[31]

Then on Sunday, March 30, 2008, Roger was getting ready for golf when he was stricken with a heart attack. Ms. Kem Lindsay, his life partner, called 911, and Roger was again rushed to the hospital. Family members converged on Sarasota: Bill, Susan, Irene, Roger's daughter Sable, and his cousin John Knapp flew in from Des Moines. Bill II drove up from Naples, Florida, and they all joined Lindsay in the hospital waiting room. A couple of hours later, the doctor came in and knelt down to tell Lindsay that Roger was gone. The family was stunned.[32]

Others arrived over the next few days, including Roger's youngest daughter Montana and her mother Amy Knapp, Ginny and Mark Haviland, and their daughter Kendy Granzow. Greg Abel, a good friend of Bill's and the chief executive officer of MidAmerican Energy Holdings Company, flew down to Sarasota for the memorial service on Wednesday and brought Governor Chet Culver, Paul Knapp, Rich McMenamin (Paul's personal assistant), Mike Knapp, and Gerry Neugent with him. The commemoration was held at TPC Prestancia, the golf club Roger loved. Friends would later plant a live oak in his honor along the third hole near his home on Prestancia-Stadium Course. Two days later, the evening of April 4, the Knapps reassembled in Des Moines and had a visitation for friends at Dunn's Funeral Home. The funeral was held the next day at the crowded Westminster Presbyterian Church, and Roger was interred at Resthaven Cemetery in West Des Moines.[33]

The death hit Bill hard. "It broke his heart," recalled Susan Knapp. Initially, he was angry and could not understand why he had outlived his son. The loss was compounded by guilt Bill carried for putting the family through the divorce and affair, which had strained his relationship with Roger. By the mid-1990s, however, the two had grown close again. They talked on the telephone several times a week and as Bill remembered, "We never ended a phone conversation without saying we loved each other," and when together, "we never shook hands, we always hugged." Bill's anger soon gave way to a profound sadness; he missed his son. Shortly after the burial, he began visiting Roger's grave two or three times a week. Bill was simply devastated by the loss, and although he continued going into his office at Knapp Properties, he was distracted and withdrawn. Transactions he usually relished were handled by others or fell by the wayside, and business lunches, which had been part of his daily regimen for years, were held far less frequently. The very active social schedule he and Susan kept slowed significantly.[34]

Then another blow: six weeks later, Bill's brother died. Paul's health had been declining over the past few years. Rheumatoid arthritis and neuropathy had confined him to a motorized scooter or wheelchair by 2006. A heart attack the next year weakened him. Paul had a pacemaker installed in the following spring of 2008, but there were complications and an infection. He apparently recovered, although several weeks later in May, back pain sent him to Iowa Methodist Medical Center. Not quite a day later, Paul slipped into a coma. He never recovered and died two days later. Still reeling from the death of his son, Bill now dealt with the loss of his brother, colleague, and confidant. Longtime friend and earth-moving contractor Dwayne McAninch commented on the close relationship Bill and Paul had enjoyed: "I don't know two brothers who ever appreciated each other more than those two."[35]

"Bill had already been walked through hell," Susan observed, "and he was already numb when Paul passed away." He suffered through these losses, and although Bill's mother once said he "was tougher than anybody," the death of his son and then brother tested his resilience. He grieved and was at once aloof, remote, and disengaged. Former Iowa attorney general and friend Bonnie Campbell noted that Bill had "a hole in his heart that would never heal" but that he would eventually learn to live with it; yet, Bill was eighty-one years old. Some wondered whether he would or could refocus and return to making deals and playing a leading role in the community.[36]

Epilogue

On a mild winter evening in January 2011, Bill Knapp took a break from the reception in his honor and sat down in an antique chair. He was at Terrace Hill, the elegant governor's mansion and former home of Frederick Marion (F. M.) Hubbell, the city's leading business figure and developer in the late nineteenth and early twentieth century. Bill had been recognized earlier that day with the Iowa Award, the state's highest civilian prize, given for "outstanding service of Iowans in the fields of science, medicine, law, religion, social welfare, education, agriculture, industry, government or other public service." It put Bill in some heady company. He was only the twenty-first person to receive the award since its inception in 1948. Previous recipients included Herbert Hoover, Jay N. "Ding" Darling, Henry A. Wallace, Norman Borlaug, Carrie Chapman Catt, John Ruan, George Washington Carver, Robert Ray, and Grant Wood.[1]

Bill had been "overwhelmed" at the award ceremony and promised to work hard to earn his place among the select group. He joked, "When I see the people who have received this honor, it makes me wonder when I'll get the call saying, 'We made a mistake.'" Of course, the award was not in error and recognized Bill's lifetime of achievements in business and community service. As he collected himself in that old chair at the reception, Christie Vilsack, a former first lady of Iowa and thus former resident of Terrace Hill, leaned in and whispered: "Did you know you're sitting in F. M. Hubbell's chair?" A smile came over Bill's face; he knew the Hubbell name and the family's long legacy in central Iowa's business and charitable circles. Few noticed the serendipitous moment, but there was something appropriate about it, bringing the past and present together as the city's leading real estate figure relaxed where Des Moines's most prominent real estate man once sat.[2]

By the time of the award, Bill had returned to public life; however, the comeback since the untimely death of Roger and then Paul in 2008 had not been easy. Sadness had pervaded him, and he remained withdrawn for months. Susan played a major role in Bill's recovery, encouraging activity and keeping him busy. The fall of 2008, for instance, she arranged a special event for family and friends, flying a small group out to Aspen where she and Bill renewed their wedding vows. It was bittersweet without Roger, but it was part of the healing process. Friends proved important as well. Michael Gartner's perspective was especially helpful. He had also dealt with the death of a son and understood Bill's profound sorrow. The two talked through their shared experiences. Others grieved with Bill. John Putney remembered playing golf with him in Sarasota a year after Roger died. They were on the TPC Prestancia's Stadium Course and stopped at the tree planted in Roger's honor. Bill had been stoic at the oak, but several holes later, he broke down. "It was hard," Putney recalled, "but I think it was an important time for him." All through the process, John Mauro had been gently coaxing Bill to get back in the game. "I told him that the community needed him; that he needed to get back into the flow because there weren't many others who could make things happen the way he could."[3]

Finally, Bill pushed through it, aided in part by a change in his spiritual beliefs. Although he had stopped attending church in the mid-1960s, Bill continued believing in God and the afterlife and prayed privately every night. Roger's death made him bitter and challenged him to reconsider his views. How, he wondered, could God allow this to happen? But he gradually revised his thinking. He decided that God did not or could not intervene in human affairs. Evidence was everywhere, he explained, because "bad things occur all the time." Meanwhile, he clung to his belief in heaven and the hope that he would eventually be reunited with his son in the afterlife.[4]

He steadily returned to the world of business and community service in 2009. The following spring, Kem Lindsay held a small memorial ceremony at the home she and Roger had shared in Florida. Bill and Susan, Gerry Neugent and his wife Mary Lou, and several other friends and family members were there as well. They lit candles and talked about Roger's life. Neugent remembered the event was hard for Bill, but he also felt it represented a kind of closure for his longtime friend and associate.[5]

Bill Knapp was back. Some felt there was an even greater determination about him. The death of a child, Gartner stressed, "changes you dramatically," but he added, it also "pushes you in directions you were going anyway." This, he believed, led Bill in an "altruistic rush to do good. It was as if he wanted Roger to be proud of him."[6]

Meanwhile, few had noticed a major change at Knapp Properties. Two years earlier in January 2008, Bill had sold the management company to Bill Knapp II and Gerry Neugent. At the same time, he sold each of them a 10 percent stake in William C. Knapp LC, the principal holding company of his family's vast property interests. The two had worked for Bill for thirty years, and he felt they had earned the right to own the firm. Actually, the shift did not make a noticeable difference. Bill II and Neugent had run Knapp Properties' day-to-day affairs for a number of years, but Bill continued in his key role when it came to big decisions and deals. Such was the case in the summer of 2007, when the firm bought 540 acres of land south and west of Des Moines along the border of Dallas and Warren counties because Bill thought development was moving in that direction.[7]

Yet the "the altruistic rush" was now his priority. He had plenty of money—a close friend estimated Bill's net worth "in the strong nine figures"—and while he still sought profitable business deals, he was much more interested in devoting his time and wealth to the community's good. He was involved in numerous projects, raising money and/or contributing to organizations such as Planned Parenthood, Des Moines's Young Women's Resource Center, and Meals for the Heartland, a local nonprofit, which packaged meals for hungry people around the world. For the latter, he donated land for a food packaging center and raised more than a million dollars to pay for the facility. But there were three other activities that stood out from the rest.[8]

One of Bill's favorite undertakings was sponsoring a Central Iowa Honor Flight, which took aging World War II veterans to Washington, D.C., to see the World War II Memorial. The Honor Flight Network had been established in 2005 to "transport America's veterans to Washington, D.C., to visit those memorials dedicated to honor their service and sacrifices." In the summer 2009, Duane Gibson, an old friend of Bill's and longtime pastor of the First Baptist Church of Des Moines, was raising funds for Iowa's honor flight organization. He and Jeff Ballenger, director of Central Iowa Honor Flight, called on Bill Knapp II to see if his uncle might be interested providing support. Before Bill II could talk with Bill, Gibson and Ballenger obtained funding from Hy-Vee Food Stores and then Casey's General Stores for the honor flights. Shortly thereafter, several other flights were scheduled, but there remained a waiting list of Iowa veterans who had not yet taken the trip. Thus the following May 2010, Gibson and Ballenger returned to Knapp Properties, asking if Bill would sponsor an honor flight.[9]

Although never one to look back, Bill had become more interested in his World War II experience since his involvement several years earlier in establishing the Iowa Veterans Cemetery in Van Meter. He readily agreed to underwrite the additional trip, which cost a total of $250,000, with the stipulation that because he had not seen the World War II Memorial, he could go along as well. On Wednesday afternoon, August 18, 2010, over 300 Iowa veterans rode in a parade through Des Moines to Prairie Meadows Racetrack and Casino where they were honored at a dinner. They rose early the next morning and boarded a Boeing 747 aircraft for their one-day excursion to see the World War II Memorial and other monuments throughout the capital. The tour brought back many memories for Bill, but he found it especially heartwarming to be among the other veterans because of "all the camaraderie we enjoyed and the conversations we had while we looked at the monuments. I've gotten more thanks from that than anything else I've done."[10]

Preparations for the trip also led to an improbable reunion. Shortly before the honor flight, Bill II searched the internet for information on any living sailors who had served with his uncle on the USS Catron. He came across a newspaper article in the *Gadsden* (Alabama) *Times* about James Penney, an eighty-three-year-old World War II veteran who had recently been on an honor flight and had served on the same ship. Bill II told Bill, who could not recall Penney, but was interested in finding out more. They located a phone number, and Bill called. When Bill asked if Penney remembered him, he responded, "Why sure I do. You were the short guy who was as tough as a pine knot."[11]

The two corresponded several times over the next eighteen months until Susan arranged a get-together for the two former shipmates. They were reunited in March 2012, when Bill and Susan added a two-hour lunch stop at the Northeast Alabama Regional Airport in Gadsden on their flight to Florida. The veterans talked of their war experiences and the different courses their lives had taken. They discussed the possibility of making a trip back to Okinawa together, but more immediately they planned for Penney and his family to be Bill's guests at the upcoming Iowa State Fair. That August, Penney, his two daughters, and a granddaughter joined Bill and Susan and friends and family for an evening at the fair Knapp style: a white-napkin, catered affair at Bill's special, well-appointed campsite.[12]

Even more unlikely than Bill's reconnection with Penney was his work with Iowa's Republican governor Terry Branstad. The governor had reached out to Bill, inviting him to discuss projects they might work on together. Bill agreed, and he, Bill II, and Gerry Neugent went to see the governor. The March 2012 meeting also included Lt. Governor Kim Reynolds, Jeff Boeyink, the governor's chief of staff, and Teresa Wahlert, head of Iowa Workforce Development.

There was some tension between the two old adversaries as the meeting started, and Bill addressed it directly, telling Branstad, "I was impressed getting a call from you because you know how much I've personally spent to keep you out of office." Branstad acknowledged the statement, and said he knew they could not agree on social issues but hoped to find common ground. Then Bill raised the subject of jobs. "We need to get people working," he said. "We need to help people get jobs." That was it; Bill had identified a shared concern. Branstad asked Wahlert to put some ideas together, which led to the Skilled Iowa Initiative announced just three months later in June. The program provided online education for job seekers to beef up their basic skills and awarded a National Career Readiness Certificate upon completion of the course. It then matched the unemployed to companies that offered training internships and hoped to hire. Interns were not paid but received unemployment benefits during their training—which was not generally the case—and participating firms pledged to consider hiring the worker once the internship ended.[13]

Bill was enthusiastic about the plan. As it was being formulated, he agreed to raise money for the Workforce Development Foundation, which would provide funds to advertise and promote public-private efforts. He put in $50,000, and then contacted colleagues in the business community. In what had become his standard practice, Bill's first calls were to his best friends, Jim Cownie and MidAmerican Energy's Greg Abel, who each matched his contribution. He relied on these two to get fundraising campaigns going, explaining their willingness to give simply: "Jim and Greg both care deeply for the community and the state." Cownie put it a little differently, "Bill's a smart guy. He's been so successful and done so much good, you'd be a damn fool not to give his proposals serious consideration."

Others stepped up as well. Principal Financial Group and Roger Brooks, retired chief executive officer (CEO) of AmerUs (now Aviva), donated $25,000 each. There were smaller gifts as well, and by the time the program was announced, Bill had raised $250,000 for the foundation. At the press conference, Bill explained that he had not been a big supporter of the governor, but he thought their partnership should "send a message across Iowa that Democrats and Republicans should start working together for the good of Iowa and make this a better place for all of us."[14]

At about the same time, Bill became involved in possibly his most significant endeavor in decades—putting together a successor group to the Des Moines Development Corporation (DMDC). As a nonprofit adjunct of the Greater Des Moines Chamber of Commerce Federation, the DMDC had been vital to the city's renewal in late 1970s and 1980s when it purchased older properties often held by several different owners, cleared the land, and made way for new development. But the organization was dissolved in 1999 when it, the Greater Des Moines Chamber, and other groups merged to become the Greater Des Moines Partnership.[15]

By 2010, a growing interest in downtown redevelopment led some to consider a new version of the DMDC. The idea first surfaced late that year during the public input phase of Capital Crossroads, a strategic plan then being drafted for metropolitan Des Moines. It picked up momentum early 2012 when Larry Zimpleman, the president and CEO of the Principal Group, became its leading advocate. The Des Moines city manager, Rick Clark, saw great potential because the city budget did not have the funds available to make large land purchases. He noted, "If there is not some way to assemble the land into usable parcels, it [redevelopment] is just not going to happen."[16]

Jim Cownie, Steve Lacy, CEO of the Meredith Corporation, Gene Meyer, president of the Greater Des Moines Partnership, and others were soon working with Zimpleman on a framework for such an organization. Bill joined the conversation and immediately embraced the idea. He had been a key member of the DMDC years earlier and knew the importance of controlling land for development, often saying, "You can't plan someone else's property." In fact, even as the details of the new organization were being nailed down, Bill was on the phone or out to lunch using his clout and connections to sell the proposal and recruit members for what would become the Des Moines Redevelopment Company (DMRC). By that fall, eighteen of central Iowa business leaders and companies had joined the new nonprofit. Besides Bill, it included his friends and business colleagues Jim Cownie, Michael Gartner, Denny Elwell, and retired ING executive Fred Hubbell. Then there were the city's leading companies—the Principal Financial Group, Meredith Corporation, the Ruan Companies, Kum & Go, Hy-Vee, EMC Insurance, MidAmerican Energy, Wellmark, Graham Group, Waldinger Corporation, Baker Group and Baker Electric, and West Bank. Each member guaranteed up to $500,000 for the group, hence providing the DMRC $9 million, which could be used to buy and assemble parcels of land for downtown development.[17]

The significance of the moment and bringing together important business leaders into the DMRC was not lost of Rick Tollakson, CEO of Hubbell Realty, who called the ongoing deliberations about downtown "50-year decisions." There was talk of relocating the downtown YMCA, adding an annex to the aging Polk County Courthouse, and building a new convention hotel. Related to these issues were questions of reusing or demolishing some of downtown Des Moines's prominent older structures in various redevelopment schemes. Such facilities included the Register Building, which would be vacated by the newspaper in 2013, the former J. C. Penney Building—owned by Wellmark but empty after the insurance company closed its offices there and consolidated operations in the firm's new headquarters on Grand Avenue in 2010—the Riverfront YMCA Building, and the outdated Polk County Convention Complex. The DMRC was in the mix on all these discussions and right in the middle was Bill Knapp.[18]

His leadership in the DMRC and the next phase of downtown renewal was typical of his unrelenting interest and involvement in the community. Although in the twilight of his career, his work on behalf of present and planned civil projects expanded. Iowa Workforce Development director Teresa Wahlert explained, "He continues to challenge us for the next step....He is still formulating the vision for twenty years out."[19]

He had already made a large and lasting imprint on the community. The ubiquitous blue and white Iowa Realty "For Sale" signs that dotted the Iowa landscape seemed symbolic of his wide influence. His many residential and commercial developments—Napa Valley, Country Club, West Lakes, or Interstate Acres, for instance—had reshaped greater Des Moines; his work downtown had kept the city's renaissance moving forward; and he had led the revitalization of the deteriorating Drake University neighborhood. At the same time, his generous giving and successful fundraising made Iowa and its capital city a better place to live.

Yet he was not finished. Bill was focused on the future and remained a man in motion, rarely pausing and impatient about getting things done. "Bill thrived on having something going," recounted Bill II, while former Iowa governor Chet Culver noted, "He never stops and never will." And so it was. Bill loved making deals and putting things together; he loved buying and selling land; and no one was better at envisioning a new or different use for a piece of property, be it virgin ground or a deteriorating building. That was Bill Knapp; still pushing, still seeing opportunities, and still getting things done. [20]

A Note on Sources

Much of this book is based on manuscript collections, which are privately held. Other important components of my research consisted of interviews and correspondence with people who have known Bill Knapp throughout his lifetime.

Manuscript Collections

Cedarstrom, Larry, Papers. Private collection, West Des Moines, Iowa.

Cleven, Roger, Papers. Private collection, Des Moines, Iowa.

Grubb, John W., Papers. Private collection, Urbandale, Iowa.

Haviland, Virginia, Papers. Private collection, West Des Moines, Iowa.

Houser, Robert, Papers. In possession of author, West Des Moines, Iowa.

Iowa Realty Papers. Private collection, West Des Moines, Iowa.

Jones, Nancy, Papers. Private collection, Allerton, Iowa.

Knapp, Bill, Papers. Private collection, West Des Moines, Iowa.

Knapp, Bill II, Papers. Private collection, West Des Moines, Iowa.

Knapp, Irene Papers. Private collection, Urbandale, Iowa.

Knapp Properties Papers. Private collection, West Des Moines, Iowa.

Leachman, John, Papers. Private collection, Des Moines, Iowa.

Penney, James, Papers. Private collection, Glencoe, Alabama.

Toomey, Margaret, Papers. Private collection, Des Moines, Iowa.

Interviews and Correspondence with Author

Ballenger, Jeff. Telephone conversation with author, 31 October 2012.

Bell, Joe. Telephone conversation with author, 3 February 2011.

Birocci, Linda. Correspondence with author, 28 December 2011.

Brooks, Roger. Telephone conversation with author, 5 March 2012.

Calvert, Les. Interview by author, West Des Moines, Iowa, 8 February 2011.

Campbell, Bonnie. Interview by author, Des Moines, Iowa, 27 December 2011. Correspondence with author, 12 March 2012.

Cedarstrom, Larry. Interview by author, West Des Moines, Iowa, 9 January 2012.

Clarkson, Lew. Interview by author, Johnston, Iowa, 10 February 2011.

Cleven, Roger. Interview by author, Des Moines, Iowa, 3 May 2011. Telephone conversations with author, 22, 28 December 2010; and 20 June 2011.

Cole, Lu Jean. Interview by author, Des Moines, Iowa, 4 June 2012.

Conlin, Roxanne. Interview by author, Des Moines, Iowa, 3 October 2012.

Cooper, James. Interview by author, Des Moines, Iowa, 5 May 2011. Telephone conversation with author, 18 May 2011.

Cownie, James. Interview by author, Des Moines, Iowa, 17 September 2012. Telephone conversation with author, 15 January 2013.

Crooks, Reva. Telephone conversation with author, 13 October 2010.

Culver, Chet. Interview by author, Des Moines, Iowa, 6 November 2012.

Dailey, Marilyn. Telephone conversations with author, 30 December 2010; and 13 September and 11 October 2011.

Dalmer, Bert. Interview by author, Des Moines, Iowa, 27 September 2012.

Davis, Billy. Telephone conversation with author, 14 October 2010.

Doggett, Carolyn. Interview by author, Allerton, Iowa, 5 October 2010. Telephone conversations with author, 28 July 2011; 1 October 2012; and 23 February 2013.

Earley, J. Michael. Telephone conversation with author, 6 April 2012.

Ferrari, Michael. Telephone conversation with author, 6 April 2012.

Fisher, Carly. Correspondence with author, 11 July, 4, 9 October 2012.

Gartner, Michael. Interview by author, Des Moines, Iowa, 3 July 2012.

Gentry, Cecelia. Interview by author, West Des Moines, Iowa, 20 June 2012.

Grandquist, Cindy. Interview by author, West Des Moines, Iowa, 17 June 2011.

Grandquist, Linda. Interview by author, West Des Moines, Iowa, 11 January 2012.

Grubb, John W. Interview by author, Urbandale, Iowa, 23 June 2011.

Gunzenhauser, Keith. Telephone conversation with author, 29 May 2012.

Haviland, Mark. Telephone conversation with author, 16 January 2012.

Haviland, Virginia. Interviews with author, West Des Moines, Iowa, 29 September 2010; and 7 September 2011.

Hawkins, Lex. Telephone conversation with author, 22 July 2011.

Hornocker, Wayne. Telephone conversation with author, 7 October 2010.

Hull, Charles. Interview by author, Des Moines, Iowa 2 July 2012.

Jenkins, Warren. Interview by author, Des Moines, Iowa, 18 September 2012.

Johnson, Renee. Telephone conversation with author, 18 December 2012.

Jones, Nancy. Interview by author, Allerton, Iowa, 5 October 2010. Telephone conversations with author, 11 November 2010; and 1 October 2012.

Kint, Ruby. Telephone conversation with author, 18 December 2010.

Kirk, Joseph, Sr. Interview by author, West Des Moines, Iowa, 5 April 2011.

Kline, Mark. Correspondence with author, 2 April 2012.

Knapp, Bill. Interviews by author, West Des Moines, Iowa, 21, 23 September, 7, 27 October 2010; 5 January, 29 April, 17 May, 16 June, 18 July, 1 August, 14 October, 22 November, 8 December 2011; 30 March, 23 May, 30 June, 11 July, 9, 24 August, 14 September, 2 November 2012; and 14 January 2013. Telephone conversations with author, 20 January, and 6 April 2012.

Knapp, Bill II. Interviews by author, West Des Moines, Iowa, 16 December 2010; 18 July, 27 September, 14 October, 8 December 2011; and 30 March, 19 April, 29 August, 26 September 2012. Correspondence with author, 21 September, 23 November 2010; 13 July, 11 October 2011; and 24 October 2012.

A Note on Sources

Knapp, Carol. Interview by author, West Des Moines, Iowa, 9 October 2012.

Knapp, Irene. Interviews by author, Urbandale, Iowa, 29 September 2010; 1 June 2011; and 22 February 2012. Telephone conversations with author, 2 June, 6, 25 July 2011; and 18 May, and 31 August 2012.

Knapp, Mike. Interview by author, West Des Moines, Iowa, December 31, 2010.

Knapp, Susan. Interview by author, Van Meter, Iowa, 5 October 2012.

Kruidenier, Elizabeth. Interview by author, Des Moines, Iowa, 8 August 2011.

Leachman, John. Interview by author, Des Moines, Iowa, 27 October 2011.

Levis, Delrein. Telephone conversation with author, 14 October 2010.

MacAllister, Jack. Telephone conversation with author, 9 October 2011.

Manley, Paul. Interview by author, Des Moines, Iowa, 5 January 2011.

Mauro, John. Interview by author, Des Moines, Iowa, 23 August 2012.

Maxwell, David. Interview by author, Des Moines, Iowa, 6 December 2012.

McCulloh, Jim. Interviews by author, Des Moines, Iowa, 3, 23 May 2012.

McEachern, Harold. Telephone conversation with author, 17 October 2011.

McKain, Virginia. Telephone conversation with author, 8 February 2011.

McWilliams, Jack. Interview by author, West Des Moines, Iowa, 28 December 2011.

Meline, Tim. Interview by author, West Des Moines, Iowa, 22 December 2011.

Miller, David. Interview by author, West Des Moines, Iowa, 24 October 2011.

Miller, Herman. Interview by author, Des Moines, Iowa, 13 April 2011.

Miller, Margaret. Interview by author, Des Moines, Iowa, 13 April 2011.

Moore, Marjorie. Interview by author, West Des Moines, Iowa, 4 December 2010.

Neugent, Gerry. Interviews by author, West Des Moines, Iowa, 30 March, 29 August, and 26 September 2012. Telephone conversation with author, 16 May 2012. Correspondence with author, 4 September 2012.

Neumann, Daryl. Interview by author, West Des Moines, Iowa, 9 August 2011.

Oman, Mark. Interview by author, West Des Moines, Iowa, 19 September 2012.

Pearson, Ron. Interview by author, West Des Moines, Iowa, 10 October 2011.

Penney, James. Interview by author, Des Moines, Iowa, 9 August 2012. Telephone conversations with author, 26, 30 September 2010.

Putney, John. Interview by author, Des Moines, Iowa, 10 July 2012. Correspondence with author, 18 September, and 4 October 2012.

Ramsay, Richard. Telephone conversation with author, 21 February 2012.

Ramsey, David. Telephone conversation with author, 19 October 2011.

Ramsey, Susan. Correspondence with author, 1 November 2012.

Riley, Roy. Telephone conversations with author, 24 May, and 2 September 2011.

Shotwell, Walt. Interview by author, Des Moines, Iowa, 9 September 2010.

Stanbrough, Gene. Interview by author, Clive, Iowa, 20 September 2011.

Stauffer, Jean. Interview by author, Urbandale, Iowa, 5 October 2011.

Stauffer, John. Telephone conversation with author, 17 May 2012.

Stauffer, William. Interview by author, Urbandale, Iowa, 5 October 2011.

Stokstad, Arden. Telephone conversation with author, 7 September 2011. Correspondence with author, 25 September 2011.

Timmins, Robert. Interview by author, West Des Moines, Iowa, 5 May 2011.

Toomey, Margaret. Interview by author, Des Moines, Iowa, 16 July 2012.

Turner, Beatrice. Interview by author, Des Moines, Iowa, 30 September 2010.

Underwood, Robert. Interview by author, Johnston, Iowa, 28 June 2011. Telephone conversation with author, 4 August 2011.

Vaudt, David. Interview by author, Des Moines, Iowa, 18 September 2012.

Wahlert, Teresa. Interview by author, Des Moines, Iowa, 8 October 2012.

Wahlig, Jack. Interview by author, Clive, Iowa, 30 August 2011. Telephone conversation with author, 1 May 2012.

Weitz, Fred. Interview by author. Des Moines, Iowa, 6 December 2011.

Wilkey, Richard. Interview by author, West Des Moines, Iowa, 26 December 2011.

Wimer, Connie. Interviews by author, Des Moines, Iowa, 31 August 2011; and 10 September 2012. Correspondence with author, 8 June, and 24 August 2012.

Notes

Introduction

1. The conversation between Bill Knapp and Gerry Neugent was heard by author, 3 December 2010.

2. *Des Moines Register*, 3 October 1983.

3. On the desire to control his life, see Bill Knapp, interview by author, West Des Moines, Iowa, 5 January 2011.

4. Ibid.

5. Tim Meline's quote is from Tim Meline, interview by author, West Des Moines, Iowa, 22 December 2011. Bill Knapp is quoted from Jack McWilliams, interview by author, West Des Moines, Iowa, 28 December 2011.

6. Jim Cownie's quote is from James Cownie, interview by author, Des Moines, Iowa, 17 September 2012; Gerry Neugent's quote is from Gerry Neugent, interview by author, West Des Moines, Iowa, 26 September 2012; Roger Brooks's quote is from Roger Brooks, telephone conversation with author, 5 March 2012; and Bill Knapp's quote is from Bill Knapp, interview, 11 July 2012.

7. Elaine Szymoniak is quoted from *Des Moines Register*, 14 January 1990.

8. Roxanne Conlin's quotation and comment about his rivals are from *Des Moines Register*, 14 January 1990. Bill's quote is from *Des Moines Register*, 26 August 2012.

9. For Bill's idea of time as the enemy, see John Putney, interview by author, Des Moines, Iowa, 10 July 2012. For more on the notion and Bill's quotation, see Bill Knapp, interview, 11 July 2012.

Chapter 1

1. For the story of creditors discussing foreclosure with the Knapps, see Bill Knapp, interview by author, West Des Moines, Iowa, 7 October 2010. Details on paying off the Union Central Life Insurance loan and obtaining a loan from the Federal Land Bank of Omaha are from Book 68, p. 278, and Book 15, p. 400, in the records of the Recorder of Wayne County, Iowa. Abstracts of these are in Bill Knapp Papers, private collection held by Bill Knapp, West Des Moines, Iowa [hereafter cited as Bill Knapp Papers]. For quotation, see *Des Moines Register*, 14 January 1983.

2. On assembling the 200-acre family farm, see Book 42, p. 240, and Book 45, p. 420, in the records of the Recorder of Wayne County, Iowa. Abstracts of these records are available in Bill Knapp Papers.

3. Nancy Jones, "Anna's Story" (privately printed manuscript, 1988), 25; and Walt Shotwell, *The Knapps and Notable Others: From Less Than Nothing to More Than Plenty* (Des Moines, IA: Walt Shotwell, 2000), 8. For more detail on Henry Ford and the $5-a-day wage, see Stephen Meyer III, *The Five Dollar Day: Labor Management and Social Control in the Ford Motor Company, 1908–1921* (Albany: State University of New York Press, 1981). On Bill Knapp at Ford Motor Company,

see Jones, "Anna's Story," 15; Shotwell, *Knapps*, 9; and Nancy Jones, interview by author, Allerton, Iowa, 5 October 2010.

4. Jones, "Anna's Story," 11-12.

5. Ibid., 12-13.

6. Ibid., 15-16. For descriptions of Bill and Anna's personalities, see Nancy Jones, interview; Bill Knapp, interviews, 21, 23 September 2010; Carolyn Doggett, interview by author, Allerton, Iowa, 5 October 2010; Reva Crooks, telephone conversation with author, 13 October 2010; and Wayne Hornocker, telephone conversation with author, 7 October 2010.

7. Birth certificate for William Clair Knapp, 18 July 1926, register number 163195, Michigan Department of Public Health, Bill Knapp Papers; Shotwell, *Knapps,* 11; and Bill Knapp, interview, 21 September 2010.

8. Jones, "Anna's Story," 15; and Nancy Jones, interview, 5 October 2010.

9. David Danbom, *Born in the Country: A History of Rural America* (Baltimore: The Johns Hopkins University Press, 2006), 163-87; and Dorothy Schwieder, *Iowa: The Middle Land* (Ames: Iowa State University Press, 1996), 256. Foreclosure is explained in District Court in and for Wayne County, Iowa, case number 11049, *Farmers National Bank vs. W. M. Knapp, Minnie Knapp, Floyd Knapp, and W. M. Knapp, Jr., W. M. Ockerman,* 11 August 1921. Sale of Knapp farm to Farmers National Bank for $4,440.04 is described in Sheriff's Deed, Record 2, p. 449, in the records of the Recorder of Wayne County, Iowa, and abstracted in Bill Knapp Papers.

10. Trustee's sale of land to Will Knapp is found in Deed Record 66, p. 440, in the records of the Recorder of Wayne County, Iowa, and abstracted in Bill Knapp Papers.

11. For Floyd Knapp's loan to his parents, see Mortgage Record 63, p. 23, in the records of the Recorder of Wayne County, Iowa, and abstracted in Bill Knapp Papers. For family story that all the children chipped in to save the farm, see Nancy Jones, telephone conversation with author, 11 November 2010.

12. Jones, "Anna's Story," 27.

13. For Floyd's lawsuit to recover the money, see District Court of the State of Iowa, case number 14095, *Floyd Knapp vs. William Knapp and Minnie Knapp,* 24 December 1930; for property being purchased by Union Central Life Insurance, see Sheriff's Deed Record 4, p. 8, in the records of the Recorder of Wayne County, Iowa; on Bill Knapp purchasing the farm and taking out the mortgage, see Deed Record 72, p. 344, and Mortgage Record 66, p. 262, in the records of the Recorder of Wayne County, Iowa, all abstracted in Bill Knapp Papers. On problems between the Knapp brothers, see Bill Knapp, interview, 26 October 2010.

14. Dwight Hoover, *A Good Day's Work: An Iowa Farm in the Great Depression* (Chicago: Ivan R. Dee, 2007), 3-4. Another memoir that offers poignant personal observations of life on a Depression-era Iowa farm is Mildred Kalish, *Little Heathens: Hard Times and High Spirits on an Iowa Farm During the Great Depression* (New York: Bantam Books, 2007).

15. Description of the Knapp family farm is taken from advertisement for the sale of Knapp farm assets, 1 September 1938, Nancy Jones Papers, private collection held by Nancy Jones, Allerton, Iowa [hereafter cited as Nancy Jones Papers]. See also Bill Knapp, interview, 26 October 2010. For the introduction of the tractor in southern Iowa, see *Des Moines Register*, 27 February 2011.

16. Irene Knapp, interview by author, Urbandale, Iowa, 29 September 2010.

17. Bill Knapp, interview, 23 September 2010.

18. Wayne Hornocker, telephone conversation; Reva Crooks, telephone conversation; and Delrein Levis, telephone conversation with author, 14 October 2010.

19. Merit badge in Knapp Family, Scrapbook, Nancy Jones Papers. On the creation of the Allerton scout troop and its facilities, see *Allerton News*, 23, 30, April, 28 May, 25 June, 9, 16 July, 10 September 1936; 7, 28 January 1937.

20. Nancy Jones, interview; Carolyn Doggett, interview; and Bill Knapp, interview, 23 September 2010.

21. Photograph of Knapp barn and story of gift of cow in Jones, "Anna's Story," 39, 34. Bill's quotation is from Bill Knapp, interview, 7 October 2010.

22. On sale of farm equipment, see advertisement for the sale of Knapp farm assets, 1 September 1938, Nancy Jones Papers; and Nancy Jones, telephone conversation.

23. Bill Knapp, interviews, 21, 23 September 2010; Bill Knapp II, correspondence with author, 23 November 2010; and Jones, "Anna's Story," 29.

24. Bill Knapp, interview, 7 October 2010. Bill's comment to Slim Richardson is from Shotwell, *Knapps*, 17.

25. For the importance of Saturday night shopping in rural America, see Dennis S. Nordin and Roy V. Scott, *From Prairie Farmer to Entrepreneur: The Transformation of Midwestern Agriculture* (Bloomington and Indianapolis: Indiana University Press, 2005), 96, and Frank Mitchell, "A People and a Place in Time: The Shared Story of an Iowa County and the American Nation," unpublished manuscript, chapter 16, 21-27. See also *Allerton News*, 21, 28 May 1936, and *Allerton, Iowa Centennial, 1874–1974* (Allerton, IA: privately printed, 1974), 61.

26. Bill Knapp, interview, 21 September 2010; and Irene Knapp, interview, 29 September 2010; "Allerton Eye: Highlights of the Class of 1944, 50th Anniversary Edition," (17 September 1994), 2, 11, Nancy Jones Papers; and Wayne Hornocker, telephone conversation.

27. "Allerton Eye Highlights," 2, Nancy Jones Papers.

28. Irene Knapp, interview, 29 September 2010; and Marjorie Moore, interview by author, West Des Moines, Iowa, 4 December 2010.

29. Bill Knapp, interview, 21 September 2010.

30. Ibid.; *Corydon Times-Republican,* 12 October 1944; and James Penney, telephone conversation with author, 26 September 2010.

31. Bill Knapp, interview, 21 September 2010; James Penney, telephone conversation; and Irene Knapp Notes, 10 November 2010, Irene Knapp Papers, private collection held by Irene Knapp, Urbandale, Iowa [hereafter cited as Irene Knapp Papers].

32. James Penney, telephone conversation, 30 September 2010.

33. Ibid.; and Bill Knapp, interview, 7 October 2010.

34. James Penney, telephone conversation, 26 September 2010; Catron Itinerary, James Penney Papers, private collection held by James Penney, Glencoe, Alabama [hereafter cited as Penney Papers]; Bill Knapp, interview, 21 September 2010; and *Des Moines Register,* 14 August 2010. Graham's letter to Bill's parents was printed on the front page of the *Corydon Times-Republican,* 21 June 1945.

35. For Bill's statements about the war, see *Des Moines Register,* 14 August 2010. The

Catron's movements can be followed in the Catron Itinerary, Penney Papers. For the story about shipping rifles and machine gun home, see Bill Knapp, interview, 23 September 2010; and Shotwell, *Knapps*, 16-17.

36. Information about the ship and the Bikini Atoll test from www.history.Navy.mil/photos/sh-usn/usnsh-c/apa71.htm, accessed on 23 September 2010. See also discharge papers for William Clair Knapp, 29 May 1946, Bill Knapp Papers.

37. Irene Knapp, interview, 29 September 2010.

38. Ibid.; Wayne Hornocker, telephone conversation; and Bill Knapp, interview, 26 October 2010.

39. Bill Knapp, interview, 21 September 2010; Irene Knapp Notes, Irene Knapp Papers; and Shotwell, *Knapps*, 22.

40. *Corydon Times-Republican,* 28 November 1946; Bill Knapp interviews, 21 September, 26 October 2010; Irene Knapp interviews, 29 September 2010 and 1 June 2011; and Marjorie Moore, interview.

Chapter 2

1. Bill Knapp, interview by author, West Des Moines, Iowa, 29 April 2011.

2. Ibid.; and Irene Knapp, interviews by author, Urbandale, Iowa, 29 September 2010 and 1 June 2011.

3. Bill Knapp, interview, 23 September 2010; Irene Knapp interview, 1 June 2011. Statement about being subject to someone else's agenda is taken from *Business Record*, Junior Achievement Section, 26 March-1 April 1990. The greasy spoon quotation is taken from *Des Moines Register,* 3 October 1983.

4. Irene Knapp Notes, 11 November 2010, Irene Knapp Papers, private collection held by Irene Knapp, Urbandale, Iowa [hereafter cited as Irene Knapp Papers]; Bill Knapp, interview, 23 September 2010; and Ruby Kint, telephone conversation with author, 18 December 2010.

5. Irene Knapp, interview, 29 September 2010.

6. Bill Knapp, interview, 21 September 2010; and Wayne Hornocker, telephone conversation with author, 7 October 2010.

7. Quotation is from Walt Shotwell, *The Knapps and Notable Others: From Less Than Nothing to More Than Plenty* (Des Moines, IA: Walt Shotwell, 2000), 23.

8. Irene Knapp Notes, Irene Knapp Papers. See *Polk's Des Moines City Directory, 1949* (Omaha: NE: R. L. Polk & Co., 1949), 410, 1146.

9. Shotwell, *Knapps*, 23-25; and Irene Knapp, interview, 29 September 2010.

10. Bill Knapp, interview, 5 January 2011; and Irene Knapp Notes, Irene Knapp Papers.

11. On Floyd Knapp, see Herman Miller, interview by author, Des Moines, Iowa, 13 April 2011 and Margaret Miller, interviewed by author, Des Moines, Iowa, 13 April 2011. See also *Des Moines Telephone Directory* (Des Moines, IA: Northwest Bell Telephone Company, 1950), 192, 193.

12. Lizabeth Cohen, *A Consumers' Republic: The Politics of Mass Consumption in Postwar America* (New York: Vintage Books, 2003), 122-23.

13. Bill Knapp, interview, 5 January 2011; and Irene Knapp, interview, 29 September 2010.

14. Irene Knapp, interviews, 29 September 2010, 1 June 2011.

15. Bill Knapp was listed as a salesman at Hollis & Company in *Polk's Des Moines City Directory, 1950* (Omaha, NE: R. L. Polk & Co., 1950), 453.

16. See Bill Knapp, interview 5 January 2011; and Paul Manley, interview by author, Des Moines, Iowa, 5 January 2011. First quotation is from *Business Record,* 3 May 1993; second quotation is from Michael Walker, "He's Sold on Des Moines," *Iowan* (Spring 1983): 32.

17. Irene Knapp, interview, 1 June 2011.

18. *Des Moines Tribune,* 11 April 1977. See also Shotwell, *Knapps,* 28.

19. See http://www.bls.gov/opub/uscs/1950.pdf, accessed on 31 March 2011. Put into today's dollars, Bill was making approximately $135, 000 to $145,000 per year.

20. Bill Knapp, interview, 5 January 2011; and Irene Knapp, interview, 29 September 2010.

21. On John R. Grubb, see, John R. Grubb, *My Life: A Memoir* (Des Moines, IA: Ink Publishing, 2000).

22. Paul Manley, interview; Bill Knapp, interview, 5 January 2011; and Virginia McKain, telephone conversation with author, 8 February 2011. The last Hollis & Company advertisement to run in the *Des Moines Sunday Register* was on 17 August 1952. Two weeks later, the first Iowa Realty advertisement appeared in the *Des Moines Sunday Register,* 31 August 1952.

23. Les Calvert, interview by author, West Des Moines, Iowa, 8 February 2011.

24. On Billy McKain and partnership, see Irene Knapp Notes, Irene Knapp Papers; Virginia McKain, telephone conversation; Lew Clarkson, interview by author, Johnston, Iowa, 10 February 2011; and Bill Knapp, interview, 5 January 2011. See also *Des Moines Sunday Register,* 1 June, 7 September 1952.

25. On naming the company Iowa Realty, see Bill Knapp II, correspondence with author, 23 November 2010; Bill Knapp, interview, 5 January 2011; Shotwell, *Knapps,* 27-28; and the *Des Moines Sunday Register,* 31 August 1952.

26. Bill Knapp, interview, 5 January 2011; Irene Knapp Notes, Irene Knapp Papers; Virginia McKain, telephone conversation; Paul Manley, interview; and Les Calvert, interview. The last time McKain's named was listed in an Iowa Realty ad was in the *Des Moines Sunday Register* 29 November 1953.

27. Paul Manley, interview.

Chapter 3

1. Story about Bill Knapp getting a client up early in the morning is taken from *Business Record*, Junior Achievement Section, 26 March-1 April 1990.

2. Paul Manley, interview by author, Des Moines, Iowa, 5 January 2011; Herman Miller, interview by author, Des Moines, Iowa, 13 April 2011; and Bill Knapp, interview by author, West Des Moines, Iowa, 5 January 2011. See also *Polk's Des Moines City Directory, 1954* (Omaha, NE: R. L. Polk & Co. 1954), 441, 543; and Iowa Realty classified advertisements in the *Des Moines Sunday Register,* 4, 11 January 1953.

3. Story of Bill meeting Grandquist and Grandquist's quotation are from Walt Shotwell, *The Knapps and Notable Others: From Less Than Nothing to More Than*

Plenty (Des Moines, IA: Walt Shotwell, 2000), 35-36. On Grandquist's personality, see Paul Manley, interview, and Herman Miller, interview. For Grandquist's first mention in an Iowa Realty advertisement, see *Des Moines Register*, 26 July 1953.

4. Calvert quotation is from Les Calvert, interview by author, West Des Moines, Iowa, 8 February 2011. See also Herman Miller, interview, and Paul Manley, interview.

5. On weekly real estate luncheon, see Les Calvert, interview. On record sales and selling a home a day, see Iowa Realty advertisement in *Des Moines Register*, 19 September 1954.

6. Roger Cleven, telephone conversation with author, 28 December 2010. On poker game and Bill's lack of interest in gambling, see Herman Miller, interview.

7. Paul Manley, interview. Quotation is from Lew Clarkson, interview by author, Johnston, Iowa, 10 February 2011.

8. Robert Underwood, interview by author, Johnston, Iowa, 28 June 2011.

9. The office was located at 3617 Beaver Avenue. Bill Knapp, interview, 29 April 2011. See *Des Moines Register,*,30 August 1953, for the first Iowa Realty advertisement using the new Beaver Avenue address. See also *Polk's Des Moines City Directory, 1954*, 391.

10. Jon C. Teaford, *The Twentieth-Century American City: Promise, Problem, and Reality* (Baltimore and London: The Johns Hopkins University Press, 1986), 98.

11. On temporary housing in Des Moines, see Orin Dahl, *Des Moines: Capital City* (Tulsa, OK: Continental Heritage, 1978), 135. For reconfiguring structures into housing, see Kenneth T. Jackson, *Crabgrass Frontier: The Suburbanization of the United States* (New York and Oxford: Oxford University Press), 232.

12. Gwendolyn Wright, *Building the Dream: A Social History of Housing in America* (New York: Pantheon Books, 1981), 240-41.

13. Teaford, *Twentieth Century City*, 84-85; Becky M. Nicolaides, *My Blue Heaven: Life and Politics in the Working-Class Suburbs of Los Angeles, 1920–1965* (Chicago and London: University of Chicago Press, 2002), 188-89.

14. For housing starts nationally through 1950, see Jackson, *Crabgrass Frontier*, 233. On housing starts nationally for 1960, see http://www.census.gov/const/www/newresconstindex.html, accessed on 27 April 2011. For housing starts in Des Moines, see U.S. Bureau of the Census, *Statistical Abstract of the United States, 1949*, 809; *Statistical Abstract of the United States, 1951*, 715; and *Statistical Abstract of the United States, 1961*, 758. For Des Moines and suburban population growth, see http://www.statelibraryofiowa.org/datacenter/archive/2011/02/citypop.pdf, accessed on 27 April 2011. From 1950 to 1960, Ankeny grew from 1,229 to 2,964; Urbandale, from 1,777 to 5,821; West Des Moines, from 5,615 to 11,949; and Windsor Heights, from 1,414 to 4,715.

15. Lew Clarkson, interview.

16. On contractors, homes built, and subdivisions, see Jackson, *Crabgrass Frontier*, 233. On Grubb, see John R. Grubb, *My Life: A Memoir* (Des Moines, IA: Ink Publishing, 2000), 59.

17. Iowa Realty advertisement, *Des Moines Register*, 19 September 1954.

18. Paul Manley, interview; Bill Knapp, interview, 29 April 2011; and Iowa Realty advertisement, *Des Moines Register*, 19 January 1958.

19. See Bill Knapp, interview, 29 April 2011; James Cooper, interview by author, Des

Moines, Iowa, 5 May 2011; Larry Cedarstrom, interview by author, West Des Moines, Iowa, 9 January 2012; Shotwell, *Knapps*, 31; and Grubb, *My Life*, 91.

20. For Cleven's quotation, see Roger Cleven, interview by author, Des Moines, Iowa, 3 May 2011. For general information about seeking financing, see Bill Knapp, interview, 29 April 2011. Quotation is from Iowa Realty advertisement, *Des Moines Register*, 19 January 1958. Bill's quotation is from Shotwell, *Knapps*, 33-34.

21. See *Des Moines Register* classified real estate advertisements, 3, 13, 20, 27 August, 7, 14, 21, 28 September 1952. Jester and Sons' innovative advertisement ran in the *Des Moines Register*, 15 March 1953; Iowa Realty's first ad with border ran the following Sunday, see *Des Moines Register,* 22 March 1953.

22. Other companies that began using borders around their ads included Ed Jones, Beaverdale, Jalbert Murphy, and Neal Adamson, see real estate classified advertisements, *Des Moines Register,* 2, 9, 16, 23, 30 January 1955. This initial Iowa Realty advertisement appeared in the *Des Moines Register*, 19 September 1954. Similar ads followed; see, for example, *Des Moines Register*, 19 January 1958 and 25 January 1959. For Iowa Realty advertisements focusing on the sale of homes in specific subdivisions, see *Des Moines Register,* 23 March, 20, 27 April 1958 and 23 August 1959.

23. Paul Manley, interview; Herman Miller, interview; and Bill Knapp, interview, 29 April 2011. Harold Knapp, Bob McCaughtry, Paul Manley, and Herman Miller were all listed with Central Realty in 1957, see *Polk's Des Moines City Directory, 1957* (Omaha, NE: R. L. Polk & Co., 1957), 183, 612, 689, 712, 754.

24. *Iowa Newsletter* 3 (November 1981): 1. This was a monthly, in-house Iowa Realty publication, Iowa Realty Papers, private collection held by Iowa Realty Company, West Des Moines, Iowa [hereafter cited as Iowa Realty Papers].

25. See *Iowa Newsletter* 3 (December 1981): 1; *Des Moines Register*, 3 October 1983, 12 October 1987; and *Polk's Des Moines City Directory, 1954* (Omaha, NE: R.L. Polk & Co., 1954), 441. For examples of Paul's part-time selling of real estate, see listings in Iowa Realty advertisements, *Des Moines Register*, 5 July, 2, 23, August, 6 September 1953.

26. *Des Moines Register*, 12 October 1987. See also *Des Moines Register*, 31 December 1972.

27. Bill Knapp, interviews, 29 April, 17 May 2011; Robert Timmins, interview by author, West Des Moines, Iowa, 5 May 2011; Irene Knapp, interviews by author, Urbandale, Iowa, 29 September 2010, 1 June 2011; Roger Cleven, telephone conversation; and Marilyn Dailey, telephone conversation with author, 30 December 2010.

28. See Iowa Realty advertisement in *Des Moines Register*, 19 January 1958. On division of labor, see Joe Bell, telephone conversation with author, 3 February 2011; Marilyn Dailey, telephone conversation; and Paul Manley, interview.

29. On Grandquist as a manager, see Roger Cleven, interview; James Cooper, interview; Paul Manley, interview; Herman Miller, interview; and Roy Riley, telephone conversation with author, 24 May 2011.

30. See Irene Knapp, interview, 1 June 2001; Iowa Realty advertisements, *Des Moines Register*, 19 January 1958 and 25 January 1959; and *Iowa Realty Home Buyers Guide*, undated company pamphlet, Iowa Realty Papers.

31. *Polk's Des Moines City Directory, 1957* (Omaha, NE: R. L. Polk & Co., 1957), 281; James Cooper, interview; James Cooper, telephone conversation with author, 18 May 2011; and Bill Knapp, interview, 17 May 2011.

32. *Des Moines Register*, 3 April 1957, 23 March 1958.

33. See *Des Moines Register*, 31 August 1958; and Iowa Realty advertisement in *Des Moines Register*, 25 January 1959. Quotation is from Roger Cleven, interview. On automobiles owned, see Shotwell, *Knapps*, 35; Paul Manley, interview; and Grubb, *My Life*, 90.

34. Bill Knapp, interview, 5 January 2011; Grubb, *My Life,* 90; and Shotwell, *Knapps*, 33. On the strike at General Motors, see *New York Times*, 7 October 1958.

35. For Grubb borrowing money to prepare Zelda Acres for development and records of the first home sales, see mortgage, John R. Grubb to Des Moines Savings and Loan, 30 December 1957, Book 3012, p. 285, and for first homes sold in subdivision, see Warranty Deeds, John R. Grubb to Des Moines Savings and Loan, 7 April 1958, Book 3025, pp. 383, 385, 387, and 389, records of the Polk County Recorder, Des Moines, Iowa, from the abstract records of Iowa Title Company, West Des Moines, Iowa. See James Cooper, interview; Roger Cleven, interview; and Roy Riley, telephone conversation. See also *Des Moines Register*, 25 May, 29 June 1958; Grubb, *My Life*, 61-62, 87, 89; and John R. Grubb Scrapbook, John W. Grubb Papers, private collection held by John W. Grubb, Urbandale, Iowa [hereafter cited as Grubb Papers].

36. See *Des Moines Register*, 22 February, 2, 23 August 1959; and Grubb Scrapbook, Grubb Papers.

37. On issue of whether or not Iowa Realty was the city's largest real estate firm by 1959, see Roy Riley, telephone conversation; and Joseph Kirk, Sr., interview by author, Des Moines, Iowa, 5 April 2011. See *Des Moines Register,* 4, 11, 18, 25 January 1953; 3, 10, 17, 24, 31 January 1954; 2, 9, 16, 23, 30 January 1955; 1, 8, 15, 22, 29 January 1956; 6, 13, 20, 27 January 1957; 5, 12, 19, 26 January 1958; 4, 11, 18, 25 January 1959; and 3, 10, 17, 24, 31 January 1960.

38. On Bill's initial purchase of Stuart Hills, see Raymond Stuart, Olive S. Olmstead, and Mark Stuart to Bill and Irene Knapp, 28 January 1959, Book 3114, p. 467; and Stuarts et al. to Bill and Irene Knapp, release of mortgage, 12 June 1959, Book 3156, p. 419, in the records of the Polk County Recorder, and from abstract records at Iowa Title Company. On Allied Development, see articles of incorporation, 18 July 1959; $50,000 mortgage note on Stuart Hills, 27 August 1959; and minutes of the first meeting of the board of directors of Allied Development, 10 September 1959, Knapp Properties Papers, private collection held by Knapp Properties, West Des Moines, Iowa. On Merle Hay Plaza's opening, see *Des Moines Register,* 16, 17 August 1959.

39. Paul Manley, interview; and Bill Knapp, interview, 5 January 2011. Bill Knapp and Kenny Grandquist purchased twenty-three lots from Benton: three lots on Bryn Mawr Drive and twenty lots along Benton Avenue in March of 1960, see Benton Development to Bill Knapp and Kenny Grandquist, 1 March 1960, Book 3228, pp. 346, 347, in the records of the Polk County Recorder. They sold the three Bryn Mawr lots to Jerry Grubb, John Grubb's brother and a builder as well, in April, and the rest of the lots to John Grubb in May 1960, see Bill Knapp to Jerry Grubb, 27 April 1960, Book 3231, p. 522; and Bill Knapp to John Grubb, 9 May 1960, Book 3233, p. 132, in the records of the Polk County Recorder, Des Moines, Iowa, and from abstract records at Iowa Title Company.

40. See Joseph Kirk, Sr., interview; Robert Timmins, interview; and Bill Knapp, interview, 17 May 2011.

Chapter 4

1. See David Halberstam, *The Fifties* (New York: Fawcett Columbine, 1993), 587. In addition to Halberstam, there are a number of fine works on American life and culture during the 1950s, including John Diggins, *The Proud Decades: America in War and Peace, 1941–1960* (New York and London: W. W. Norton & Company, 1988); J. Ronald Oakley, *God's Country: America in the Fifties* (New York: Dembner Books, 1986); and William O'Neill, *American High: The Years of Confidence* (New York: Free Press, 1986). Stephanie Coontz, *The Way We Never Were: American Families and the Nostalgia Trap* (New York: Basic Books, 2000), debunks many myths about the period as a golden age for American families. See also the memoirs, Doris Kearns Goodwin, *Wait Till Next Year* (New York: Simon & Schuster, 1997) and Bill Bryson, *The Life and Times of the Thunderbolt Kid* (New York: Broadway Books, 2006), which is a humorous account of growing up in Des Moines in the 1950s and 1960s.

2. U.S. Bureau of the Census, *Statistical Abstract of the United States, 1965* (Washington, D.C., 1965), 326, 344.

3. Population numbers from *Statistical Abstract, 1965,* 9. On church and synagogue membership and participation in civic organizations during the 1950s and early 1960s, see Robert Putnam, *Bowling Alone: The Collapse and Revival of American Community* (New York: Simon and Schuster, 2001).

4. Cheever quoted in McNeill, *American High*, 23. For statement by Diggins and percentage of Americans living in suburbia, see Diggins, *Proud Decades*, 183.

5. Irene Knapp, interview by author, Urbandale, Iowa, 1 June 2011.

6. Irene Knapp, telephone conversation with author, 25 July 2011.

7. Bill Knapp, interview by author, West Des Moines, Iowa, 16 June 2011; Irene Knapp, interview, 29 September 2010; Virginia Haviland, interview by author, Urbandale, Iowa, 29 September 2010; and Cindy Grandquist, interview by author, West Des Moines, Iowa, 17 June 2011. On number of television sets in the United States, see Goodwin, *Wait Till Next Year*, 121.

8. Irene Knapp, interview, 29 September 2010; and Haviland, interview, 29 September 2010.

9. John W. Grubb, interview by author, Urbandale, Iowa, 23 June 2011; Cindy Grandquist, interview; Irene Knapp, interview, 1 June 2011; and Bill Knapp, interview, 16 June 2011.

10. Irene Knapp, interview, 29 September 2010; and Beatrice Turner, interview by author, Des Moines, Iowa, 30 September 2010.

11. Marilyn Dailey, telephone conversation with author, 6 July 2011; and Irene Knapp, telephone conversation with author, 6 July 2011.

12. Irene Knapp, interview, 1 June 2011; and Bill Knapp, interview, 16 June 2011.

13. Beatrice Turner, interview; Virginia Haviland, interview, 7 September 2011; and Irene Knapp, interview, 29 September 2010. Critchett Piano Company was located at 1409 Forest Avenue, north and slightly west of downtown Des Moines, see *Polk's Des Moines City Directory, 1962* (Kansas City, MO: R. L. Polk & Co., 1962), 175. For Evelynne Wheaton and Beaverdale Dance School, see *Polk's Des Moines City Directory, 1964*, 895.

14. Beatrice Turner, interview; Virginia Haviland, interview, 7 September 2011; and Irene Knapp, interview, 29 September 2010.

15. Herman Miller, interview by author, Des Moines, Iowa, 13 April 2011; Margaret Miller, interview by author, Des Moines, Iowa, 13 April 2011; and Irene Knapp, interview, 1 June 2011. Highland Park Presbyterian Church is located north of downtown Des Moines on Euclid Avenue. St. Andrews Evangelical United Brethren Church, located north and west of downtown Des Moines on Thirty-first and Iola Avenue, became St. Andrews United Methodist Church when the two denominations merged in 1968. Six years later, the congregation moved to West Des Moines, starting Valley United Methodist Church on Ashworth Road.

16. Bill Knapp, interview, 21 September 2010; Irene Knapp, interview, 29 September 2010; and Virginia Haviland interview, 29 September 2010.

17. Bill Knapp, interview, 16 June 2011; Roger Cleven, interview by author, Des Moines, Iowa, 3 May 2011; and Cindy Grandquist, interview.

18. On Bill's interest in exercise, see Bill Knapp, interview, 16 June 2011; Irene Knapp interview, 2 June 2011; and *Des Moines Register,* 12 October 1987, 30 March 1990. For Grandquist story, see *Des Moines Register*, 3 October 1983. On basement workout room, see Roger Cleven, interview; James Cooper, interview by author, Des Moines, Iowa, 5 May 2011; Cindy Grandquist, interview; John W. Grubb, interview; and Roy Riley, telephone conversation with author, 24 May 2011.

19. See Ginger Kuhl-Davis, "Bill Knapp Gets It Done," *Des Moines*, March 1986, 16.

20. Bill Knapp, interview, 16 June 2011; and Irene Knapp, telephone conversation with author, 25 July 2011.

21. Bill Knapp, interview, 29 April 2011; John W. Grubb, interview; and Cindy Grandquist, interview.

22. Ibid.; and John R. Grubb, *My Life: A Memoir* (Des Moines, IA: Ink Publishing, 2000), 93-94.

23. Allan Brandt, *The Cigarette Century: The Rise, Fall, and Deadly Persistence of the Product that Defined America* (New York: Basic Books, 2007), 91, 131-57, 160-61.

24. Nancy Jones, "Anna's Story" (privately printed manuscript, 1988), 47; and Carolyn Doggett telephone conversation with author, 28 July 2011.

25. Jones, "Anna's Story," 47.

26. Bill Knapp, interview, 16 June 2011.

27. Ibid.

28. Bill Knapp, interview, 18 July 2011.

29. Ibid.; and Cindy Grandquist, interview; John W. Grubb, interview; and Robert Underwood, interview by author, Johnston, Iowa, 28 June 2011. See also Putnam, *Bowling Alone,* 440-45.

30. Irene Knapp, telephone conversation, 25 July 2011; and Robert Underwood, telephone conversation with author, 4 August 2011.

31. *Des Moines Tribune*, 10 October 1969; and Bill Knapp II, correspondence with author, 23 November 2010.

32. Walt Shotwell, *The Knapps and Notable Others: From Less Than Nothing to More Than Plenty* (Des Moines, IA: Walt Shotwell, 2000), 48-9. For story about Urbandale City Council and quote, see *Des Moines Tribune*, 11 April 1977. Politicians were frequent visitors at Iowa Realty's office. Former Iowa Realty agent Jim Cooper remembered local politicians "being in and out of the Beaver [Avenue] office all the time" to talk with Bill Knapp, see James Cooper, interview.

33. Michael Walker, "He's Sold on Des Moines," *Iowan* (Spring 1983): 32.

34. For Hughes-Knapp meeting, see Lex Hawkins, telephone conversation with author, 22 July 2011; for Bill's quote about Hughes, see *Des Moines Tribune*, 11 April 1977; for donation, see Shotwell, *Knapps,* 89; and for "must-see" reference, see *Des Moines Register*, 14 January 1990. For more on Hughes, see Harold Hughes and Dick Schneider, *The Man from Ida Grove: A Senator's Personal Story* (Lincoln, VA: Chosen Books, 1979).

35. Susan Rugh, *Are We There Yet? The Golden Age of American Family Vacations* (Lawrence: University of Kansas Press, 2008), 3.

36. Virginia Haviland, interview, 29 September 2010.

37. Bill Knapp, interview, 16 June 2011.

38. Virginia Haviland, interview, 7 September 2011.

39. Cindy Grandquist, interview; John W. Grubb, interview; Bill Knapp II, interview by author, West Des Moines, Iowa, 18 July 2011; Irene Knapp, interview, 1 June 2011; and Bill Knapp, interview, 29 April 2011.

40. Rugh, *Are We There Yet?,* 12-13.

41. Irene Knapp Notes, 11 November 2010, Irene Knapp Papers, private collection held by Irene Knapp, Urbandale, Iowa; Cindy Grandquist, interview; and John W. Grubb, interview.

42. Roger Cleven, interview.

43. *Des Moines Register,* 12 October 1987.

Chapter 5

1. Jack Wahlig, interview by author, Clive, Iowa, 30 August 2011.

2. Quotation is from Gene Stanbrough, interview by author, Clive, Iowa, 20 September 2011. On Bill giving stock to Grandquist and Paul, see Bill Knapp, interview by author, West Des Moines, Iowa, 8 December 2011; and Bill Knapp II, interview by author, West Des Moines, Iowa, 8 December 2011.

3. Marilyn Dailey, telephone conversation with author, 13 September 2011.

4. Connie Wimer, interview by author, Des Moines, Iowa, 31 August 2011; Roy Riley, telephone conversation with author, 2 September 2011; Bill Knapp, interview, 16 June 2011; and Richard Ramsay, telephone conversation with author, 21 February, 2012. For 1963 reference to law firm, see *Polk's Des Moines City Directory, 1963* (Kansas City, MO: R. L. Polk and Company, 1963), 760.

5. Jack Wahlig, interview; Robert Timmins, interview by author, West Des Moines, Iowa, 5 May 2011; Bill Knapp, interview, 1 August 2011; and Dailey, telephone conversation, 13 September 2011.

6. Story of Bill hiring George Benson is from Walt Shotwell, *The Knapps and Notable Others: From Less Than Nothing to More Than Plenty* (Des Moines, IA: Walt Shotwell, 2000), 32. Quotation about Iowa Realty's supply of apartments is from undated *Iowa Realty Home Buyers Guide,* ca. 1962–1964, Iowa Realty Papers, private collection held by Iowa Realty Company, West Des Moines, Iowa [hereafter cited as Iowa Realty Papers].

7. Transcript of Bill Knapp speech at the Celebrity Roast for Sid Bradley and Pat Greene, Des Moines, Iowa, 17 January 1992, "Iowa Realty Volume Two," Scrapbook,

Iowa Realty Papers. On the Des Moines Industrial Bureau, see *Des Moines Tribune*, 9 March 1982.

8. Gene Stanbrough, interview; *Des Moines Register*, 8 August 1994; and *Polk's Des Moines City Directory, 1957* (Kansas City, MO: R. L. Polk and Company, 1957), 55, 1041.

9. Gene Stanbrough, interview; *Polk's Des Moines City Directory, 1959*, 961; and *Polk's Des Moines City Directory, 1961*, 1264.

10. Gene Stanbrough, interview. For the first mention of "The Home Show" in a local newspaper, see *Des Moines Register*, 12 March 1961.

11. *Des Moines Register*, 3 January 1965; 2 January 1966; 13 August 1967; and 17 December 2010.

12. James Cooper, interview by author, Des Moines, Iowa, 5 May 2011.

13. Marilyn Dailey, telephone conversation, 11 October 2011; Bill Knapp, interview, 1 August 2011; and Roger Cleven, interview by author, Des Moines, Iowa, 3 May 2011. More on Dee Sullivan can be found in *Des Moines Register*, 27 June 1984. Eleanor Leachman is first listed as working at Iowa Realty in January 1967, see *Des Moines Register*, 8 January 1967. For Iowa Realty's million-dollar producers in 1972, see *Real Estate in Des Moines*, an Iowa Realty brochure, 1973, Bill Knapp Papers, private collection held by Bill Knapp, West Des Moines, Iowa [hereafter cited as Bill Knapp Papers].

14. Gene Stanbrough, interview. See also *Des Moines Register*, 16 October 1967, 7 April, 11 September 1968, and 8 August 1994.

15. For fire, see *Des Moines Register*, 25 June 1967; for temporary office space, see *Des Moines Register*, 9 July 1967; and for move into new building, see *Des Moines Register*, 15, 17 August 1967. For more on the fire and move, see Marilyn Dailey, telephone conversation, 11 October 2011; Bill Knapp, interview, 14 October 2011; and Bill Knapp II, interview, 14 October 2011.

16. Iowa Realty's new computer program is described in the *Des Moines Register*, 29 October 1967. Quotations are from Iowa Realty classified advertisement, *Des Moines Register*, 24 November, 1967. For the service being available in West Des Moines, see Iowa Realty classified advertisement, *Des Moines Register*, 11 September 1968. Neal Adamson, a rival real estate firm in Des Moines, began offering a similar service at roughly the same time.

17. Information on new Iowa Realty offices from *Polk's Des Moines City Directory, 1972*, 414, and *Polk's Des Moines City Directory, 1973*, 415. See also *Real Estate in Des Moines*, an Iowa Realty brochure, 1973, Bill Knapp Papers. The 1958 sales figures from Iowa Realty advertisement, *Des Moines Register*, 25 January 1959; 1970 sales figures from Iowa Realty Fact Sheet, 1996, "Iowa Realty Volume Two," Scrapbook, Iowa Realty Papers.

18. Gene Stanbrough, interview.

19. Hy-Vee moved its corporate offices to West Des Moines in April 1995. Harold "Mac" McEachern, telephone conversation with author, 17 October 2011; Bill Knapp, interview, 14 October 2011; Ron Pearson, interview by author, West Des Moines, Iowa, 10 October 2011; *Des Moines Register*, 2 January 1961; and Kathleen Gilbert, *The History of Hy-Vee: 75 Years of "A Helpful Smile"* (Phoenix, AZ: Heritage Publishers, Inc., 2004), 30, 112-13, 118, 121, 123.

20. On profitability of Hy-Vee leases, see Ron Pearson, interview, and Bill Knapp, interview, 14 October 2011.

21. On the Meredith farm see R. M. Gow, *The Jersey: An Outline of Her History During Two Centuries—1734–1935* (New York: American Jersey Cattle Club, 1936), 539, and http://www.stmarysdsm.org/Parish_History.html, accessed on 18 October 2011. More on E. T. Meredith can be found in Peter Lewis Peterson, "A Publisher in Politics: Edwin T. Meredith, Progressive Reform, and the Democratic Party, 1912–1928," (PhD dissertation, University of Iowa, 1971).

22. For Grubb's quotation, see John R. Grubb, *My Life: A Memoir* (Des Moines, IA: Ink Publishing, 2000), 92. On sale of Meredith farm, see *Des Moines Register*, 11 July 1963. Meredith gave fifty acres of the original farm to the Des Moines Community School District in 1957. The district built Herbert Hoover High School and Meredith Junior High School on this land. For skepticism about Bill and Grubb's purchase, see *Des Moines Tribune,* 11 April 1977.

23. Grubb, *My Life,* 92; Bill Knapp, interviews, 29 April, 14 October 2011; Bill Knapp II, interview, 8 December 2011; and John W. Grubb, interview by author, Urbandale, Iowa, 23 June 2011.

24. John W. Grubb, interview.

25. On Interstate 35 and Interstate 80, see William H. Thompson, *Transportation in Iowa: A Historical Summary* (Ames: Iowa Department of Transportation, 1989), 245. On significance of interstates for area and particular interchange, see Bill Knapp, interviews, 1 August, 14 October 2011, and Philip Orbanes, *The Game Makers: The Story of Parker Brothers from Tiddledy Winks to Trivial Pursuit* (Boston: Harvard Business School Press, 2004), 138-139.

26. Iowa Realty offer to buy 77.7 acres from Dalo, Inc., 15 October 1962; Iowa Realty offer to buy 200 acres from executors of estate of Edith Anderson Noble, 20 December 1967; Interstate Acres plat map, 28 February 1967; and map of Interstate Acres, marked "Exhibit A," Bill Knapp offer to buy and from Iowa Realty, 1 June 1983, in Interstate Acres file, Bill Knapp Papers. See also Bill Knapp II, interview, 14 October 2011.

27. *Des Moines Tribune*, 10 May 1966, 24 April 1969; *Des Moines Register*, 19 October 1967. See also, *Iowa Newsletter* 2 (November 1980): 1. This was an internal publication of Iowa Realty, Iowa Realty Papers.

28. Daryl Neumann, interview by author, West Des Moines, Iowa, 9 August 2011; Bill Knapp II, correspondence with author, 11 October 2011; William Stauffer, interview by author, Urbandale, Iowa, 5 October 2011; Jack MacAllister, telephone conversation with author, 15 October 2011; and Paul Cremer to William Knapp, 13 February 1976, Bill Knapp Papers.

29. *Des Moines Tribune*, 15 February 1970; Bill Knapp, interview, 14 October 2011; Bill Knapp II, interview, 14 October 2011; and David Ramsey, telephone conversation with author, 19 October 2011.

30. Bill Knapp, interview, 1 August 2011; and *Des Moines Tribune,* 18 March 1972.

31. Shotwell, *Knapps,* 115-16. Quotation is from Bill Knapp, interview, 14 October 2011.

32. Michael Walker, "He's Sold on Des Moines," *Iowan* (Spring 1983): 32.

33. Hughes's statement about "letting his hair down" is from *Des Moines Tribune,* 11 April 1977; and Bill Knapp's quote is from Shotwell, *Knapps,* 91. For Hughes's interest in hunting and fishing, see James C. Larew, *A Party Reborn: The Democrats of Iowa, 1950–1974* (Iowa City: Iowa State Historical Department, 1980), 82.

34. Bill Knapp, interview, 21 September 2010.

35. Bill Knapp's quotation is from Shotwell, *Knapps*, 93.

36. Grubb, *My Life*, 118-19.

37. On the Oakridge neighborhood, see http://www.oakridgeneighborhood.org/main. htm, accessed on 6 November 2011, and *Des Moines Register*, 6 November 2011. Joe Wall's quotation is from Hughes obituary, *New York Times*, 25 October 1996. On Robert Kennedy recruiting Hughes to run for the Senate, see Harold Hughes and Dick Schneider, *Harold E. Hughes: The Man from Ida Grove: A Senator's Personal Story* (Lincoln, VA: Chosen Books, 1979), 237-240. For Bill Knapp's statement, see Bill Knapp, interview, 14 October 2011.

38. See Bill Knapp, interview, 8 December 2011; Bill Knapp II, interview 14 October 2011; and Joe Kirk, Sr., interview by author, Windsor Heights, Iowa, 5 April 2011; Hughes's quotation is from *Des Moines Tribune*, 11 April 1977. Ed Campbell's views and idea of rumors are from Shotwell, *Knapps*, 90. Bill bought land at the Bondurant interchange in July 1968; Interstate 80 had been built through the area by November 1960. His purchase of land by an Iowa City interchange took place in October 1967, four years after the highway ran through the area. His acquisition of land at Kamrar and Randall off of I-35 took place in1968 and 1970, respectively, while the highway through the area was opened in December 1967. He also bought land near the Marne I-80 interchange in September 1972, but the highway was opened through the area in December 1963. The only property he bought ahead of the opening of a stretch of road was at the I-35 Roland interchange; he purchased it in September 1967 and that stretch of highway was completed three months later in December 1967, see Iowa Completion Status of Interstate System as of 1 January 1982, Iowa Department of Transportation website, www.iowadot.gov/50thpages/pdf/interstatemap.pdf, accessed on 10 October 2011; and Paul Cremer to William Knapp, 13 February 1976, Bill Knapp Papers.

39. *Des Moines Register*, 14 December 1969. For Bill's quotation about Hughes and his establishing Hughes for President office in Des Moines, see Bill Knapp, interview, 14 October 2011. On Hughes setting up a Washington, D.C., office, see Hughes and Schneider, *Harold E. Hughes*, 291.

40. Connie Wimer, interview; and Bill Knapp, interviews, 16 June, 14 October 2011.

41. Hughes and Schneider, *Harold E. Hughes*, 298; Bill Knapp, interview, 14 October 2011; and David Miller, interview by author, West Des Moines, Iowa, 24 October 2011. On Bill's involvement in the Hughes for President effort, see William Knapp to Diane Roupe, 30 March 1971, "Charitable Contributions, etc.," Scrapbook, Bill Knapp II Papers, private collection held by Bill Knapp II, West Des Moines, Iowa.

42. Bill Knapp's first quotation is from Shotwell, *Knapps*, 93. For Hughes quotation and Bill's second quotation, see Bill Knapp, interview, 14 October 2011.

43. On Hughes's affiliation with the Spiritual Frontiers Fellowship, see Mary Lynn Kolz, "Hughes Family Finds a 'Most Rewarding' Life in a Woodsy Suburb of the National Capital," *Picture* magazine, *Des Moines Sunday Register*, 21 June 1970, 5. On communicating with his dead brother and quotation, see *New York Times*, July 1971. For *Register* interview, see *Des Moines Register,* 11 July 1971. On Hughes's pulling out of race for the presidential nomination, see *New York Times*, 15, 16 July 1971; and *Des Moines Register,* 15 July 1971, for story and Frank Miller editorial cartoon about Hughes's withdrawing from race. Bill's ball game quote is from Bill Knapp, interview, 14 October 2011; and Bill's quote about Hughes not living up to potential is from Shotwell, *Knapps*, 93. For Hughes's decision not to seek another Senate term, see Hughes and Schneider, *Harold E. Hughes*, 313-20; and for his activities after leaving the Senate, see obituary, the *New York Times*, 25 October 1996.

44. Jack Wahlig, interview; Bill Knapp, interview, 1 August 2011; John Leachman interview by author, Des Moines, Iowa, 27 October 2011; and Breakfast Club roster, 1962–1997, John Leachman Papers, private collection held by John Leachman, Des Moines, Iowa [hereafter cited as Leachman Papers].

45. David Miller, interview; and *Des Moines Register*, 8 January, 3 October 1983.

46. John Leachman, interview; handwritten notes of parties in Breakfast Club files, Leachman Papers.

47. Ibid.; David Miller, interview; and Bill Knapp, interview, 14 October 2011.

48. Virginia Haviland, interview by author, West Des Moines, Iowa, 7 September 2011.

49. On decision to install a tennis court and Roger taking up tennis, see *Des Moines Tribune,* 22 April 1975, 29 April 1976; Irene Knapp, interview by author, Urbandale, Iowa, 1 June 2011; and Bill Knapp, interview, 18 July 2011. Stokstad quotation is from Arden Stokstad, telephone conversation with author, 7 September 2011. Tennis match story and Ginny Knapp's quotation are from Virginia Haviland, interview.

50. Arden Stokstad, telephone conversation; "Knapp Returns Home to Head Tennis Program," unmarked clipping, "Roger Knapp," Scrapbook, Virginia Haviland Papers, private collection held by Virginia Haviland, West Des Moines, Iowa [hereafter cited as Haviland Papers].

51. Jean Stauffer, interview by author, Urbandale, Iowa, 5 October 2011; Irene Knapp, interview, 1 June 2011; and unmarked *Des Moines Register* clipping, "Roger Knapp," Scrapbook, Haviland Papers.

52. On the Mandarin for lunch, see Daryl Neumann, interview.

53. Ibid.; for John R. Grubb's quote, see Shotwell, *Knapps*, 39.

54. Story and Paul Knapp's quotation are from Shotwell, *Knapps*, 39.

55. Bill Knapp, interviews, 1 August, 14 October 2011. For quotation and announcement of realignment, see *Des Moines Register*, 31 December 1972.

Chapter 6

1. James Hubbell III quotation is from *Des Moines Register*, 3 October 1983; and Fred Weitz quotation is from Fred Weitz, interview by author, Des Moines, Iowa, 6 December 2011. For statement about Bill being the godfather of downtown housing, see *Des Moines Register,* 1 September 1985.

2. Quotation is from Walt Shotwell, *The Knapps and Notable Others: From Less Than Nothing to More Than Plenty* (Des Moines, IA: Walt Shotwell, 2000), 40. For more on Grandquist's reaction, see Cindy Grandquist, interview by author, West Des Moines, Iowa, 17 June 2011; Larry Cedarstrom, interview by author, West Des Moines, Iowa, 9 January 2012; and Bill Knapp, interview by author, West Des Moines, Iowa, 22 November 2011.

3. Bill Knapp, interview, 22 November 2011.

4. For comparisons of Kenny Grandquist and Paul Knapp, see Jack McWilliams, interview by author, Des Moines, Iowa, 28 December 2011; Tim Meline, interview by author, West Des Moines, Iowa, 22 December 2011; and Gene Stanbrough, interview by author, Clive, Iowa, 20 September 2011. Quotation is from Daryl Neumann, interview by author, West Des Moines, Iowa, 9 August 2011.

5. On expansion, see Jack McWilliams, interview; *Real Estate in Des Moines*, Iowa

Realty brochures, 1973 and 1976, Bill Knapp Papers, private collection held by
Bill Knapp, West Des Moines, Iowa [hereafter cited as Bill Knapp Papers]; and
unmarked clippings of Iowa Realty classified advertisements, 1976 and 1977, *Des
Moines Register,* in "Newspaper Clippings," Scrapbook, Bill Knapp Papers.

6. See unmarked clippings of Iowa Realty classified advertisements, 1979 and 1980,
Des Moines Register, in "Newspaper Clippings," Scrapbook, Bill Knapp Papers.
Sales figures and number of agents from Iowa Realty Fact Sheet, 1996, "Iowa Realty
Volume Two," Scrapbook, Iowa Realty Papers, private collection held by Iowa
Realty, West Des Moines, Iowa [hereafter cited as Iowa Realty Papers].

7. Tim Meline, interview. For quotation and more on Meline and training program,
see *Des Moines Register,* 13 November 1989.

8. Ibid.

9. Jack McWilliams, interview; Bill Knapp II, interview by author, West Des Moines,
Iowa, 8 December 2011; Gene Stanbrough, interview; Stanbrough classified
advertisement, *Des Moines Register,* 5 March 1978; *Des Moines Tribune,* 29 January
1979; and unmarked 1980 *Des Moines Register* clipping, "Newspaper Clippings,"
Scrapbook, Bill Knapp Papers.

10. Jack McWilliams, interview; and "Iowa Realty/Knapp's Milestones and Interesting
Events, 1979 through 1989," unpublished typescript, Bill Knapp Papers.

11. Ibid. See also *Iowa Newsletter* 2 (March 1980): 1. This was an in-house publication
of Iowa Realty, Iowa Realty Papers. New franchises added included offices in Sac
City, Storm Lake, Carroll, Webster City, and Mason City. In addition, Iowa Realty
branch offices in Perry and Boone were purchased by agents and became franchises,
see *Iowa Newsletter* 2 (April 1980): 1; 2 (July 1980): 3; 2 (August 1980): 3; and 2
(September 1980): 2.

12. Mike Knapp, interview by author, West Des Moines, Iowa, 31 December 2010.

13. Bill Knapp II, interview, 16 December 2010; Bonnie Campbell, interview by author,
Des Moines, Iowa, 27 December 2011; and Shotwell, *Knapps,* 64. On name change,
see *Des Moines Tribune,* 15 November 1978.

14. *Des Moines Tribune,* 2 January 1977; Cindy Grandquist, interview; Bill Knapp,
interview, 22 November 2011; Bill Knapp II, interview, 8 December 2011; and Larry
Cedarstrom, interview.

15. Universal Realty classified advertisement, *Des Moines Register,* 9 October 1977;
and unmarked Universal Realty advertisement, *Des Moines Register,* in Larry
Cedarstrom Scrapbook, Larry Cedarstrom Papers, private collection held by Larry
Cedarstrom, West Des Moines, Iowa. 16 *Des Moines Tribune,* 15 May 1978; Larry
Cedarstrom, interview; and Shotwell, *Knapps,* 40.

17. Jack Wahlig quotation is recounted by Bill Knapp II in Bill Knapp II, interview,
8 December 2011. For settlement, see Memorandum of Agreement between
Grandquist and Iowa Realty, 1 February 1979, Bill Knapp Papers.

18. *Des Moines Register,* 27 April 1999; Linda Grandquist, interview by author, West
Des Moines, Iowa, 11 January 2012; Bill Knapp, interview, 8 December 2011; and
Polk's Des Moines City Directory, 1980 (Kansas City, MO: R. L. Polk and Co. 1980),
97. On the sale of Ken Grandquist and Associates, see *Des Moines Register,* 24
January 1985.

19. Bill Knapp II, interview, 8 December 2011; *Des Moines Tribune,* 11 April 1977; and
Bill Knapp, interview, 8 December 2011.

20. Ibid.; see also *Des Moines Tribune,* 6 March 1972; and *Des Moines Register,* 4 June 1976.

21. Bill Knapp II, interview, 8 December 2011. See also *Polk's Des Moines City Directory, 1971* (Kansas City, MO: R. L. Polk and Co. 1971), 574. Bill eventually sold the remainder of his Fort Des Moines land (which included frontage on Army Post Road) in 1985 and 1986 for retail development; see "Iowa Realty/Knapp's Milestones," Bill Knapp Papers.

22. Mark Haviland, Bill's son-in law, was hired to oversee the growing property management division. For more on Iowa Realty's apartments, see *Iowa Newsletter* 2 (December 1980): 2; and Mark Haviland, telephone conversation with author, 16 January 2012. For units converted to condominiums, see "Iowa Realty/Knapp's Milestones," Bill Knapp Papers.

23. Ron Pearson, interview by author, West Des Moines, Iowa, 10 October 2011; Bill Knapp II, interview, 8 December 2011; Bill Knapp, interview, 8 December 2011; and "Iowa Realty/Knapp Milestones," Bill Knapp Papers.

24. Quotation is from *Des Moines Tribune,* 4 September 1980. See also *Des Moines Tribune,* 5 December 1980; and *Iowa Newsletter* 11 (November 1980): 1.

25. Linda Birocci, Iowa Title Company, West Des Moines, Iowa, correspondence with author, 28 December 2011.

26. On John Ruan, see William Friedricks, *In for the Long Haul: The Life of John Ruan* (Ames: Iowa State Press, 2003). On Rosenfield bringing the two together, see Bill Knapp, interview, 22 November 2011.

27. Ruan quotation is from Friedricks, *In for Long Haul,* 132; on Greater Des Moines Committee, see "Corporate Overview," unpublished typescript, Greater Des Moines Partnership Papers, private collection held Greater Des Moines Partnership, Des Moines Iowa. On appointing Bill to Bankers Trust and GDMC, see *Des Moines Register,* 14 January 1990.

28. Bill's quotation is from *Des Moines Register,* 1 September 1985. Dave Elbert refers to "Dead Moines" nickname in *Des Moines Register,* 27 November 2011. For information on downtown's early redevelopment, see Orin Dahl, *Des Moines: Capital City* (Tulsa, OK: Continental Heritage, Inc., 1978), 182-83; and Robert Houser, "Some Significant Dates in History of Des Moines," Robert Houser Papers, private collection held by author, West Des Moines, Iowa [hereafter cited as Houser Papers].

29. Friedricks, *In for Long Haul,* 132-33.

30. Ibid., 133; William Friedricks, *Covering Iowa: The History of the Des Moines Register and Tribune Company, 1849–1985* (Ames: Iowa State University Press, 2000), 193-94; and *Des Moines Register,* 11 November 1975.

31. Bill Knapp quoted in *Des Moines Register,* 16 May 1976. For more on the effort to buy Merle Hay Mall, see also *Des Moines Register,* 18 May 1976 and 12, 19 June 2000; and Bill Knapp, telephone conversation with author, 20 January 2012.

32. Ibid.

33. "The Powers That Be" articles ran in the *Des Moines Register,* 3, 10, 17 October 1976. The listing of the twenty-five most powerful, the methodology, and the quotation about Bill are taken from *Des Moines Register,* 3 October 1976.

34. Friedricks, *In for Long Haul,* 134-39; *Des Moines Register,* 19, 24 March, 7 May, 20, 27 October 1978; and Bill Knapp, telephone conversation.

35. *Des Moines Register* 1, 28 October, 1 November 1978; Linda Birocci, correspondence with author.

36. On Paul Knapp worrying about the Savery purchase, see *Des Moines Register*, 12 October 1987. Bill's quotation is from *Des Moines Register*, 14 January 1990. On renovations, see *Des Moines Tribune* 28 September 1978; and Shotwell, *Knapps*, 80.

37. Unmarked clippings, "Newspaper Clippings," Scrapbook, Bill Knapp Papers; *Des Moines Tribune*, 13 February 1981; Shotwell, *Knapps*, 80; and *Iowa Newsletter* 3 (April 1981): 2.

38. *Des Moines Tribune*, 15 October 1979.

39. For Nahas's quotation and Bill's negotiating techniques, see *Des Moines Register*, 3 October 1983.

40. Des Moines Development Corporation mission statement and typescript history, Houser Papers, and *Des Moines Register*, 1 September 1985. See also *Des Moines Tribune*, 9 March 1982.

41. Unmarked *Des Moines Register* clipping, "Newspaper Clippings," Scrapbook, Bill Knapp Papers.

42. *Des Moines Tribune*, 3 December 1979, 7 April 1980. For the Valley National Bank Building situation and Ray quotation, see *Des Moines Tribune,* 21 February 1980; for McCausland quotation and more on vacating bank building, see Ginger Kuhl-Davis, "Bill Knapp Gets It Done," *Des Moines,* March 1986, 15.

43. For the Ginsberg Building, see *Des Moines Tribune*, 19 September 1980. For proposals and quotations, see *Des Moines Tribune,* 22 April 1980.

44. Richard Wilkey, interview by author, West Des Moines, Iowa, 26 December 2011; and *Des Moines Tribune*, 4, 5, 17 June 1980. Quotation is from *Des Moines Tribune*, 7 October 1980.

45. Bill Knapp, interview, 8 December 2011; Richard Wilkey, interview; and *Des Moines Tribune*, 31 July, 18 December 1980. For more on UFS leasing space and quotation, see *Des Moines Tribune*, 18 November 1980.

46. Bill Knapp, interview, 8 December 2011; Richard Wilkey, interview; and *Des Moines Tribune*, 24 March, 15, 16 April, 1981. On opening of Capital Square, see *Des Moines Register,* 20 March 1983. Quotations and more on Capital Square are from *Des Moines Register*, 24 April 1983.

47. *Des Moines Register*, 1 November 1980; Richard Wilkey, interview; and Bill Knapp, interview, 8 December 2011. See also *Business Record*, 13-19 May 1991.

48. Bill's quotation is from *Des Moines Register*, 17 September 1980.

49. *Des Moines Tribune*, 3 September 1980.

50. Ibid. For quotation and more information on project, see unmarked 1980 *Des Moines Tribune* clipping, "Newspaper Clippings," Scrapbook, Bill Knapp Papers.

51. Ibid.; and *Des Moines Tribune,* 5 October 1980, 12 December 1981, and 8 March 1982. For more on Elsie Mason Manor and quotation, see *Des Moines Tribune*, 6 October 1980.

52. Besides Iowa Realty, Civic Center Court's investors included, for example, Bankers Life, Northwestern Bell, Iowa Resources, Pioneer Hi-Bred, United Federal Savings, United Central Bank, Central Life Assurance, Kirke-Van Orsdel, Inc., American Federal Savings and Loan, Iowa-Des Moines National Bank, Brenton Banks, Weitz Companies, Employers Mutual, Bankers Trust, Dial Corporation, and Valley National Bank. For a complete list and more on the project, see *Des Moines Tribune,* 9 September 1981 and *Des Moines Register*, 11 September 1981. See also *Des Moines*

Tribune, 11 August, 1, 10, 11 September 1981; Civic Center Court, Inc. Projected Financial Statement, 15 July 1981, Bill Knapp Papers; and Kuhl-Davis, "Knapp Gets It Done," 17. For more on apartments and quotation, see *Des Moines Register,* 9 September 1981.

53. *Des Moines Register* 2, 16, October 1981. On Architectural Review Committee and quotation, see *Des Moines Tribune,* 19 October 1981.

54. For Bill's first quotation, see *Des Moines Register,* 3 October 1983. For Bill's second quotation and more on Epstein's proposal and extension, see *Des Moines Register,* 13 October 1981. On council selecting Bill's proposal, see *Des Moines Register,* 15 October 1981; and on completion, see *Iowa Newsletter* 4 (June 1982): 1, 4.

55. For origins of the Des Moines skywalk system, see Friedricks, *In for Long Haul,* 136-38. Bill's quotation is from unmarked *Des Moines Tribune* clipping, "Newspaper Clippings," Scrapbook, Bill Knapp Papers. On tour of Minneapolis skywalks and Glasrud story, see Richard Wilkey, interview; Bill Knapp, interview, 8 December 2011; and Bill Knapp II, interview, 8 December 2011.

56. *Iowa Newsletter* 3 (January 1981): 1-2; and unmarked clippings, "Newspaper Clippings," Scrapbook, Bill Knapp Papers.

57. Bill Knapp, interview, 8 December 2011; Bill Knapp II, interview, 8 December 2011; and Richard Wilkey, interview. For details and quotations, see *Des Moines Tribune,* 10 September 1981.

58. Bill's quotation is from Bill Knapp, interview, 8 December 2011; and Wilkey's quotation is from Kuhl-Davis, "Knapp Gets It Done," 17. For more on The Plaza, see *Des Moines Register,* 24 December 1982, 16 August 1985; and *Iowa Newsletter* 5 (February 1983): 3; 5 (August 1983): 2; 5 (September 1983): 4; and 7 (February 1984): 4.

59. See *Des Moines Tribune,* 15 October 1979; and Michael Walker, "He's Sold on Des Moines," *Iowan* (Spring 1983): 33.

60. *Des Moines Register,* 12 May 1983.

61. On his downtown activity, see *Des Moines Tribune,* 24 October 1978, 8 March 1982. Quotation is from Bill Knapp, telephone conversation.

Chapter 7

1. Bill Knapp, interview by author, West Des Moines, Iowa, 14 October 2011; and Connie Wimer, interview by author, Des Moines, Iowa, 31 August 2011.

2. Ibid.

3. Ibid.

4. *Des Moines Register,* 28 August 1977; Wimer, interview; *Business Record: 25th Anniversary Special Edition* (13 October 2008), 5; *Business Record,* 20 October 2003; and Walt Shotwell, *The Knapps and Notable Others: From Less Than Nothing to More Than Plenty* (Des Moines, IA: Walt Shotwell, 2000), 74-75.

5. *Drake Sports* (Summer 1989) unmarked clipping, and *Des Moines Tribune,* 1973, unmarked clipping, "Roger Knapp," Scrapbook, Virginia Haviland Papers, private collection held by Virginia Haviland, West Des Moines, Iowa [hereafter cited as Haviland Papers]. See also *Des Moines Tribune,* 22 April 1975.

6. *Des Moines Register,* 18, 25 May 1975.

7. John Stauffer, telephone conversation with author, 17 May 2012; and Irene Knapp, telephone conversation with author, 18 May 2012.

8. Arden Stokstad, telephone conversation with author, 7 September 2011; Irene Knapp, interview by author, Urbandale, Iowa, 22 February 2012; Bill Knapp, interview, 14 October 2011; and *Des Moines Tribune*, July 1975, unmarked clipping, "Roger Knapp," Scrapbook, Haviland Papers. Roger's quotation is from *Des Moines Register*, 18 May 1975.

9. Arden Stokstad, telephone conversation. Segura's quotation is from *Des Moines Tribune*, 29 April 1976.

10. Irene Knapp, interview, 22 February 2012. On state championship and Roger's quotation, see *Des Moines Register*, 30 May 1976.

11. *Des Moines Tribune*, 25 March 1980. Irene Knapp, interview, 1 June 2011; and Beatrice Turner, interview by author, Des Moines, Iowa, 30 September 2010.

12. Bill Knapp, interview, 14 October 2011; Connie Wimer, interview; Irene Knapp, interview, 22 February 2012; and Bonnie Campbell, interview by author, Des Moines, Iowa, 27 December 2011.

13. Mike Knapp, interview by author, West Des Moines, Iowa, 31 December 2010; Bonnie Campbell, interview; Irene Knapp, interview, 22, February 2012; and Bill Knapp, interview, 23 May 2012.

14. *Des Moines Tribune*, 1 June 1982; (Sarasota) *Herald-Tribune*, 2 April 2008; *Des Moines Register*, 28 November 1983, 1 July 1986. Irene Knapp Notes, 11 November 2010, Irene Knapp Papers, private collection held by Irene Knapp, Urbandale, Iowa; and Virginia Haviland, interview by author, West Des Moines, Iowa, 7 September 2011.

15. *Iowa Newsletter* 5 (September 1983): 4. This was a monthly, in-house Iowa Realty publication, Iowa Realty Papers, private collection held by Iowa Realty Company, West Des Moines, Iowa. See also Irene Knapp, interview, 22 February 2012.

16. Ibid. See also Shotwell, *Knapps*, 119-20; and Charles Hull, interview by author, Des Moines, Iowa, 2 July 2012. Roger's quotation is taken from *Des Moines Register,* 1 March 1985. See also *Des Moines Register,* 28 November 1983 and 1 July 1986.

17. Roger's first quotation is from *Des Moines Register*, 1 March 1985; and second quotation is from *Des Moines Register*, 1 July 1986. On beating Leconte, see *Des Moines Register*, 21 June 1985. See also *Des Moines Register*, 30 January, 9 June 1985; and *International Tennis Weekly*, 5 July 1985. See also Bill Knapp, interview, 22 November 2011; and Irene Knapp, interview, 22 February 2012.

18. See *Des Moines Register*, 29 October, 17 November, 1985, and 4 April 1989. Roger's quotation is from *Des Moines Register*, 2 November 1989.

19. Bill Knapp, interview, 11 November 2011; and Irene Knapp interview, 22 February 2012. Roger's quotation about his mother is from Shotwell, *Knapps*, 120-21.

20. See Bill Knapp interview, 23 May 2012; Connie Wimer, interview; and Bonnie Campbell, interview. Roger's quotation is from *Daily Trojan*, 9 April 1987.

21. On divorce settlement, see Bill Knapp II, interviews by author, West Des Moines, Iowa, 30 March, 29 August, 26 September 2012; Irene Knapp, interviews, 29 September 2010 and 22 February 2012; Gerry Neugent, interviews by author, West Des Moines, Iowa, 29 August, 26 September 2012; Bill Knapp, telephone conversation with author, 20 January 2012; and *Des Moines Register*, 4 April 1987. Irene Knapp's quotation is from Shotwell, *Knapps*, 123.

22. Power couple reference is from *Des Moines Register*, 14 January 1990. Bill Knapp's quotation is from Bill Knapp, telephone conversation, 20 January 2012.

23. Michael Ferrari, telephone conversation with author, 6 April 2012; and Bill Knapp, telephone conversation, 6 April 2012. Roger Knapp's quotation is from *Des Moines Register,* 18 September 1990.

24. Ibid. For more on Roger taking the Drake job and his quotation, see *Des Moines Register*, 4 April 1989. See also *Des Moines Register*, 18 September 1990.

25. Connie Wimer, interview. For quotation, story of Roger walking out of party, and more on the relationship between Roger and Bill, see Bonnie Campbell, interview.

26. On Timberline Tennis Ranch, and Hansen's quote, see *Des Moines Register,* 2 November 1989. For more on facility, see *Des Moines Register*, 23 November 1989 and *Timberline Tennis Ranch,* brochure, Bill Knapp Papers, privately held by Bill Knapp, West Des Moines, Iowa.

27. Bill Knapp, interview, 30 March 2012; Connie Wimer, interview; and *Des Moines Register*, 10 August 1989.

28. Bill Knapp II, interview, 19 April 2012; Gerry Neugent, telephone conversation with author, 16 May 2012; and *Business Record*, 4-9 September 1989.

29. Bill Knapp, interview, 23 May 2012.

Chapter 8

1. Inflation and housing starts information from U.S. Bureau of the Census, *Statistical Abstract of the United States, 1985* (Washington, D.C., 1985), xxi, 467, 725; unemployment rates from Bureau of Labor Statistics website, http://www.bls.gov/cps/prev_yrs.htm, accessed on 22 February 2012; and interest rate figures from http://www.freddiemac.com/pmms/pmms30.htm, accessed on 22 February 2012. Bill Knapp's quotation is from *Des Moines Tribune,* 17 May 1980. See also *Des Moines Register,* 18 May 1980.

2. Jack Wahlig, interview by author, Clive, Iowa, 30 August 2011; and Bill Knapp, interviews by author, West Des Moines Iowa, 29 April, 22 November 2011.

3. Ibid. Bill Knapp's quote is from Bill Knapp, interview, 22 November 2011; Wahlig's quotation is from Jack Wahlig, interview.

4. On home buying, see *Des Moines Tribune,* 2 November 1981. For impact of recession on Des Moines and Bell's quote, see *Des Moines Tribune*, unmarked 1980 clipping, "Newspaper Clippings," Scrapbook, Bill Knapp Papers, private collection held by Bill Knapp, West Des Moines, Iowa [hereafter cited as Bill Knapp Papers]; Iowa Realty sales figures from company spreadsheet in Central Life, Iowa Realty recapitalization folder, Bill Knapp Papers; and Meline's quote from Tim Meline, interview by author, West Des Moines, Iowa, 22 December 2011. On Camelot West, see *Des Moines Register,* 16 February, 3 March 1983, and *Iowa Newsletter* 5 (March 1983): 2. This was a monthly in-house Iowa Realty publication, Iowa Realty Papers, private collection held by Iowa Realty Company, West Des Moines, Iowa [hereafter cited as Iowa Realty Papers].

5. *Iowa Newsletter* 2 (February 1980): 2; 2 (June 1980): 1; 2 (October 1980): 1. On Bill Knapp II and his first quotation, see *Business Record*, 13 June 1994. Bill Knapp II's second quotation is from Bill Knapp II, interview by author, West Des Moines, Iowa, 23 May 2012.

6. *Iowa Newsletter* 2 (June 1980): 1; 2 (December 1980), 2.

7. *Des Moines Register*, 18 November 1979; and *Des Moines Tribune,* 9 October 1981.

8. *Iowa Newsletter* 2 (December 1980): 1; 3 (August 1981): 2; *Des Moines Tribune,* 6 November 1980, 13 April 1981; and *Des Moines Register,* 7, 9 November 1980. On not campaigning, see *Des Moines Register,* 15 June 1980; for possible change of heart and quote, see *Des Moines Register,* 28 August 1981; and for early speculation of Hughes running for governor, see *Des Moines Register,* 9 December 1980.

9. *Des Moines Register,* 25 October, 20 November 1981. See also Bill Knapp, interview, 30 March 2012.

10. On Mary Jane Odell, see *Des Moines Register,* 17 December 2010. Coincidentally, Odell was the former Mary Jane Chinn, the television personality who had hosted Iowa Realty's television program, "The Home Show" in the 1960s. She went on to be a newscaster in Chicago and then worked for Iowa Public Television before being appointed secretary of state by Governor Robert Ray in 1980. For Hughes's residence question, see *Des Moines Tribune,* 28 December 1981; and *Des Moines Register,* 29 December 1981. For Hughes withdrawal from race and Bill's quote, see *Des Moines Register,* 8 January 1982.

11. See Bonnie Campbell, interview by author, Des Moines, Iowa, 27 December 2011; Bonnie Campbell, correspondence with author, 12 March 2012; *Des Moines Register,* 29 January 1982; and *Des Moines Tribune,* 3 May 1982. For Hughes joining the Campbell campaign, see *Des Moines Tribune,* 3 March 1982.

12. For impression that Campbell's association with Hughes and Bill was a problem and Elbert quotation, see *Des Moines Tribune,* 3 May 1982. See also *Iowa Newsletter* 4 (March 1982): 1; and 4 (May 1982): 1.

13. See *Des Moines Register,* 29 April 1982.

14. *Des Moines Tribune,* 3, 7 May, 9 June 1982.

15. Michal Walker, "He's Sold on Des Moines," *Iowan* (Spring 1983): 32; Ginger Kuhl-Davis, "Bill Knapp Gets It Done," *Des Moines,* March 1986, 14; *Des Moines Register,* 14 January 1990; *Cityview,* 1 December 2005; Bill Knapp, interview, 14 January 2013; Bonnie Campbell, interview; and Richard Wilkey, interview by author, West Des Moines, Iowa, 26 December 2011. Quotation is from *Des Moines Register,* 12 December 2011.

16. On Iowa Mortgage Corporation, see *Iowa Newsletter* 2 (October 1980): 1; 2 (November 1980): 4; 3 (June 1981): 2; *Business Record,* 20-26 May 1983; and Iowa Realty 1987 Annual Report, "Iowa Realty Volume One," Scrapbook, Iowa Realty Papers.

17. Bill Knapp, interview, 30 March 2012; Bill Knapp II, interview, 30 March 2012; Daryl Neumann, interview by author, West Des Moines, Iowa, 9 August 2011; and "Iowa Realty/Knapp's Milestones and Interesting Events, 1979–1989," Bill Knapp Papers.

18. Iowa Realty sales volume figures are from company spreadsheet in Central Life, Iowa Realty recapitalization folder, Bill Knapp Papers; and Bill Knapp, interview, 30 March 2012. Quotation is from Daryl Neumann, interview.

19. Bill Knapp, interview, 30 March 2012; and Bill Knapp II, interview, 30 March 2012. See also *Des Moines Register,* 25 February 1983 and 21 September 1984.

20. Bill Knapp, interview, 30 March 2012; Bill Knapp II, interview, 30 March 2012; and Mark Kline, correspondence with author, 2 April 2012.

21. On Grandquist purchase, see *Des Moines Register,* 24 January 1985.

22. Bill Knapp, interview, 30 March 2012; Roger Brooks, telephone conversation with author, 5 March 2012; and Bill Knapp II, interview, 30 March 2012.

23. *Des Moines Register*, 5 January 1985; and *Business Record*, 17-23 June 1985.

24. Roger Brooks, telephone conversation; *Business Record*, 27 February-4 March 1984; *Des Moines Register*, 21 February, 7 March, 12 December 1984; and *Iowa Newsletter* 7 (March 1984): 1.

25. *Business Record*, 24-30 December 1984; *Des Moines Register*, 22 December 1984; *Iowa Newsletter* 8 (February 1985): 1-2; and Roger Brooks, telephone conversation.

26. *Des Moines Register*, 22 December 1984; *Business Record*, 24-30 December 1984; and *Iowa Newsletter*, 8 (February 1985): 1-2.

27. J. Michael Earley, telephone conversation with author, 6 April 2012.

28. Ibid. For quotation and more on bus tour, see *Business Record*, 31 March-6 April 1986. For more on trustees getting involved and statement about building a moat around campus, see Bill Knapp, telephone conversation, 6 April 2012.

29. J Michael Earley, telephone conversation; Bill Knapp, telephone conversation, 6 April 2012; and Michael Ferrari, telephone conversation with author, 6 April 2012.

30. *Des Moines Register*, 24 September, 4 October 1984; 30 January, 3 August 1985; *Business Record*, 31 March-6 April 1986; Michael Ferrari, telephone conversation; Bill Knapp, telephone conversation, 6 April 2012; and J. Michael Earley, telephone conversation. On Pat Greene's role and quotation, see text of Bill Knapp's remarks at Pat Greene's retirement, 17 January 1992, "Iowa Realty Volume Two," Scrapbook, Iowa Realty Papers.

31. *Business Record*, 31 August-6 September, 9-15 November 1987; *Des Moines Register*, 7, 26 March 1986; 30 March, 5 July, 31 August 1987; and *Iowa Realty Newsletter* 9 (December 1986): 1-2. This was a continuation of Iowa Realty's in-house *Iowa Newsletter*; the name was evidently changed sometime in 1985. See also Bill Knapp, interview, 30 March 2012.

32. Bill Knapp, interview, 30 March 2012; Michael Ferrari, telephone conversation; *Des Moines Register*, 20 October 1986; 24 February, 12 May, 26 October, 3, 19 November 1987; and *Business Record*, 31 August-6 September 1987.

33. Quotations from Ferrari and Lozano are from *Business Record*, 31 August-6 September 1987. "Breathing new life" quotation is from a program for Boy Scouts, Twelfth Annual Distinguished Iowa Citizen Dinner Honoring Bill Knapp, 23 June 1994, in "Iowa Business Hall of Fame, etc.," Scrapbook, Bill Knapp II Papers, private collection held by Bill Knapp II, West Des Moines, Iowa [hereafter cited as Bill Knapp II Papers].

34. *In the Manner of the Bankruptcy of Crawford Cox Hubbell, United States Bankruptcy Court for the Southern District of Iowa, 24 December 1986,* in Abstract of Title, Lot 2 in Napa Valley Estates Plat 1, Dallas County, in Bill Knapp Papers. See also *Des Moines Register*, 27 October 1987; 11 February 1990; and *Business Record*, 20-26 June 1988. On naming of Napa Valley and Haviland quotation, see *Des Moines Register,* 4 May 1990.

35. *Des Moines Register*, 11 February 1990. See also invitations to Napa Valley wine tastings, and Napa Valley brochure, all in "Charitable Contributions, etc.," Scrapbook, Bill Knapp II Papers.

36. *Business Record*, 20-26 June 1988. For the two homes, see *Des Moines Register*, 13, 22 October 1989 and 24 June 1990.

37. Bill Knapp II, interview, 30 March 2012; Gerry Neugent, interview by author, West Des Moines, Iowa, 30 March 2012. For a list of developments, see "Iowa Realty News Update, July 1987," in "Iowa Realty Volume Two," Scrapbook, Iowa Realty Papers.

38. See *Des Moines Register*, 12 September 1990; *Business Record* 25-31 July 1988; and "Iowa Realty New Update, 8 April 1987," "Iowa Realty Volume Two," Scrapbook, Iowa Realty Papers.

39. *Business Record*, 19-25 September 1988. On the Clive annexation, see *Des Moines Register*, 18 June, 7 July, 20 August, 24 September, 19, 26 November 1986. See also Abstract of Clive Special Annexation Election, 25 November 1986, City Clerk's Office, Clive, Iowa.

40. Bill Knapp II, interview, 19 April 2012; *Des Moines Register*, 1 August 1988, 7 September 1990; and Jim McCulloh, interview by author, Des Moines, Iowa, 3 May 2012. For more on Country Club development and Haviland's quotation, see *Des Moines Register*, 29 February 1988.

41. On sale of lots and Bryant's quotation, see *Business Record*, 25-31 July 1988. For more on sale and Mike Knapp's quotation, see *Des Moines Register*, 1 August 1988.

42. On bidding for Home Show Expo, see *Business Record*, 25-31 July, 1-7 August, 3-9 October 1988; *Des Moines Register*, 1 August 1988, 31 July 1989. See also Home Show Expo 1989 program, "Iowa Realty Volume Two," Scrapbook, Iowa Realty Papers.

43. *Des Moines Register*, 2 July 1990; 31 January, 15 March 1991; 24 August 1994.

44. *Business Record*, 3-8 August, 1987, 12-18 June, 28 August-3 September 1989.

45. On Hy-Vee purchase, see *Business Record*, 26 December 1988-1 January 1989; and on the Iowa Methodist purchase, see *Des Moines Register*,15 June 1988 and *Business Record*, 28 August-3 September 1989; *Des Moines Register*, 4 June 1990.

46. On deal and quotation about size of project, see *Des Moines Register,* 4 December 1989. On joint venture and Bill's quotation, see *Des Moines Register*, 23 February 1989.

47. Iowa Realty Press Release, 4 May 1990, "Iowa Realty Volume Two," Scrapbook, Iowa Realty Papers; *Business Record*, 7-13 May 1990; *Des Moines Register,* 5 May 1990; and *Business Record*, 15-21 July 1991. On purchase of LakePoint, see *Business Record*, 16-22 September 1991; and *Des Moines Register*, 18 September 1991.

48. *Business Record*, 14-20 October 1991.

49. *Des Moines Register*, 31 March 1985.

50. Number of agents in 1987 is from Iowa Realty 1987 Annual Report, "Iowa Realty Volume One," Scrapbook, Iowa Realty Papers; number of agents in 1988 from *Des Moines Register*, 26 December 1988. Iowa Realty sales volume figures from company spreadsheet in Central Life, Iowa Realty recapitalization folder, Bill Knapp Papers. Paul Knapp quotation is from *Des Moines Register,* 21 October 1990.

51. For market share ad campaign battle, see *Business Record,* 14-20 December 1987, and *Des Moines Register*, 11 January 1988. For Stanbrough's concession that his company had been losing market share since 1985, see *Des Moines Register*, 26 December 1988.

52. Gene Stanbrough, interview by author, 20 September 2011, Urbandale, Iowa; *Des Moines Register*, 29 December 1988; and *Business Record*, 7-13 August 1989. For quotation and more on Stanbrough's problems, see *Des Moines Register*, 26 December 1988.

53. Gene Stanbrough, interview; and Bill Knapp, telephone conversation, 6 April 2012. For specifics of partnership and Paul Knapp's quotation, see *Des Moines Register,* 26 December 1988.

54. Bill Knapp II, interviews, 30 March, 19 April 2012; Bill Knapp, interview, 30 March

2012; Jack Wahlig, telephone conversation with author, 1 May 2012; Roger Brooks, telephone conversation; Keith Gunzenhauser, telephone conservation with author, 29 May 2012; and Keith Gunzenhauser to William Knapp, 19 December 1984, Bill Knapp Papers.

55. Ibid.

56. Rubber chicken incident and meeting described in Bill Knapp, interview, 30 March 2012; Bill Knapp II, interview, 30 March 2012; and Jack Wahlig, telephone conversation. Sale amount from Iowa Realty stockholder spreadsheet, 1989 recapitalization folder, Bill Knapp Papers. Reported stories about sale include *Des Moines Register*, 30 August 1989; and *Business Record*, 4-10 September 1989.

57. Bill was named the city's most powerful in "The Powers That Be" poll, which ran in the *Des Moines Register*, 15 January 1990. His comment about being embarrassed by the selection is from Walt Shotwell, *The Knapps and Notable Others: From Less Than Nothing to More Than Plenty* (Des Moines, IA: Walt Shotwell, 2000), 145, and quotation about retirement is from *Des Moines Register*, 3 October 1983.

Chapter 9

1. *Des Moines Register*, 3 October 1983. Kruidenier's quotation is from unmarked *Des Moines Register* clipping, Virginia Haviland Scrapbook, Virginia Haviland Papers, private collection held by Virginia Haviland, West Des Moines, Iowa [hereafter cited as Haviland Papers].

2. See Bill Knapp, interview by author, West Des Moines, Iowa, 30 March 2012. On Kruidenier, see Walt Shotwell, *The Knapps and Notable Others: From Less Than Nothing to More Than Plenty* (Des Moines, IA: Walt Shotwell, 2000), 130. On Naples office, see "Iowa Realty/Knapp's Milestones and Interesting Events, 1979-1989," Bill Knapp Papers, private collection held by Bill Knapp, West Des Moines, Iowa [hereafter cited as Bill Knapp Papers].

3. Cecilia Gentry, interview by author, West Des Moines, Iowa, 20 June 2012.

4. Ibid.; and Bill Knapp, interview, 11 July 2012. For more on Bill's use of the telephone, see Renee Johnson, telephone conversation with author, 18 December 2012.

5. Shotwell, *Knapps*, 130. Bill Knapp II's quotation is from *Business Record,* 15 December 1997; and Michael Gartner's quotation is from Michael Gartner, interview by author, Des Moines, Iowa, 3 July 2012.

6. Connie Wimer, correspondence with author, 8 June 2012; and Michael Gartner, interview.

7. *Des Moines Register*, 20 April 1983.

8. Bill's quotation is from Bill Knapp, interview, 11 July 2012.

9. *Des Moines Register*, 7, 21 September 1984; Lu Jean Cole, interview by author, Des Moines, Iowa, 5 June 2012; and Bill Knapp, interview, 30 June 2012.

10. Michael Gartner, interview; Lu Jean Cole, interview; Bill Knapp, interview, 30 June 2012; and *Des Moines Register,* 2 October 1984; 22 September 1991. See also Lu Jean Cole to Bill Knapp, 12 September 1984; and John James to Bill Knapp, 13 September 1984, both in "Charitable Contributions, etc.," Scrapbook, Bill Knapp II Papers, private collection held by Bill Knapp II, West Des Moines, Iowa [hereafter cited as Bill Knapp II Papers]. Colston's quotation is from Monroe Colston to Bill

Knapp, 13 August 1990, in "Charitable Contributions, etc.," Scrapbook, Bill Knapp II Papers. Davis's quotation is from Evelyn Davis to Bill Knapp, 29 December 1986, in "Charitable Contributions, etc.," Scrapbook, Bill Knapp II Papers.

11. *Des Moines Register,* 8 July 1984.

12. Ibid.; see also (Corydon) *Times-Republic,* 17 September 1985.

13. Elizabeth Kruidenier, interview by author, Des Moines, Iowa, 8 August 2011; Connie Wimer, interview by author, Des Moines, Iowa, 31 August 2011; and Michael Gartner, interview. For more on David Kruidenier, see William Friedricks, *Covering Iowa: The History of the Des Moines Register and Tribune Company, 1849–1985* (Ames: Iowa State University Press, 2000), 126-28, 140-41.

14. Elizabeth Kruidenier's quotation is from Elizabeth Kruidenier, interview. See also *Des Moines Register,* 18 July 1998, 13 July 2001. Invitation to 2001 party located in Virginia Haviland Scrapbook, Haviland Papers.

15. See Elizabeth Kruidenier, interview; and Connie Wimer, interview, 31 August 2011.

16. Bill Knapp, interview, 30 March 2012; and Connie Wimer, interview, 10 September 2012. On creation of Iowa Realty Foundation, see "Iowa Realty/Knapp's Milestones and Interesting Events, 1979–1989," Bill Knapp Papers; and for list of Iowa Realty donations, see Iowa Realty Contributions, 1987, 1988, 1989, and 1990, in "Iowa Realty Volume Two," Scrapbook, Iowa Realty Papers, private collection held by Iowa Realty, West Des Moines, Iowa [hereafter cited as Iowa Realty Papers].

17. *Des Moines Register,* 20, 28 May, 7 June, 9 August, 4, 6 October 1986; 23, 27 June 1987; 15 March 1988; *Business Record* 2-7 November 1987; and Ralph Huff to William Knapp, 2 December 1986, "Charitable Contributions, etc.," Scrapbook, Bill Knapp II Papers.

18. Cecilia Gentry, interview; and Margaret Toomey, interview by author, Des Moines, Iowa, 16 July 2012.

19. Bill Knapp, interview, 11 July 2012; and Fred Weitz, interview by author, Des Moines, Iowa, 6 December 2011; and *Des Moines Register,* 9 August 1989.

20. Ibid.; Toomey's quotation is from *Des Moines Register,* 14 January 1990. For more on establishing the Variety Center, see groundbreaking invitation, 29 June 1989, "Evelyn Davis, etc.," scrapbook, Bill Knapp II Papers, and *Des Moines Register,* 30 March, 18 April 1989.

21. On Toomey and dream of center, see *Des Moines Register,* 30 March 1989. Connie Cook's quotation is from Connie Cook to Bill Knapp, 27 January 1989, "Evelyn Davis, etc.,"Scrapbook, Bill Knapp II Papers.

22. Transcript of Bill's address at childcare news conference, 3 October 1996, in "Charitable Contributions, etc.," Scrapbook, Bill Knapp II Papers; *Des Moines Register,* 9 August, 3 October 1996; *Des Moines Register* quotation is from *Des Moines Register,* 12 October 1994.

23. "Church United Breaks Ground on Shelter," press release, 14 November 1994 in "Charitable Contributions, etc.," Scrapbook, Bill Knapp II Papers. Quotation is from *Des Moines Register* 12 October 1994.

24. Bill Knapp, interview, 11 July 2012; Michael Ferrari, telephone conversation with author, 6 April 2012.

25. Ibid.; and *On Campus* 42 (18 January 1991): 1-2. This is a Drake University newsletter, "Iowa Hall of Fame, etc.," Scrapbook, Bill Knapp II Papers.

26. *Des Moines Register,* 13 January 1991. For editorial on Bill's gift, see *Des Moines Register,* 15 January 1991. For Bill's quotation, see his handwritten notes for comments at announcement 12 January 1991; and Eliot Nusbaum story is from unmarked *Des Moines Register* clipping. Both are in "Iowa Business Hall of Fame, etc.," Scrapbook, Bill Knapp II Papers.

27. Drake University press release, 29 July 1991, and text of Bill Knapp speech, "Iowa Business Hall of Fame, etc.," Scrapbook, Bill Knapp II Papers.

28. White was convicted on two counts of first-degree murder and sentenced to life in prison without the possibility of parole. He was initially sent to the Iowa State Penitentiary in Fort Madison but became violent, and officials decided to move him to an out-of-state prison. He briefly escaped during transport, which was a federal offense, and is now held in a maximum security federal prison in Colorado. For more on the Drake Diner murders and its impact on the community, see *Des Moines Register,* 30 November, 2, 8, 31 December 1992; 2, 31 March, 18 May, 19 June 1993; 29 August 1996; 16 March 2000; and 25 November 2012. See also Bill Knapp, interview, 11 July 2012.

29. On rumors on the naming of the sports arena, see *Business Record,* 7-13 December 1992. Ferrari's desire to name the building the Knapp Center is explained in Michael Ferrari to Drake Board of Governors and Board of Trustees, 19 November 1992, in "Iowa Business Hall of Fame, etc.," Scrapbook, Bill Knapp II Papers; and Ferrari, telephone conversation.

30. For story on Roger's resignation and quotations, see *Des Moines Register,* 18 December 1993. See also *Des Moines Register,* 24 June 1994. On Bill giving $5 million to Drake in 1998, see *Des Moines Register,* 29 July 1998.

31. Cecilia Gentry, interview. On Mike Knapp's and Bill Knapp II's promotions, see *Des Moines Register,* 21 January 1991. On corporate reorganization and additional promotions, see *Business Record,* 27 April-3 May 1992; *Des Moines Register,* 25 April 1992; and William Knapp to All Iowa Realty Employees, 23 April 1992, "Iowa Realty Volume Two," Scrapbook, Iowa Realty Papers.

32. *Des Moines Register,* 25 April 1992; Bill Knapp II, correspondence with author, 21 September 2010; and Bill Knapp II, interviews by author, West Des Moines, Iowa, 16 December 2010 and 30 March 2012. In 2004, Knapp Properties left its building at 5000 Westown Parkway and moved across Fiftieth Street (just a block to the north and east) to another building it owned at 4949 Westown Parkway in West Des Moines, but it leased this space to a customer and returned to its 5000 Westown Parkway address in July 2013.

33. Bill's quotation is from Shotwell, *Knapps,* 157. On heart problem see *Des Moines Register,* 30 March 1991.

34. On Moore's discontent, see Shotwell, *Knapps,* 81-82. For more on the situation and Bill's views, see Bill Knapp, interview, 24 August 2012; and Bill Knapp II, interview, 29 August 2012.

35. Bill Knapp, interview, 24 August 2012. See also Bill Knapp II, interview, 29 August 2012; and Gerry Neugent, interview by author, West Des Moines, Iowa, 29 August 2012. Rumors of Baumgarten leaving her position at Prairie Meadows were reported in *Des Moines Register,* 21 May 1991. For Bill's hiring of Baumgarten, see *Des Moines Register,* 13 November 1991, and for lawsuit, see *Des Moines Register,* 23 January 1992.

36. Bill Knapp II, interview, 29 August 2012; Gerry Neugent, interview; and *Des Moines Register,* 6 March 1993. Bill's quote is from Bill Knapp, interview, 24 August 2012.

37. Bill Knapp, interview, 24 August 2012; Bill Knapp II, interview, 29 August 2012; Gerry Neugent, interview; and *Des Moines Register*, 24 September 1993.

38. On merger of Central Life and American Mutual, see *Des Moines Register*, 22, 25 July, 11, 14 November 1994. On name change, see *Des Moines Register,* 20 February, 3 April 1995. Once Stanbrough lost First Realty in 1988, it was purchased by Edina Realty of Minneapolis before Hubbell Realty bought it in the spring of 1990. More on purchase of First Realty may be found in *Des Moines Register*, 8 August 1995. On other acquisitions and Bill stepping down as chairman, see Iowa Realty press release, 12 December 1995, "Iowa Realty Volume Two," Scrapbook, Iowa Realty Papers. On Paul's retirement and Mike Knapp becoming chairman, see *Des Moines Register*, 17 July 1997.

39. *Des Moines Register,* 28 November 1999.

40. On "cash register business" phrase and decision to get out of these businesses, see Bill Knapp, interview, 24 August 2012 ; Bill Knapp II, interview, 29 August 2012; and Gerry Neugent, interview. On selling the Savery and Bill's quotation, see Bill Knapp, interview, 24 August 2012. Mike Knapp's quotation is from Mike Knapp, interview by author, West Des Moines, Iowa, 31 December 2010. For more on sale of Savery, see Bill Knapp II, interview, 29 August 2012; *Business Record*, 1 April 1996; and *Des Moines Register*, 29 May, 3 June 1996; and 15 October 1997. As the sale was being finalized, Carole Baumgarten stepped down as the Savery's manager, and as Knapp Properties moved to sell the rest of its hotels, Baumgarten left the company in early 1997, see *Des Moines Register*, 10 May 1996, 14 March 1997.

41. Roger Brooks, telephone conversation with author, 5 March 2012. For more on sale and Bill's quotation, see *Des Moines Register*, 7 April 1998.

42. Bill Knapp interview, 24 August 2012; and Connie Wimer, interview, 31 August 2011.

43. Bill Knapp, interview, 24 August 2012; and Cecilia Gentry, interview.

44. Susan Knapp, interview by author, Van Meter, Iowa, 5 October 2012; and *Des Moines Register*, 5 October, 1987.

45. *Des Moines Register,* 16 June 1988; 22 September, 3 October, 24 November 1989; 16, 27, 31 January 1990; Bill Knapp, interview, 24 August 2012; and Susan Knapp, interview. Quotation about structuring is from *Houston Chronicle*, 21 January 1990.

46. The Harkers struck a plea deal. Dennis Harker pleaded guilty to one count of tax evasion and one count of conspiracy to defraud the federal government. He received one year in jail and three years of supervised release. Mary Ann Harker pleaded guilty to tax evasion and was sentenced to three years of probation and one year of community service. Together, the Harkers were ordered to pay $245,900 in back taxes, see *Des Moines Register* 17 January, 14 July 1990. On Susan's case and the sentence, see *Des Moines Register* 16, 25, 26, 27, 31 January, 1 February, 13, 14, 17 March 1990. See also Susan Knapp, interview.

47. Bill Knapp, interview, 24 August 2012; Susan Knapp, interview; and Gerry Neugent, correspondence with author, 4 September 2012. Susan's quotation is from Shotwell, *Knapps,* 163.

48. Susan Knapp, interview; and John Putney, interview by author, Des Moines, Iowa, 10 July 2012.

49. *Des Moines Register,* 18 August 1998.

50. John Putney, interview; and Bill Knapp, interview, 24 August 2012. For more on gift and Bill's quotation, see *Des Moines Register*, 12 February 1997.

51. John Putney, interview; on the renaming and dedication of the Varied Industries Building, see *Des Moines Register*, 9, 10 August 2001. For more on the building and Swift's statement about the size of the facility, see *Des Moines Register,* August 2001.

52. Bill's original attitude toward golf is explained in Bill Knapp, interview, 16 June 2011. The Roger Cleven incident was recalled by Tim Meline, see Tim Meline, interview by author, West Des Moines, Iowa, 22 December 2011.

53. Bill Knapp, interview, 24 August 2012; and Cecilia Gentry, interview.

54. On rotator cuff surgeries, see Bill Knapp, interview, 11 July 2012; and Carly Fisher, correspondence with author, 11 July 2012; John Mauro, interview by author, Des Moines, Iowa, 23 August 2012; and Michael Gartner, interview.

55. Bill Knapp, interview, 24 August 2012; Susan Knapp, interview; Irene Knapp, telephone conversation with author, 31 August 2012; and Gerry Neugent, correspondence.

56. Bill Knapp interview, 24 August 2012; Susan Knapp, interview; and Roger Brooks, telephone conversation with author, 5 March 2012.

57. On Bill and Susan Knapp, see Roger Brooks, telephone conversation; Cecilia Gentry, interview; Linda Grandquist, interview by author, West Des Moines, Iowa, 11 January 2012; Bill Knapp II, interview, 29 August 2012; James Cownie, interview by author, Des Moines, Iowa, 17 September 2012; Mark Oman, interview by author, West Des Moines, Iowa, 19 September 2012; Roxanne Conlin, interview by author, Des Moines, Iowa, 3 October 2012; Elizabeth Kruidenier, interview; and John Mauro, interview. Putney's quotation is from John Putney, interview.

58. *Des Moines Register,* 19, 22, 27 April 1999. See also Linda Grandquist, interview.

59. For Anna Knapp's death see *Des Moines Register,* 7 October 1995; Carolyn Doggett, telephone conversation with author, 1 October 2012; and Nancy Jones, telephone conversation with author, 1 October 2012. On Hughes's death, see *New York Times,* 25 October 1996. Bill's quotation is from Bill Knapp, interview, 24 August 2012.

Chapter 10

1. *Des Moines Register,* 3 October 1983.

2. See *Des Moines Register,* 8 February 1984; "The Greater Des Moines Committee, Inc., Iowa Business Hall of Fame" program, 2 December 1991; *Business Record,* clipping, 28 June 1993; and Robert Kemp to Bill Knapp, 28 June 1994; all in "Iowa Business Hall of Fame, etc.," Scrapbook, Bill Knapp II Papers, private collection held by Bill Knapp II, West Des Moines, Iowa; *Des Moines Register,* 20 January 2004; and "William C. Knapp Biography—Iowa Hall of Pride," typescript, in possession of author.

3. Bill Knapp II's quotation is from *Business Record*, 15 December 1997. On his daily schedule, see Cecilia Gentry, interview by author, West Des Moines, Iowa, 20 June 2012.

4. For Bill's routine at the Hotel Savery, see Bill Knapp, interview by author, West Des Moines,Iowa, 22 November 2011, and Cecilia Gentry, interview. On his use of the telephone to gather information, see John Putney, interview by author, Des Moines, Iowa, 10 July 2012, and James Cownie, interview by author, Des Moines, Iowa, 17 September 2012.

5. Bill Knapp, interview, 24 August 2012. James Hubbell III's quotation is from *Business Record*, 13 June 1994. Bill's quote is from *Des Moines Register,* 28 November 1999.

6. See articles on Des Moines's new leadership in *Des Moines Register*, 9 March 2003, 15 October 2006. Latter article lists Des Moines's civic and business leaders by age; Bill was the oldest and the only one listed in his eighties. There were only two in their seventies (Marvin Pomerantz and John Pappajohn).

7. Weitz's statement about Bill serving as a "spark plug" is taken from *Business Record*, 26 March-1 April 1990.

8. "Gray's Lake History," on the City of Des Moines Parks and Recreation webpage, www.dmgov.org/Departments/Parks/GraysLakeHistory.apex, accessed on 13 September 2012. See also Dan Martin and Helene Berlin, "Quarries' Next Quest," *Planning*, February 2012, 42.

9. Bill Knapp, interview, 14 September 2012; John R. Grubb, *My Life: A Memoir* (Des Moines, IA: Ink Publishing, 2000), 138; and Walt Shotwell, *The Knapps and Notable Others: From Less Than Nothing to More Than Plenty* (Des Moines, IA: Walt Shotwell, 2000), 44-45.

10. Ibid.; *Des Moines Register,* 1 March 1999; and Bill Knapp II, interview by author, West Des Moines, Iowa, 26 September 2012.

11. *Des Moines Register*, 19 May, 6 August 2001, 4 October 2011.

12. *Des Moines Register*, 17 January 1999. Bill's quote is taken from *Des Moines Register*, 11 November 1999. See also *Des Moines Register,* 12 November 2001; and 17 October 2004. Early in the midst of its fundraising campaign, Choose Des Moines joined with the Des Moines Chamber Federation, Des Moines Development Corporation, and the Downtown Alliance in the creation of the umbrella organization, the Greater Des Moines Partnership. Choose Des Moines was eventually folded into the economic development operation of the new partnership.

13. John Putney, interview; and Bill Knapp, interview, 24 August 2012. For Bill and Susan's service as parade marshals, see *Des Moines Register,* 5 August 2007. Quotations are from *Des Moines Register,* 15 August 2010.

14. Putney's quotation is from John Putney, interview. On Bill's continued support of the fair, see *Des Moines Register,* 6 August, 2006, 5 August 2007, 15 August 2010; John Putney, interview; Bill Knapp, interview, 24 August 2012; and Don Greiman with Jane Cox, *A Blue Ribbon Life: Memories of the Iowa State Fair* (Des Moines, IA: The Blue Ribbon Foundation), 44-45.

15. James Cownie, interview; John Putney, interview; John Putney, correspondence with author, 18 September 2012; and *Des Moines Register*, 19 August 2012.

16. *Des Moines Register,* 23 July 2004; 4 February, 18 August 2006; and Bill Knapp II, correspondence with author, 21 September 2010.

17. See https://va.iowa.gov./vetcemetery/history.html, accessed on 18 September 2012.

18. Bill Knapp, interview, 24 August 2012; and *Des Moines Register*, 29 June 2008.

19. Ibid.; see also *Des Moines Register*, 22 February, 12 November 2006.

20. *Des Moines Register*, 22 April, 3 May 2000; and Bill Knapp, interview, 14 September 2012. For more information and Bill's quotation, see *Des Moines Register*, 12 November 2000.

21. On Bill's acquisition of the Polk City land, see *Business Record,* 19-25 September 1988, and Bill Knapp II, correspondence with author. See also *Des Moines Register*, 2 March, 16 May 2001. On the development and golf course, see *Des Moines Register*, 16 February, 22 May, 20, 31 August 2002; and 26, 19 June April 2003. Arnold Palmer's quotation is taken from *Des Moines Register,* 20 August 2002. For *Golf Digest* magazine's recognition, see www.tcofiowa.com, accessed on 18 September 2012.

22. Mark Oman, interview by author, West Des Moines, Iowa, 19 September 2012; Bill Knapp, interview, 14 September 2012; and *Des Moines Register*, 16 January 2005.

23. Bill Knapp, interview, 14 September 2012. For more on negotiating the deal and Siedenburg's quotation, see Gerry Neugent, interview by author, West Des Moines, Iowa, 26 September 2012.

24. Ibid.; Bill Knapp's quotation is from *Des Moines* Register, 26 August 2012. For more on these deals and Bill Knapp II's quotation, see *Des Moines Register*, 16 January 2005. For more on Wells Fargo deal and Galleria, see *Des Moines Register*, 1 August, 26 September, 18 October 2003, 31 December 2004, 7 May 2011; CRE: The Counselors of Real Estate, "Case Study Wells Fargo Home Mortgage Chooses West Des Moines, Iowa for New Campus," webpage, http://www.cre.org/counseling_projects/case_article.cfm?projectID=1108, and Siedenburg Group webpage, http://www.siedenburg.com/projects/completed, both accessed on 22 September 2012. See also Bill Knapp II, interview, 26 September 2012.

25. *Des Moines Register*, 23, 29 July 1999; 23 February 2000; 9 March 2001; and 9, 18, 19, 25 February, 4 March 2005.

26. *Des Moines Register*, 13, 16 November 2005.

27. Ibid.; and *Des Moines Register,* 19, 25, February, 14 December 2005.

28. See Bill Knapp, interview, 14 September 2012. For Bill's guest editorial, see *Des Moines Register,* 11 December 2005. On the attorney general's probe and Vaudt's quote, see *Des Moines Register,* 3 December 2005.

29. *Des Moines Register*, 22 April 2006. For more on investigation and its conclusion, see David Vaudt, interview by author, Des Moines, Iowa, 18 September 2012; Warren Jenkins, interview by author, Des Moines, Iowa, 18 September 2012; and David Vaudt to Thomas Miller, 7 August 2007, copy in possession of author. For *Des Moines Register*'s story on closing the investigation and quotation, see *Des Moines Register,* 25 September 2007.

30. *Des Moines Register*, 8 June 2000; 28 October 2001; 3 June 2004; and 10 January 2006.

31. Bill Knapp, interview, 24 August, 2012; Irene Knapp, interview by author, Urbandale, Iowa, 22 February 2012; Bill Knapp II, interviews, 30 March, 26 September 2012; *Cityview,* 5 June 2008; and *Des Moines Register*, 5 April 2008.

32. Ibid. See also Susan Knapp, interview by author, Van Meter, Iowa, 5 October 2012.

33. Bill Knapp II, interview, 26 September 2012; Gerry Neugent, interview, 26 September 2012; John Putney, correspondence with author, 4 October 2012; Carly Fisher, correspondence with author, 4, 9 October 2012; *Des Moines Register,* 5 April 2008.

34. Susan Knapp's quotation is from Susan Knapp, interview. Bill Knapp's quotation is from *Des Moines Register*, 5 April 2008. See also Bill Knapp, interview, 24 August 2012; Bill Knapp II, interview, 26 September 2012; Gerry Neugent, interview, 26 September 2012; Susan Knapp, interview; James Cownie, interview; Michael Gartner, interview by author, Des Moines, Iowa, 3 July 2012; Mark Oman, interview; Roxanne Conlin, interview by author, Des Moines, Iowa, 3 October 2012; Bonnie Campbell, interview by author, Des Moines, Iowa, 27 December 2011; Roger Brooks, telephone conversation with author, 5 March 2012; and John Putney, interview.

35. Bill Knapp II, interview, 26 September 2012; Carol Knapp, interview by author, West Des Moines, Iowa, 9 October 2012; and Gerry Neugent, interview 26

September 2012. For obituary and McAninch's quotation, see *Des Moines Register,* 15 May 2008. In December 2009, a little over a year and a half after Paul's death, Bill's sister Mary Louise Cawthorn died as well, leaving him with one living sibling, younger sister Carolyn Doggett. For Cawthorn's obituary, see *Des Moines Register*, 3 January 2010.

36. Susan Knapp's quotation is from Susan Knapp, interview; Anna Knapp's statement about Bill's toughness is quoted from Shotwell, *Knapps*, 166; and Bonnie Campbell's quotation is from Bonnie Campbell, interview.

Epilogue

1. For more on the Iowa Award, previous winners, and quotation, see "The Iowa Award Program," 8 January 2011. A copy is in possession of the author. Other significant awards followed, including the Variety Club's Humanitarian Award in 2011 and the Bravo Award for his support of the arts. See Invitation to Bravo Awards, 4 February 2012, in possession of the author; and "William C. Knapp Biography—Iowa Hall of Pride," in possession of the author.

2. Bill's quotations are from *Des Moines Register,* 9 January 2012. Christie Vilsack's quotation is recalled by author, who was present at the reception, 8 January 2011. For more on F. M. Hubbell and his significance, see William Friedricks, *Investing in Iowa: The Life and Times of F. M. Hubbell* (Des Moines: The Iowan Books, 2007).

3. Susan Knapp, interview by author, Van Meter, Iowa, 5 October 2012; Michael Gartner, interview by author, Des Moines, Iowa, 3 July 2012; John Putney, interview by author, Des Moines, Iowa, 10 July 2012; and John Mauro, interview by author, Des Moines, Iowa, 9 August 2012.

4. Bill Knapp, interview by author, Van Meter, Iowa, 24 August 2012.

5. Gerry Neugent, interview by author, West Des Moines, Iowa, 26 September 2012; and Bill Knapp II, interview by author, West Des Moines, Iowa, 26 September 2012.

6. Michael Gartner, interview.

7. *Des Moines Register,* 19 January 2008; Bill Knapp II, interview, 29 August 2012; Gerry Neugent, interview, 29 August 2012; and Gerry Neugent, correspondence with author, 4 September 2012.

8. Bill Knapp, interview, 30 March 2012; Bill Knapp II, interview, 29 August 2012; Bill Knapp II, correspondence with author, 21 September 2010; and *Cityview,* 10 October 2012. For estimate of Bill's worth, see James Cownie, telephone conversation with author, 15 January 2013.

9. Jeff Ballenger, telephone conversation with author, 31 October 2012; Bill Knapp II, correspondence with author, 24 October 2012; and Bill Knapp, interview, 14 September 2012. For quotation on the honor flight's mission, see http://www.honorflight.org/about/mission.cfm, accessed on 23 October 2012.

10. Jeff Ballenger, telephone conversation; Bill Knapp II, correspondence, 24 October 2012; *Des Moines Register,* 14, 15, 20, 31 August 2010. For quotation and more on the honor flight trip to Washington, D.C., see Bill Knapp, interview, 14 September 2012.

11. Bill Knapp II, interview, 8 December 2011; and Bill Knapp, interviews, 5 January, 22 November 2011. For Penney's quotation and more on initial phone conversation with Bill, see James Penney, telephone conversation with author, 26 September 2010.

12. Bill Knapp, interview 14 September 2012. For lunch in Alabama, see *Gadsden*

(Alabama) *Times*, 11 March 2012 and *Des Moines Register,* 27 March 2012. For Iowa State Fair visit, see Bill Knapp, interview, 9 August 2012; James Penney, interview 9 August 2012; and *Des Moines Register,* 11 August 2012.

13. For Bill's quotation and initial meeting, see Teresa Wahlert, interview by author, Des Moines, Iowa, 8 October 2012. For more on the development of the Skilled Iowa Initiative, see Bill Knapp, interview, 11 July 2012; Bill Knapp II, interview, 29 August 2012; and *Des Moines Register*, 12 June 2012.

14. Bill's first quotation is from Bill Knapp, interview, 14 January 2013. Jim Cownie's quotation is from James Cownie, telephone conversation. Bill's press conference quotation is from Radio Iowa.com., http://www.radioiowa.com/2012/06/11/governor-unveils-program-to-help-workers-improve-their-skills, accessed on 11 November 2012.

15. On dissolution of the DMDC, see Susan Ramsey, correspondence with author, 1 November 2012.

16. Ibid. See also Bill Knapp, interview, 2 November 2012; Bill Knapp II, interview, 29 August 2012; Gerry Neugent, interview, 29 August 2012; Michael Gartner, interview; and James Cownie, interview by author, Des Moines, Iowa, 17 September 2012. For quotation and more on creation of Des Moines Redevelopment Company, see *Des Moines Register,* 24 June 2012.

17. Ibid. Bill's quotation is from Bill Knapp, interview, 2 November 2012. For more on Des Moines Redevelopment, see *Des Moines Register*, 26 August 2012. See also "Des Moines Redevelopment Company Committed Guarantors," Knapp Properties Papers, private collection held by Knapp Properties, West Des Moines, Iowa.

18. For discussion of these downtown issues and Rick Tollakson's quotation, see *Des Moines Register*, 24 June 2012. See also Bill Knapp, interview, 2 November 2012; *Des Moines Register*, 24 June 2012; and *Cityview*, 24 October 2012;

19. Teresa Wahlert, interview.

20. Bill Knapp II, interview, 29 August 2012; Chet Culver, interview by author, Des Moines, Iowa, 6 November 2012.

Index

Throughout this index, the abbreviation WK will be used to indicate references to William Clair Knapp, "Bill."

Page numbers appearing in italic type refer to pages that contain photographs.

Index

Index

Index

Index

Index